AF593379

# AIRBRIDGE TO BERLIN

# AIRBRIDGE TO BERLIN

## The Berlin Crisis of 1948, its Origins and Aftermath

D. M. Giangreco
and Robert E. Griffin

PRESIDIO

Copyright © 1988 by D. M. Giangreco and Robert E. Griffin
First Edition

All rights reserved

No part of this book may be reproduced in any form without written permission from the publisher
Published by Presidio Press, 31 Pamaron Way, Novato, California 94947

Printed in the United States of America by Standard-Hart Printing of Topeka, Kansas. Type by Lopez Graphics, Inc. of Kansas City, Missouri.

**Library of Congress Cataloging-in-Publication Data**

Giangreco, D.M., 1952–
Airbridge to Berlin.

Includes index.
1. Berlin (Germany)–Blockade, 1948–1949.
I. Griffin, Robert E. II. Title.
DD881.G53 1988 943.1'5540874 88–15159
ISBN 0-89141-329-4

# Acknowledgments

I would like to thank the many people who made this book possible. In late 1980 I requested assistance in The Retired Officer magazine from veterans of the Berlin Airlift and others who had knowledge of the events that occurred in 1948-49 in Germany. I gratefully acknowledge the contributions and assistance of Colonel Robert E. Wood, USAF, (retired), Colonel Arthur Eve, Jr., USAF (retired), Lt. Colonel Guy B. Dunn, USAF, (retired), Major Jeff Warren, USAF, (retired), Colonel John C. O'Connor, USAF, (retired), Lt. Colonel Kenneth Slaker, USAF (retired), Commander Herman T. Krol, USN (retired), and Mrs. Lillian B. Petranek. Also, CWO Bernard Desmond, USAF, (retired), Major Clifford T. Lloyd, USAF (retired), Lt. Colonel Harold E. Runyon, USAF (retired), Lt. Colonel James E. Lee, USAF (retired), Lt. Colonel Alfred T. Sadler, USAF (retired), Charles F. Messmer, Mrs. Barbara Merrill, John Gayer, and Colonel Bernard J. Humes, USA (retired). The above individuals are all veterans of the Berlin Airlift or witnesses to the events that transpired.

Research assistance was provided by the staff of the Military Field Branch, Military Archives Division, National Archives, to include William G. Lewis, Richard L. Boylan, and Amy Schmidt. Photo research was provided by the Still Pictures Branch, National Archives, the Defense Audio-Visual Agency, the Harry S Truman Library, Department of Defense Public Affairs, John Westcott of Air Power Journal at the Air War College and the staff of the Landesbildstelle Berlin. Textual assistance was provided by Lt. Colonel Tom Conrad, Major Terry Griswold, Margaret M. Blue and Cynthia L. Teare of the US Army's Command and General Staff College.

Every writer needs encouragement and constant reinforcement and for this I owe a special thanks to Arthur Hecker of Forest Hills, New York, Frank Berger of Lakehurst, New Jersey, Wolf J. Pelikan of Bonn, Germany, and especially my co-author, D. M. Giangreco. Finally, an extra special thanks to my wife, Christel, a native *Berlinerin*, who experienced the blockade and the airlift as a young girl. She assisted in translations and most importantly always lent moral support. Her love for her city and my experiences in Berlin made me constantly want to learn as much as possible about this unique city and its history.

Robert E. Griffin
December 15, 1987

# Contents

(*Below*) A young girl runs from the area of burning houses set fire by tanks of the US 45th Division in Aschaffenburg, Germany, 28 March 1945. (*Opposite*) US 30th Division forces in Magdeburg, 18 April.

# Collapse in the West

As the armies of the Western Allies pummelled their way eastward through Germany in the spring of 1945, they completed the job begun years before by heavy bombers raiding from England. Behind them, ugly scars that were once proud cities gave testament to the folly of Adolf Hitler's dreams of conquest. The German nation and the armies raised by Hitler were crushed.

The end of World War II in Europe found ten Western Allied armies, two British, one Canadian, one French and six American, spread from Trieste on the Adriatic Sea to Wismar on the Baltic. Many of their soldiers had been fighting for two, three and even four years, many more had been relatively new to the fighting. Almost to a man they agreed with the statement of the Supreme Allied Commander, General Dwight D. Eisenhower, that, "Clearly Berlin is the main prize." However, on April 15, two days before General William H. Simpson's US Ninth Army was to begin its assault on the capital, he was ordered to halt the advance.

Simpson's leading spearhead was at Zerbst, only 48 miles from Berlin, and patrols were reaching as far as Potsdam. He demanded to know "where in the hell" the order to stop had come from. The bearer of the bad news, General Omar N. Bradley,

(*Below*) The results of the Allied bombardment of Cologne.

simply replied, "From Ike." The Ninth Army commander later recalled that he was so shocked he was unable to "even remember half of the things Brad said from then on. . . . I got back on the plane in a kind of daze. All I could think of was, How am I going to tell my staff, my corps commanders and my troops? Above all, How am I going to tell my troops?"

While the capture of the Third Reich's capital had always held an attraction for the supreme commander, his directive from Washington was to destroy the German Army—an aim which didn't necessarily have anything to do with Berlin. As the war drew to an end, Eisenhower was less interested in the postwar political implications of who captured the capital than he was at getting the war over quickly with the least possible loss of American lives. Both his superior in Washington, General George C. Marshall, and his army group

(*Left*) US 3rd Division soldiers cautiously advance past a flaming building in Zweibrücken, as they search for snipers, 20 March 1945. (*Right*) US 11th Armored Division troops take Wernberg, 22 April. (*Bottom*) US 82nd Airborne Division soldiers outside Ludwigslust, 2 May 1945.

commander in central Germany, Bradley, agreed with him.

The German army defending the western approaches to Berlin had been shattered by the speed and violence of the US thrust from the Rhine River and Bradley felt that Simpson's army would suffer few casualties getting to the city. He stated, however, that he "was convinced that the Germans would fight hard for the capital" and, in a phone conversation with Eisenhower, estimated that the city "might cost us 100,000 men." Berlin, moreover, was slated to be within the Soviet Union's postwar occupation zone which prompted Bradley to add, "It would be a pretty stiff price to pay for a prestige objective, especially when we know that we've got to pull back and let the other fellow take over."

(*Below*) 14-year-old members of the "Air Guard" captured near Giessen, April 1945. (*Bottom*) A temporary prisoner of war enclosure outside Remagen, 25 April.

With Eisenhower's order not to move on Berlin, US forces settled down along their "stop line" running generally from Ludwigulust to Karl Marx Stadt deep in present day East Germany. The vicious, but sporatic fighting at places like Leipzig, Magdeburg, the Harz Mountains, Erfurt, and the disastrous attempt to establish a bridgehead across the Elbe River at Westerhusen took its toll of Americans in the area the Soviets would soon occupy. Later that year, after permission to cross back into eastern Germany was obtained from Soviet authorities, US graves registration teams entered the former combat zone to recover the bodies of the 2,000 Americans hastily interred during the fighting—roughly one fiftieth the number of Soviet troops killed during the Battle of Berlin.

# *Die Götterdämmerung*
# The Fall of Berlin

(*Top*) Soviet artillery pounds Berlin. (*Center*) Soviet infantry and assault-guns. (*Bottom*) Soviet armor crossing a pontoon bridge over the Spree River near Berlin.

Berlin had been the beating heart of the German nation ever since unification of the odd conglomeration of Germanic states, principalities, duchies, grand duchies, and free cities was achieved by Prussia's "iron chancellor," Otto von Bismarck, in 1871. Before World War II, nearly 4.5 million people had lived and worked in the capital. By mid April 1945, barely 2 million remained and many of those refugees who had fled the fighting further east. The migration of Berliners away from their city had begun in earnest a year earlier when it became clear the massed attacks of US and British bombers was not going to let up and the tempo of the exodus further increased as the bombing became heavier and Soviet armies grew closer. By the time of the final Soviet offensive, in April 1945, 52,000 Berliners had died in the air raids which had ground 6,340 city acres into rubble and severely damaged several times that amount.

After nearly four years of fighting that had seen the Soviets driven all the way back to the gates of Moscow, the Red Army had pushed, shoved and slashed its way over a thousand miles to the Oder River, within 40 miles of Berlin. All told, roughly 20 million Soviet citizens were said to have died in the war and only one more battle would be required to crush Hitler's Third Reich forever.

Generals Ivan S. Konev and Georgi K. Zhukov had amassed nearly 2.5 million men against 1 million German defenders and outnumbered them four to one in artillery and tanks and nearly three to one in operational aircraft. Their offensive exploded across the Oder on Monday, April 16, but initially made little progress against ferocious resistance. The German front, however, soon began to disintegrate under the weight of the attack. On Tuesday, April 24, 400,000 men were isolated in two large pockets with approximately half

Soviet soldiers help a wounded comrade (*top*), take cover from sniper fire (*center*) and capture a German soldier who had used a sewer as a defensive position (*bottom*).

of the troops falling back into Berlin and the rest surrounded southeast of the city.

Counter attacks to relieve the capital, made up of units drawn from the stationary front facing the Americans, proved to be futile and brutal street fighting raged among the ruins for more than a week. The city was formally surrendered by its garrison commander, General Karl Weidling, on Wednesday, May 2, 1945.

The Red Army suffered 304,000 casualties during the Battle of Berlin, a third of whom were killed during the fighting or died later of wounds. German military casualties neared a million men when the huge number of prisoners taken by the Soviets is included. Close to 100,000 civilians were killed by shelling, heart attacks, summary executions, and as the fighting rolled mercilessly over them. This number includes roughly 6,000 suicides.

Wholesale raping and looting was conducted by Soviet troops during the battle and well after the city was taken. Figures on the number of rapes vary widely from a minimum of 20,000 up to 100,000 by

(*Below*) Soviet artillery of all types engages in direct fire to crush German resistance.

(*Top* and *center*) Scenes from the vicious street fighting in the center of the city. (*Bottom*) the final assault on the *Reichstag* which had been turned into a fortress by its German defenders.

Berlin doctors who were unofficially permitted to perform abortions. Soviet authorities do not deny rapes occurred and their attitude is best summed up by the words of an editor of the army newspaper, *Red Star:* "War is war, and what we did was nothing in comparison with what the Germans did in Russia." As for Joseph Stalin, when the head of the Yugoslav Military Mission to Moscow complained about rapes committed in his country—a country closely allied to the Soviet Union—Stalin replied: "Can't you understand it if a soldier who has crossed thousands of kilometers through blood and fire has fun with a woman or takes a trifle?"

(*Opposite top*) Soviet soldier distributing food to Berliners, 3 May 1945. (*Opposite bottom*) German garrison commander in Berlin, General Karl Weidling, shortly after he surrendered the city on 2 May 1945. (*Below*) Soviet tankers watch as a column of German prisoners is led from the city. Shipped to the Soviet Union to help repair its massive war damage, most were not returned to Germany until well into the 1950s.

Prime Minister Winston Churchill, President Harry S Truman and Premier Joseph Stalin at the Potsdam Conference, 23 July 1945.

## ONE

# The Stage is Set

*This war is not as in the past; whoever occupies a territory also imposes on it his own social system. Everyone imposes his own social system as far as his army has power to do so. It cannot be otherwise.* —Joseph Stalin[1]

It was the Western Allies finest hour in the immediate post-World War II years. It was a magnificent logistical effort, unparalleled in aviation history; to feed and support a city of more than two million people completely by air for more than ten months. It was a fateful time for the citizens of Berlin as they were given the opportunity to actively participate in an effort that would determine their political future and destiny. Because the Soviet Union had already subverted most of Eastern Europe, the success of the airlift in foiling Soviet attempts to force the Western Allies out of Berlin was a tremendous victory that signaled America's intention to stand firm against further Soviet expansion in Europe.

The relentless westward march of Soviet Communism since the end of World War II by political intrigue and the weight of the Soviet armies was stopped at the Brandenburg Gate in 1948. Some forty years later, they have advanced no further. One must ask, had the Allies surrendered their right to be in Berlin, would the history of post-war Western Europe have been different?

On June 25, 1948, after the Soviets had closed all road, rail, and barge traffic routes to Berlin, General Lucius D. Clay, Commander-in-Chief, US Forces in Europe, and US Military Governor for Germany, telephoned General Curtis LeMay, Commanding General, US Air Forces in Europe (USAFE). Clay asked LeMay if he could fly 45 tons of supplies to Berlin. The next day, USAFE delivered 80 tons to Berlin and the Berlin Airlift was under way.[2] A year later the Americans and British were delivering more than 8,000 tons of food and supplies to Berlin each day, the blockade had been broken, and a tremendous victory had been won without a shot being fired.

One generation of Americans can tell you where they were and what they were doing on December 7, 1941 and on V-J Day in 1945. Another generation can tell you the same for the day President John F. Kennedy was shot. By the same token, there are hundreds of US Air Force pilots and crewman, stationed in such far off places as the Panama Canal Zone, Alaska, Hawaii, Alabama, California, and Montana, who can tell you exactly what they were doing in late June and July 1948 when they received orders to depart for Germany to participate in the Berlin Airlift. The same is true for British aircrews who may have come from Australia, New Zealand, India, or South Africa. No Berliner who resided in the former German capital in 1948-49 will ever

forget the experience of living through the Soviet blockade. Nor will they ever forget the brave men and women, some of whom made the ultimate sacrifice, who made it possible for them to have the freedom to choose the form of government they desired.

What precipitated the Soviet blockade of Berlin? Why did the Soviets believe they could force the Western Allies out or, at least, impose their will by making the Allies admit that all of Berlin was a part of the Soviet Zone of Germany and subject to Soviet occupation orders and laws? Why did the Allies choose to stand in the former German capital completely surrounded by the Soviet Zone and the numerically vastly superior Soviet armies? Berlin was militarily indefensible and of little tactical value. It consisted primarily of a pile of bombed out rubble with no industry to speak of remaining, and two million plus people who had historically obtained their food and supplies from the areas now occupied by the Soviets. Berlin, in June 1948, was truly "an island in the Red Sea," an apt description which later became a well-worn cliché.

Even before the end of World War II, the Soviet Union was making certain that the buffer states on its western borders would be friendly and under their control.

Stalin did not attempt to set up pure Communist states immediately, but used the "National Front" policy proclaimed by the Comintern in 1941. This policy called for the Communists to unite with Socialists, and other liberal democratic "anti-Fascists." The *modus operandi* for the establishment of a Soviet puppet government varied only slightly in Rumania, Bulgaria, Hungary, Poland, and Czechoslovakia. After the Soviet armies moved in and executed or imprisoned any potential political opposition, a "democratic peoples" provisional government was installed. This provisional government usually consisted of "anti-Fascist non-Communists" and Communists controlled the key positions and the government. Only the Yugoslavs, who under Marshal Josip Tito had been able to liberate much of their country themselves, were able to retain some independence.

The case of Poland was especially bitter for the United States, but even more so for the British. Great Britain had gone to war in 1939 for Poland, had housed the Polish government-in-exile for five years, and had armed and supported a Polish Army of some 190,000 troops who had

Polish patriots with a German prisoner during the uprising in Warsaw, August 1944.

fought valiantly on several Western fronts for the Allied cause in the hopes of returning to their liberated homeland. The United States had also recognized the London Polish government and had several million Polish-American citizens who primarily supported a democratic free Poland independent of Germany and the Soviet Union.

The Soviets, however, were determined that Poland, the historical corridor for military assault on Russia from the west, would be friendly and, if possible, Communist. In April 1943, the Germans discovered large mass graves of Polish officers in the Katayn forest near Smolensk, and accused the Soviets of mass murder. These officers had been missing since the joint Soviet-German operations against Poland in 1939. The London Polish government-in-exile called for an investigation by the International Red Cross. The Soviet Union took offense and broke off relations with the London Polish government on April 25, 1943.

In late July 1944, Soviet armies were poised just outside Warsaw with the apparent intention of shortly capturing the city. On July 29, 1944, a Moscow radio station broadcast an appeal by Polish Communists to the people of Warsaw to rise up and help throw the Germans out. The Polish Underground, a large force whose basic loyalty was to the London Polish government, believing a Soviet attack was imminent, called for a general uprising on August 1 to assist in the liberation of their capital. Strangely, no Soviet attack came and the Germans proceeded to annihilate the Polish Underground.

The Soviet armies did not take Warsaw until mid-January of the following year. In the meantime, the Soviets established and recognized a Polish Provisional Government (known as the Lublin Committee) consisting of veteran Polish Communists. They refused to deal with the London Polish Government in spite of appeals and protests from the British, supported by the United States.

Many sessions at Yalta and Potsdam were devoted to the Polish question. The Soviets went through the charade of allowing some London Polish officials to join a Polish Government of National Unity in June 1945, but this was mere window dressing and it soon became apparent that Poland had become a Soviet satellite state. By 1947, the London Poles had been terrorized into silence, arrested, or forced to flee their homeland.

The pattern of transition from a broad-based National Front type government to a Communist state was similar in Rumania, Hungary, Bulgaria, and Czechoslovakia and by early 1948 was complete.

> These processes did not take place in public. Only their final results could not be kept secret from the world and occasionally shed a lurid light on the customary semi-darkness behind the Iron Curtain. Thus, for example, the fall of the Nagy Cabinet in Hungary in May 1947 alarmed the world; in September the Bulgarian and Rumanian opposition leaders, Petkov and Maniu, and by the end of the year the Polish and Hungarian opposition leaders, Mikolajszyk and Pfeiffer, had to flee in order to escape arrest. When A. Y. Vishinski, the Kremlin's special envoy, forced King Michael of Rumania to abdicate, Rumania was ready to become a so-called people's democratic republic. The final act in this logical development was a Communist coup d'état which was dramatically carried out in Prague in February 1948 and led to the death of Jan Masaryk, the son of the founder of the Czechoslovak state, followed by the integration of the country into the Bolshevik system. A system of pacts considerably strengthened the political and economic ties between East-Central European states and the Soviet Union.[3]

Long before World War II ended, Winston Churchill recognized the war-time alliance of the Western democracies and the Communist Soviet Union would have problems once Nazi Germany was defeated. Each feared the other might make a separate peace with Germany and these fears were one of the principal reasons for the "unconditional surrender" policy proclaimed by Franklin D. Roosevelt and supported by Churchill at the Casablanca conference in early 1943.

This mutual suspicion of a separate peace had a sound historical basis. After World War I, in 1922, the Soviet Union and Germany, then the two "outcasts" of Europe, signed a treaty at Rapallo which offset the British-French European pact. The Soviet Union had permitted the German *Reichswehr* to secretly establish experimental training centers on Russian soil. New military equipment and tech-

Soviet foreign minister Vyacheslav Molotov with Adolph Hitler and an interpreter during the brief Nazi-Soviet alliance.

niques were tested at these sites during the 1920s and early 1930s in violation of the Versailles Treaty.

Even after Adolf Hitler came to power, and despite his anti-Bolshevik tirades and outlawing of the German Communist Party, commercial cooperation continued to prosper. Then, in August 1939, the Nazi-Soviet Non-Aggression Pact gave Hitler a free hand to attack Poland and plunge the world into a conflagration which would ultimately consume more than 55 million lives. The Soviet Union's reward for standing aside during the Nazi invasion was the acquisition of eastern Polish lands formerly belonging to Czarist Russia.

The Soviet Union's suspicions of the Western Allies were based on the fact that both the United States and Great Britain had intervened in the Russian Revolution against the Bolsheviks. Over the years, Churchill had made many anti-Communist statements and the United States had not even recognized the Soviet Union until 1933, after the election of Roosevelt. Great Britain and the United States had promised an invasion of France in 1942 when the Soviet armies had been pushed back to the Volga River in Stalingrad and again in 1943. The Western Allies were unable to mount the promised operation until June 1944. Did the United States and Great Britain really care if the Nazis and the Communists killed each other off? Even as the Western Allied armies approached the Rhine in 1944-45, only one-third of Germany's total forces faced the West while the other two-thirds fought over every inch of ground while retreating before the Soviets.

Through propaganda broadcasts and disinformation spread by agents in neutral countries, the Germans attempted to play on the Soviet's suspicions and met with some degree of success. In February 1945, a German SS general met with US and British officials in Switzerland and attempted to negotiate the surrender of German armies in Italy. Although the Germans were informed that only an unconditional surrender would be accepted and the Soviets were notified of the meetings by the Allies, Molotov, the Soviet Foreign Minister, accused the Americans and British of negotiating behind the back of the Soviet Union.[4]

Churchill recognized, as did Stalin, that initial military control over the liberated Eastern European countries would be decisive in determining their future political make-up. He continually advocated a strike by Allied forces from Italy onto the Istrian Peninsula through Trieste and Vienna into the Balkans and later attempted to get the US and British armies to advance as far to the east as possible.

Churchill wanted to see the royalist regimes reinstated in Greece and Yugoslavia and, if this was not possible, at least democratic republics. In an attempt to come to some *modus vivendi* with Stalin on the future of the Balkans and Central Europe, Churchill, in a meeting in Moscow in October 1944 with Stalin, agreed to recognize the Soviet Union's influence in Rumania and Bulgaria in return for Stalin's recognition of Great Britain's influence in Greece. Churchill also proposed the Soviet Union and Great Britain split their influence 50-50 in Hungary and Yugoslavia. Stalin readily agreed to this proposal and allowed the British wide latitude in Greece by not protesting directly when the British moved successfully against the Greek Communists in 1944-45.[5]

During the latter stages of World War II, the United States was almost as suspicious of Churchill as it was of Stalin. Roosevelt, and later Harry S Truman, feared that both the Soviet Union and Great Britain were bent on reestablishing the old European game of dividing up the smaller states into "spheres of influence." The US policy was to allow each of the liberated countries the opportunity to choose their form of government by free democratic elections.

US military leaders were suspicious of Churchill's attempts to get them involved in a Balkan campaign. They felt this would be a diversion from the main thrust of defeat-

Yugoslav soldiers file past a brigade headquarters of the New Zealand Division in Trieste, Italy, 5 May 1945. The New Zealanders of the British Eighth Army accepted the surrender of the German garrison in that important Balkan city when the Germans refused to capitulate to the Yugoslav Army.

ing Germany by a frontal assault across the Rhine. When Churchill attempted to encourage General Dwight D. Eisenhower to take Berlin and Prague, Eisenhower resisted and only agreed to these objectives if they became necessary as required by the military situation. Eisenhower, as the military commander, saw his duty to meet and destroy the enemy with a minimum loss of manpower and equipment. Churchill, the experienced world statesman, recognized the potential political significance.

Truman, new to the world political scene, was advised to be cautious in his dealings with Churchill so as not to give the impression that the United States and Great Britain were conspiring against the Soviet Union. When Churchill proposed Truman visit Great Britain before the Potsdam Conference for a few days to receive the adulation of the English people for America's support and to consult on the upcoming meeting with Stalin, Truman declined because he did not want it to appear that he and Churchill were going to "gang up" on Stalin.[6] The US policy was to attempt to come to an honest accommodation with the Soviets and to mediate differences between the Soviet Union and Great Britain.

In October 1943, prior to the meeting of Churchill, Stalin, and Roosevelt at Teheran, the foreign ministers of Great Britain, the Soviet Union, and the United States met in Moscow. One of the topics they discussed was the organization of Europe after the war. No concrete decisions were made, but it was decided to form the European Advisory Committee (EAC) in London to study the problem and make recommendations. The three principal members of the EAC were John Winant, US Ambassador to Great Britain; Feodor Gusez, the Soviet Ambassador to Great Britain; and William Strang, a British Foreign Ministry official.

Prior to the formation of the EAC, the United States and Great Britain had been studying the future of Germany after its surrender. During 1942-43, a US State Department committee, headed by Under Secretary Sumner Welles, had discussed the possible partitioning of Germany. A hypothetical map had been drawn up which showed a Germany divided into three states: a Northwest Germany with a population of 26,000,000, a South Germany with 23,000,000 inhabitants; and a Northeast Germany with a population of 18,200,000.

There was general agreement that Germany would have to be broken up into three to five states, along with the possible internationalization of the Saar and Ruhr areas, to preclude Germany from reuniting and again becoming a threat to peace. Enroute to the Teheran Conference, Roosevelt suggested tying the post-war occupation zones to the final pattern of partition with US forces controlling whatever entity was created in the northwest.[7]

By late 1943, the US State Department had developed a draft study concerning the future occupation of Germany. This plan called for the three occupation zones to form a junction at Berlin, thereby guaranteeing access to the city by US and British forces. This proposal was never acted upon or forwarded to Winant for consideration by the EAC. Under the British plan formulated by a cabinet committee under Deputy Prime Minister Clement Attlee, Berlin lay completely in the proposed Soviet occupation zone. Their plan was presented to the EAC in January 1944 and was readily agreed to by the Soviet Union.[8]

## "Cease fire, *tovarisch!*... Do you have anyone there who speaks English?"

—2nd Lieutenant William Robertson, Torgau, Germany, 25 April 1945

Pressed by armies driving from east and west, the Third Reich had become a withered trunk that was finally cut in half when US and Soviet forces met at the Elbe River south of Berlin on Wednesday afternoon, April 25, 1945.

The reaction of the troops involved tended to be mixed. At Torgau, where Lieutenant Robertson and Soviet soldiers crawled out on the girders of a destroyed bridge to meet each other, things were all smiles and backslapping. Hours earlier, at Strehla, Americans encountered a massacred refugee column extending for hundreds of yards along the shore line near an unfinished pontoon bridge. Everywhere could be seen upturned wagons and carts with ransacked baggage and the bodies of men, women, and children strewn about. Here, the Soviet troops were less than happy about the arrival of the US patrol.

(*Opposite*) A recently liberated Russian POW translates messages between the US 83rd Division and oncoming Soviet forces, 23 April 1945. (*Left*) Lieutenants Robertson of the US 69th Division and Alexander Sylvashko of the Soviet 5th Guards Army, Torgau, Germany, 25 April. (*Right*) Army group commanders Marshal Ivan Konev of the 1st Ukranian Front and General Omar N. Bradley, US XII Army Group with US 9th Air Force commander, General Hoyt S. Vandenberg, at right, Torgau, 5 May. (*Bottom*) US 82nd Airborne Division soldiers meet troops of the Soviet 49th Army at Grabow as a lone German soldier with a bicycle looks on, 3 May.

(*Top*) Photos of Roosevelt and Stalin look down on a party as US and Soviet soldiers (*bottom*) gather around a T-34 tank, Torgau, Germany, 27 April 1945.

Soldiers of the German 21st Army moving west to surrender to the US forces, Grabow, 5 May 1945.

Roosevelt's concept of postwar occupation zones drawn in pencil by the president himself on a *National Geographic* map while en route to the Cairo Conference, November 1943.

In late February 1944, the US War Department proposed a change, strikingly similar to that in the earlier State Department draft study, with occupation zones radiating like a wheel with Berlin the hub. But the proposal would have only allocated 22 percent of the land area, population, and resources of pre-war Germany to the Soviet Union and the US State Department was of the opinion that it would be rejected by both the Soviet and British governments. The proposal was never made.[9]

Winant returned to the United States for consultations in May 1944. During his visit, he met with War Department officials and the question of access to Berlin was raised. Winant, at that time, desired to clarify the question of access to Berlin and felt he could get the Soviet EAC representative to accept a written agreement. The War Department officials did not wish, at that early date, to commit themselves to specific routes. War Department officials maintained this was a military matter and would be resolved "at the military level" when the time came. Winant accepted this argument.[10]

On September 12, 1944, the EAC in London published a draft agreement signed by the representatives of the United States, Great Britain, and the Soviet Union stating that Germany was to be divided for the purposes of occupation into three zones and a special Berlin area, which would be under the occupation by the three powers. The boundaries were published for the three zones of Germany and the three sectors of Berlin, but which power was to occupy which zone and sector was left blank pending further negotiations.[11]

Later in September 1944 at the Quebec Conference, Roosevelt agreed to accept the south/southwest occupation zone provided that the United States also have control of an enclave in the British zone which included the North Sea ports of Bremen and Bremerhaven.[12] Still later that month US State Department officials had some second thoughts and proposed a change be made in the occupation zones similar to the wheel proposal which would guarantee all three powers land access to Berlin. Winant reacted vehemently because the draft by all three powers had been agreed upon. He maintained that British and American access to Berlin was implicit in their right to be there.[13]

On November 14, 1944, the EAC published an additional agreement which set up the control authority for postwar Germany. It called for the commanders-in-chief of the three powers to constitute a supreme power authority called the Control Council. It authorized the Control Council to direct the administration of Greater Berlin through appropriate agencies.[14]

Another not entirely unexpected development came with the liberation of Paris in August 1944 and the formation of a French Provisional Government under General Charles deGaulle in October 1944. DeGaulle pressed for a French occupation zone in post-war Germany and Churchill was very receptive to the idea of French participation. Churchill realized that the American and British publics would probably not permit large occupation forces for a long period of time and a strong France would be a barrier against any German military resurgence.[15]

At the Yalta Conference in February 1945, the end of the war in Europe was in sight. The EAC agreements of September and November 1944 were ratified by the three heads of state. Churchill advocated the three powers allocate France an occupation zone and a seat on the Control Council. After considerable discussion, all three leaders

Prime Minister Winston Churchill, President Franklin D. Roosevelt and Premier Joseph Stalin on the patio of the palace in Yalta, where the "Big Three" met. In the rear are: Admiral Sir Andrew Cunningham, Admiral Ernest King, Air Marshal Portal and Admiral William D. Leahy, with high ranking Soviet officers, February 1945

agreed France should have an occupation zone carved from the US and British zones, but Roosevelt and Stalin opposed giving France a Control Council seat. The matter was then referred to the foreign ministers who were also present at Yalta.

Anthony Eden, the British foreign minister, insisted France would not accept a zone of occupation without membership in the Control Council, but the foreign ministers could not resolve the issue. Roosevelt then reversed himself and supported the British position. Stalin then relented and concurred.[16] The negotiations on the boundaries of the French zone were left to the EAC. An amended agreement was signed on May 2, 1945, to indicate the French occupation zone. The French Sector of Berlin was not defined, although it was understood that it would come from either the British or US sectors.[17]

It was at Yalta that Roosevelt made the serious mistake of telling Stalin that the US occupation of Germany would be limited to two years.[18] With this statement, did Roosevelt sow the seed for future Soviet actions regarding Berlin in 1948?

Two months after Yalta, Roosevelt was dead and Truman was the president of the United States. The Soviet armies had captured Berlin and the US and British armies

US truck entering the Soviet Occupation Zone on its way to Berlin

had advanced far into what had been designated as the future Soviet zone of Germany. On May 7, 1945, Germany surrendered.

The four Allied commanders—Eisenhower (USA), Bernard Law Montgomery (Great Britain), Georgi K. Zhukov (USSR), and Jean de Lattre de Tassigny (France)—met at Zhukov's headquarters in Berlin on Tuesday, June 5, 1945. As called for in the EAC agreements ratified at Yalta, the four commanders signed the declaration of the defeat of Germany and the agreement for the control of post-war Germany. They affirmed the boundaries of the four occupation zones as previously agreed upon and that each of the four powers would have a sector in Berlin, the French, however, had still not been allocated a specific occupation sector in Berlin.

These commanders who, with the exception of de Tassigny, were to become their government's initial representatives on the Control Council, decreed that the administration of Greater Berlin would be directed by an Inter-Allied Governing Authority (Kommandatura in Russian) and would operate under the general direction of the Control Council. The Kommandatura was to consist of four commanders, each of whom would serve in rotation as chief commandant.[19]

The next step was to arrange the pullback of US and British forces from the Soviet Zone in Thuringia, Saxony, and Mecklenburg and the entry of US, British, and French forces into Berlin to assume control of their respective sectors. This exchange of territory proved to be complicated and, again, Western Power access to Berlin came into question. Truman and Churchill proposed to Stalin that these movements be accomplished simultaneously beginning the middle of June 1945. Stalin agreed, but postponed the movements until July 1, 1945. Prior to the movements, Clay, then Eisenhower's deputy; Robert Murphy, a US State Department official

Marshal Georgi K. Zhukov

acting as Eisenhower's political advisor; and General Floyd Parks, the US Berlin Commandant designate, along with their British counterparts, met with Zhukov on Friday, June 29 to make the final arrangements. Clay reported:

The discussions were directed principally to the taking over of Berlin and the withdrawal of Allied troops to their agreed occupation zones. We fixed quickly the number of troops to be quartered in Berlin at approximately 25,000 each. We had previously discussed with Soviet field commanders the time required for the withdrawal of our troops and the movement of Soviet troops to replace them, and had agreed to tentatively accomplish it in a nine-day period. Zhukov believed this much too long. I agreed with him, particularly because I knew we could certainly move as rapidly as he could. Therefore, we arranged for a four-day period starting July 1, which would enable our men to enter Berlin on the Fourth of July. Soviet troops were to follow our withdrawing troops at intervals of not less than one kilometer. Liaison representatives were to be exchanged directly between field commanders responsible for the movements. Soviet reconnaissance parties were permitted to enter the areas to be occupied by Soviet troops at once, and our reconnaissance parties were permitted to enter Berlin.

. . . The remaining matters we discussed were not so easy to resolve. We had explained our intent to move into Berlin utilizing three rail lines and two highways and such air space as we needed. Zhukov would not recognize that these routes were essential and pointed out that the demobilization of Soviet forces was taxing existing facilities. I countered that we were not demanding exclusive use of these routes but merely access over them without restrictions other than normal traffic control and regulations which the Soviet administration would establish for its own use. General Weeks (British representative) supported my contentions strongly. We both knew there was no provision covering access to Berlin in the agreement reached by the European Advisory Commission. We did not wish to accept specific routes which might be interpreted as a denial of our right of access over all routes but there was merit to the Soviet contention that existing routes were needed for demobilization purposes. We had already found transport a bottleneck to our own redeployment. Therefore Weeks and I accepted as a temporary arrangement the allocation of a main highway and rail line and two air corridors, reserving the right to reopen the question in the Allied Control Council. I must admit that we did not then fully realize that the requirement of unanimous consent would enable a Soviet veto in the Allied

(*Opposite top*) the opening of the third day session of the Potsdam Conference, 19 July 45. Stalin and Molotov are at left, Truman is on the far side of the table facing the camera with Churchill and Anthony Eden at right. (*Opposite bottom*) Occupation leaders after the first meeting of the Allied Control Council in its new headquarters. Left to right: General Sokolovsky, USSR, Ambassador Murphy, US, Field Marshal Montgomery, GB, Marshal Zhukov, USSR, General Eisenhower, US, General Koenig, Fr, and Ambassador Seminov, USSR.

> Control Council to block all of our future efforts. While no record was kept at this meeting, I dictated my notes that evening and they include the following:
>
> It was agreed that all traffic—air, road, and rail, . . .would be free from border search or control by customs or military authorities.
>
> I had no way of knowing that Soviet insistence on border and customs control would serve as the excuse for the initial imposition of the blockade of Berlin.
>
> I think now that I was mistaken in not at this time making free access to Berlin a condition to our withdrawing into our occupation zone. The importance of the issue was recognized but I did not want an agreement in writing which established anything less than the right of unrestricted access. We were sincere in our desire to move into Berlin for the purpose of establishing quadripartite government, which we hoped would develop better understanding and solve many problems. Also we had a large and combat-experienced army in Germany which at that moment prevented us from having any worries over the possibility of being blockaded there. However, I doubt very much if anything in writing would have done any more to prevent events which took place than the verbal agreement which we made. The Soviet Government seems to be able to find technical reasons at will to justify the violation of understandings whether verbal or written. In any event General Eisenhower had delegated full authority to me to conduct the negotiations and the responsibility for the decision was mine. The die had been cast and for better or worse the Western Allies were not committed to withdrawal to their separate zones of occupation and to start the move into Berlin on July 1 . . .[20]

And so, on such decisions history is made. The US EAC representative believed he could have obtained a written agreement from the Soviet EAC representative guaranteeing US access to Berlin, but, no decision was made because the War Department decreed it should be resolved "at the military level" when the time came. Clay, with Murphy at his side and the concurrence of his British counterpart, made the decision "at the military level." He opted for an oral agreement because a written agreement might have restricted access to certain routes when the US and British goal was unrestricted access.

The Western Powers never got unrestricted access and even the restricted access could be questioned because there was nothing in writing. The Western Powers were left with the nebulous argument that by their presence in Berlin, access was implicit. Clay was possibly correct in his statement about the Soviet's willingness to circumvent any agreement, oral or written, but the US, British, and French legal position before international bodies would have been much stronger with a written agreement.

The first US forces moved into Berlin on Sunday, July 1, 1945, and on the Fourth of July, celebrated with a parade at the new US headquarters in Berlin. Three days later, Clay, Weeks, and Zhukov met and agreed to the formation of the Berlin Kommandatura and for it to commence functioning on July 11. Although the French entered Berlin with US forces, they still had not been assigned a sector and did not join the Kommandatura until later in July.

The Allied Control Council held its first official meeting on Monday, July 30, in its headquarters in the US Sector. In the meantime, the Potsdam Conference had commenced just outside Berlin with Truman, Stalin, and Churchill in attendance. Before the conference was completed on August 2, 1945, Clement Attlee had succeeded Churchill as Prime Minister of Great Britain. The principal topics at Potsdam were Poland (as it had been at Yalta), the administration of occupied Germany, and how to proceed with the war against Imperial Japan. This last topic was resolved two weeks later when the Soviet invasion of Manchuria and the dropping of atomic bombs on the cities of Hiroshima and Nagasaki forced Japan to come to terms.

And finally on August 12, 1945, French forces in Berlin moved into their assigned sector after the British agreed to cede the Wedding and Reinickendorf boroughs.

The occupation of Germany was now well underway with each of the Four Powers supreme in their respective zones, pursuing separate, sometimes nationalistic, goals. The difficult task of formulating overall German policy was left to the Allied Control Council which could only enact such policy when there was unanimous agreement of the Four Powers. In Berlin, this policy and its problems were mirrored by the Four Powers Kommandatura which attempted to administer the city as a whole. The unity of the Four Powers in defeating Nazi Germany, which had already displayed strains at Yalta and Potsdam, soon disintegrated as their respective goals for Germany and post-war Europe clashed.

Soviet soldiers place road signs alongside those of the Americans they are replacing in the Leipzig area, 4 July 1945.

# Out of Leipzig...

By April of 1945, Winston Churchill's unease over Soviet intentions in the post-war world turned to alarm at Soviet moves to exclusively control developments in Poland. Churchill had long advocated that Allied armies should move as far into the projected Soviet Occupation Zone as possible to use the areas under their control as a bargaining chip to ensure Soviet compliance with earlier agreements. Having failed in his efforts to get US forces into Berlin ahead of the Red Army, he now told President Harry S Truman that, "the Allies ought not to retreat from their present positions to the occupational line until we are satisfied about Poland, and also about the temporary character of the Russian occupation of Germany."

Truman was sympathetic to Churchill's arguments, but was concerned that if the United States did not keep its pledged word on the occupation zones, the Soviet Union would not honor its promise to join the war against Japan. Truman decided to abide by the earlier agreements and hoped his actions would encourage Stalin to do likewise.

On June 14, Truman asked Stalin for free access to Berlin "as part of the withdrawal of [US] troops previously agreed to" and details of the land swap were worked out between Generals Clay and Zhukov on June 29. The US Army, which had already conducted a partial withdrawal in the Chemnitz (Karl Marx Stadt) area, envisioned a gradual pull back lasting until July 10. The Soviets, however, were anxious to have the Allied forces move out of the remaining 16,400 square miles* of the Soviet zone they still possessed as expeditiously as possible. This would ensure that the withdrawal would not be delayed and conceivably spill over into the time frame of the upcoming conference at Potsdam.

*This area contained roughly 8 million inhabitants and much undamaged industrial plant that the Soviets intended to dismantle and ship east.

Soviet forces enter Leipzig, 2 July 1945

(*Below*) Curious Berliners gather around a US 2nd Armored Division tank crew on the Hauptstrasse, 4 July 1945. (*Opposite right*) "Destruction?" pulls up to its Potsdamer Strasse guard post at the junction of the US and British Sectors of Berlin where its crew is assisted by a policeman and, apparently, a little boy. The sign facing the elevated train station reads: "The Red Army is free from any feeling of race hatred. It is free of such degrading feelings because it has been educated in the spirit of equality of rights of the races and the respect of the rights of other peoples—Stalin."

# ...and into Berlin

A quicker pace was agreed upon (see page 26) and the movement of the Red Army into the rest of their occupation zone proceeded uneventfully. The efforts of US and British forces to get into Berlin proved much more interesting.

Early in June, a reconnaissance party, formed to survey the site and set up accommodations for the US delegation at the Potsdam Conference, was only allowed to travel the 60 miles to Berlin after US officials hinted strongly that the entire conference might have to be postponed if the soldiers were not allowed to proceed with their job. Even then, a portion of the group had to be left behind at the insistance of the Soviets because of previously undiscussed transit restrictions imposed from Moscow.

On July 3, it was the turn of the US contingent of Berlin's occupation troops, the 2d Armored Division, to experience the "technical problems" that would plague Western access to Berlin for decades to

Soviet trucks leav'ng the US Sector piled high with loot.

come. Generals Clay and Zhukov had agreed that the division would use the Halle-Berlin *Autobahn* for its entry into the city, but when an advance column pulled up to the Elbe River's Dessau Bridge at the edge of Soviet occupied territory, it was halted by guards who stated that the bridge was unsafe. Elements of the division were then rerouted north to Helmstedt to get to the Magdeburg-Berlin *Autobahn*. At Helmstedt, though, they found themselves embroiled in a terrific traffic jam with the Berlin bound occupation forces of Great Britain. They had been routed south because their agreed upon access route was also blocked by Soviet guards at an "unsafe" bridge.

Once in Berlin, the US commander, Colonel Frank Howley, soon found that the Soviets were reluctant to leave the US Sector, were tearing down the newly posted US occupation proclamations, and were presenting various excuses as to why withdrawal had to be delayed. Howley believed the Soviets were simply stalling for time so they could continue stripping the area of anything of value. The US occupation forces, who had originally been instructed not to press disagreements to the point of dissension, were getting rather tired of the shenanigans. As Lieutenant Colonel John J. Maginnis later put it: "All of us were so fed up that we were ready to take on any kind of trouble the Russians might offer—almost welcome it."

With negotiations between the two sides going nowhere, Howley was ordered to take over the sector "without causing," according to Maginnis, "too much trouble doing it." Early on the morning of Thursday, July 5, the American flag was raised in each US Sector borough with fully armed guards posted at all key points. The Russians, being notoriously late risers, did not get around to protesting until about eleven o'clock and proceeded to post their own soldiers along side those of the US. The ritual of establishing double guard contingents went on for several days before the Soviets tired of sending troops back into the US sector.

(*Left*) Double guard contingents in the US Sector. (*Right*) Soviet soldier and German woman disagreeing over the ownership of a bicycle. (*Bottom*) Another woman caring for the grave of a German soldier, who was buried where he was killed, as Soviet troops pass alongside on their way out of the US Sector.

German refugees moving west, Bamberg, 13 July 1945.

TWO

# Road to Confrontation

*Whoever has Germany has Europe.* —Vladimir Ilyich Lenin

The geographical location of Germany in the middle of Europe, with its industrial base and its hard working people, has long been the key to the control of the continent. Since German unification in 1870, the other European powers had attempted to hold Germany in check by a series of alliances. The breakdown of the "balance of power" and other factors had led to World War I. Despite a tremendous loss of manpower and territory, Germany had been able to recover sufficiently within 20 years to conquer most of Europe before going down to defeat by the combined forces of the Soviet Union, Great Britain, and the United States. Under the proper conditions, who could assure that Germany could not rise again?

At Teheran in 1943, Roosevelt, Churchill, and Stalin all advocated some form of partition of Germany into three to five separate states. By the time of the Potsdam Conference in July 1945, the strategic goals of the war-time allies had changed. The Soviet Union had annexed portions of eastern Germany territory. Although the United States and Great Britain maintained these annexations could not be recognized until a German peace treaty was signed, they acknowledged that little could be changed by this *fait accompli.*

Although the Soviet Union had agreed to allow France to participate in the German occupation, Great Britain and the United States were not even consulted about the fact that Poland was also, in effect, granted status as an occupying power. The 10.7 million Germans residing in the territories annexed by Poland and the Soviet Union were forced from their homes with another 2. 9 million ethnic Germans expelled from Czechoslovakia. Most ended up in the US and British zones of occupation after suffering incredible hardships during their flight west. Nearly 2. 2 million died of starvation and exposure along the roads, as the fighting ran over them, and at the hands of vengeful Poles and Russians.[1] These refugees further aggravated the problem of feeding the German population which had traditionally received most of their foodstuffs from what was now the Soviet Zone of occupation and the territories now annexed by the Poles and the Soviets.

US equipped troops of the French First Army advance cautiously into the town of Colmar, France, 2 February 1945.

The French were the one power whose policy from 1945 to 1948 remained constant for German partition. Based on its experience of three wars in the previous 70 years, France continued to fear a potential resurgent Germany even after the threat of a Communist Europe became the greater danger. The policies of the United States and Great Britain on one side and the Soviet Union on the other changed gradually (or radically depending on one's viewpoint) to advocating a unified German state, however, only on the condition that such unified state be aligned in their respective camps. Because neither side could permit the other to gain such an advantage, the partitioning of Germany became inevitable, but not as proposed by any of the wartime plans.

The Soviet Communists, being good students of Lenin, set out to insure that, if possible, Germany would eventually be a Communist state. Their theorists did not believe this would be immediately possible during the occupation period, but they believed that the United States and Great Britain would not support a long occupation. When the United States and Great Britain pulled out, the Communists believed they would come to power, perhaps in a coalition with the Socialists, but as the dominant force with the powerful armies of the Soviet Union on Germany's eastern borders exerting the necessary pressure.[2]

The Communists had good reason to believe they would be successful in Germany. Prior to 1933, the German Socialist party (SPD) and the German Communist Party (KPD) had been two of the largest political parties in Germany. But how could the two worker's parties, whose views on the proper methods of attaining socialist goals were so

Karl Liebknecht orating at the graves of followers killed during a failed coup attempt in January 1919. Several days after this photo was taken, he and colleague, Rosa Luxemburg, were murdered.

different, possibly coexist, much less unite?

Socialism in Germany can be traced to the Revolution of 1848 and the teaching and writings of Karl Marx and Friedrich Engels. In 1863, Ferdinand Lassale founded the first German worker's political party, forerunner of the SPD. Because this party basically came to support Bismarck's policies, a dissident faction led by August Bebel and Wilhelm Liebknecht formed a rival party in 1869. Persecution by German police and courts brought the two rival factions together in 1875 when the unified SPD was born.

Prior to 1914, the SPD was outlawed at various times, but gradually gained strength and by 1912 was the largest single party in the German *Reichstag*. Although the SPD proclaimed its belief in Marxist revolution, a majority faction came to believe and advocate "social democracy" and attainment of power by the electoral ballot. When the majority of the Socialists, if somewhat reluctantly, supported the war credits of the German Imperialist government in 1914, a minority led by Karl Liebknecht, the son of Wilhelm Liebknecht, and Rosa Luxemburg broke party discipline and voted no. In 1916, Liebknecht and Luxemburg were expelled from the SPD and formed the Spartacus League and the Independent Social Democratic Party (USPD).

In December 1918, one month after the armistice ending World War I, Liebknecht and Luxemburg withdrew from the USPD and formed the KPD. With the German capitulation in November 1918 and the Kaiser's abdication in December 1918, the majority SPD, as the leading party in the *Reichstag,* inherited the German government. During the period from December 1918 to June 1919, Germany was rocked by political strikes and armed insurrections fomented by the Communist policy of civil war. In Berlin, the Communists attempted to overthrow the SPD government which was forced to call for military support. The revolt was brutally put down. Liebknecht and Luxemburg were murdered. Another leader, Wilhelm Pieck, was arrested but later released.

With the death of its two principal leaders, the KPD split again over policy and tactics, but eventually its left wing reorganized under Ernst Thaelmann, the leader of the abortive Communist uprising in Hamburg in 1923. Other, more conservative elements drifted back to the SPD. During the entire history of the German Weimar Republic, the major aim of the KPD was to destroy the SPD. Stalin set the policy on February 5, 1925, when he wrote in *Die Rote Fahne*, the KPD newspaper:

> It is most essential for the German Communist Party to represent the majority of the working class and it is, therefore, the prime task of German Communists to smash the Social Democratic Party and to reduce it to an insignificant minority. . . . If there are within the working class two rival parties of equal strength then the lasting and firm triumph of the revolution, even under the most favorable conditions, is impossible.[3]

After the *Reichstag* fire in February 1933, which Hitler pinned on the Communists, the KPD and the SPD were banned. Leading Communists and Socialists were swept into concentration camps or forced to flee to other parts of Europe. Thaelmann perished in a German concentration camp in 1944, Pieck and Walter Ulbricht eventually made their way to the Soviet Union, and a young Communist organizer, named Erich Honecker, was thrown into Bran-

Walter Ulbricht (*left*) and Wilhelm Pieck circa 1948.

denburg prison where he remained until freed by Soviet troops in 1945. From 1933 to 1945, the "Popular Front" and later "National Front" strategies became Communist doctrine. These strategies basically called for the unification of all "anti-Fascists" to defeat the Nazis and the Fascists.

In 1939, the KPD held its last party congress before World War II in Bern, Switzerland. The final resolution adopted was "that a unified revolutionary party of the German working class must be organized" and both the Communists and Social Democrats were called upon "to organize the future unity party of the German working class."[4] Of course, the KPD, without saying, wanted this unity on their terms and under their leadership. The SPD remained cool to any such unification on KPD terms.

During the closing days of World War II, on Monday, April 30, 1945, ten German Communists led by Ulbricht and including Wolfgang Leonhard* were transported from the Soviet Union by airplane to join Zhukov's army just outside Berlin. Another ten German Communists under Anton Ackermann were detailed to Marshall Konev's armies then approaching Dresden. A third group was detailed to the Soviet armies in Mecklenburg. Each of these groups had the mission of setting up local German government in their areas as soon as the fighting stopped. The Ulbricht group was responsible for Berlin and the surrounding areas.

On Wednesday, May 2, 1945, the very day of Berlin's surrender, the Ulbricht group, accompanied by Soviet Army political officers, entered Berlin. Each group member was detailed to one or two Berlin boroughs to assist the Soviet commanders and to lay the groundwork for a local German administration. Several days later, Ulbricht directed the installation of local German mayors and other officials for all Berlin boroughs. Ulbricht ordered "anti-Fascist bourgeois" be installed as mayors in all districts other than the worker's boroughs of Wedding, Neukoelln, Friedrichshain, and Lichtenberg. In the other boroughs, a Communist was selected to be first deputy mayor. In addition, Communists were installed as heads of education and the police in each district. Ulbricht stated: "It is crystal clear: It must appear democratic, but we must have all the strings in our hands."[5]

By mid-May 1945, a German language radio station had been set up under Communist control and a city-wide government was installed. Dr. Arthur Werner, an independent "anti-Fascist" was named Lord Mayor of Berlin, but Karl Maron, a veteran German Communist and one of the Ulbricht group, was named as First Deputy Lord Mayor. Of

Bread being distributed from a trailer in the residential Zehlendorf section of Berlin. The ration was two-thirds of a pound per day for employed persons and one-half pound for the unemployed.

*Evidence of the Soviet Union's plans for Germany after World War II came to light in the early 1950s with the publication of Wolfgang Leonhard *Die Revolution Entlaesst Ihre Kinder*. Leonhard, the son of a German Communist mother, grew up in the Soviet Union in the 1930s and 1940s, returned to Germany in 1945, and defected to Yugoslavia in 1948. His first hand account gives us insight on Communist plans and policy during the 1945-48 period.

(*Below*) Under the direction of Soviet soldiers, civilians clear rubble away from the Unter den Linden 4 May 1945. (*Left*) Berlin woman cooking on a makeshift stove.

the 18 city officials named, nine were former KPD members.

In early June 1945, Pieck arrived from Moscow with instructions. There would be no unified Socialist party. The KPD and the SPD would be reorganized as separate parties. At least two "bourgeois center" political parties would be formed and all political parties would form an "Anti-Fascist Democratic Bloc." A land reform would be administered during the summer of 1945 in the Soviet occupation zone.[6] Ulbricht and Pieck also tasked Honecker to form the Free German Youth (FDJ), a group that would later form the vanguard of Communist mob actions.[7]

On June 10, 1945, Zhukov issued Soviet Military Order No. 2 which permitted the organization of "anti-Fascist democratic" political parties at a time when the United States, Great Britain and France had prohibited all political activity in their own occupation zones. The very next day, June 11, the KPD issued its organization proclamation and on June 15 the SPD was formed, even though most of its elected leaders were still in exile in England. This was followed by the formation of the Christian Democratic Union (CDU) and the German Liberal Party (LPD).

As it pertains to Berlin, all of these actions had been instituted before the Americans, British, and French arrived in Berlin during the first week of July 1945. Even though the Soviet Union knew and had accepted in 1944 that

General Lucius D. Clay

Berlin was to be jointly governed by all occupation powers, they and their German Communist allies had unilaterally installed a pro-Soviet city government. On Wednesday, July 11, 1945, at the first meeting of the Berlin Kommandatura, all previous appointments and ordinances approved by the Soviet Army were unanimously agreed upon. It is evident the Western members of the Kommandatura did not fully understand the significance of this agreement made in the flush of victory celebrations and the spirit of Allied cooperation. They soon learned to regret their hasty decision.

The first military governors of occupied Germany were the three victorious Allied combat commanders, Zhukov, Montgomery, and Eisenhower who all soon left the scene completely or delegated the day to day functions to deputies.

The principal Soviet player at the Allied Control Council in Berlin soon became General Vassily Sokolovsky. The victor of Smolensk was a former school teacher who had joined the Red Army during the civil war of 1918-20 and rose rapidly through the ranks to serve as Zhukov's deputy. Sokolovsky was very intelligent, capable, and "one who could quote the Bible frequently and accurately"[8], a rather unique trait for a dedicated Communist officer. General Sir Brian Robertson represented Great Britain. Robertson is described as "a brilliant officer, who could look back at both a successful army and international business career."[9] The French member was General Pierre Koenig, who gained fame as a brigade commander in Libya in 1942 for the Free France movement[10] and later became one of General Charles de Gaulle's principal lieutenants during the liberation of France.

The US representative was General Lucius D. Clay. Clay was the son of a former US senator from Georgia, a distant relative to Henry Clay, "the great compromiser," and among his close friends was James Byrnes, Truman's Secretary of State from 1945 to 1947. Although Clay had political connections, he was not a political general, but a professional officer and engineer. He graduated from West Point in 1918 and served in a variety of engineer officer assignments between the wars. Soon after Pearl Harbor, he, as many of his classmates who had languished for 20 years in the peacetime army, was rapidly promoted to brigadier general and became Director of Materiel of the Armed Service Forces. Later he was appointed as Byrnes' deputy at the Of-

The Kaiser Wilhelm Memorial Church circa 1946.

fice of War Mobilization and Reconversion. Eisenhower, with whom Clay had served in the Philippines, asked for him when the supply bottleneck at Cherbourg, France caused a major problem. Clay quickly resolved it.

Although Clay constantly strove for a combat command, his superiors consistently desired to use his talents in other areas. He was described as "a brilliant administrator and leader, a sparkling, always turned up dynamo who worked incredibly long hours, with a retentive mind and the knack of extracting the essence of a memo at a glance." On the minus side, "he was considered unyielding when opposed and—sometimes to his detriment—given to trigger quick decisions."[11]

When Eisenhower returned to Washington in November 1945, he was succeeded by General Joseph T. McNarney. Eisenhower had delegated responsibility for military government to Clay, but McNarney, who displayed little interest in German affairs, insisted on command prerogatives.[12] Clay requested relief and retirement twice during 1946. However, after visits to Germany by Walter Bedell Smith, then US Ambassador to the Soviet Union and Eisenhower's wartime Chief of Staff, and Eisenhower, then Army Chief of Staff, it was decided McNarney would leave and Clay would get the title along with the responsibilities he had been performing for almost two years. On March 15, 1947, Clay was named Military Governor and US Commander in Chief in Europe. From then until his departure in May 1949, he was America's *proconsul* in Europe with almost unlimited authority.

Clay was able to exercise this authority because of a power vacuum in Washington. In theory, the State Department was supposed to develop American policy toward Germany and the Department of the Army was supposed to carry it out. In practice, the two departments were often unwilling or unable to make a firm decision so Clay filled in and made them "Like General MacArthur, America's *proconsul* in Japan, Clay was nearly an independent sovereign in relation to the State Department, which could negotiate with him but was never able to issue orders to him."[13] Clay's admirers commended him for his calm assurance, the marked absence of anxiety, the skill and decisiveness with which he acted. His critics saw him as an imperious and impulsive figure whose overbearing self-confidence led him to make snap decisions and tended to create a climate uncongenial to negotiations.[14]

# Wasteland

The extent of destruction in Berlin was enormous. The previous year and a half of Allied bombing and final two-week battle for the city had resulted in whole districts being flattened. Only a few areas in the city had even periodic electric power and sewers dumped raw sewage directly into Berlin's water system. As one American officer put it: "There was no drinking of water without boiling—and no fuel to boil it." Dysentery was killing 65 out of every 100 newborns, with typhoid and diphtheria rapidly increasing among the city's weakened population.

Berlin's physical infrastructure was almost totally destroyed and, with the rest of Germany nearly as bad off and unable to offer any help, little could be done to put the city back in order. Even two months after the fighting had ended, one of the first American's into the city, Colonel H. G. Sheen, reported that: "The bomb damage in the heart of the city is difficult to describe. In certain areas the stench of unburied dead is almost overpowering. From Tempelhof to the Wilhelmsstrasse not one undamaged building is standing; roofs, floors, and windows are gone, and in many cases the fragments of only one or two walls are standing. Many of the streets remain passable, but rubble covers the sidewalks and large numbers of side streets are still blocked off because of bomb craters and debris."

Lieutenant Colonel John J. Maginnis, who was put in charge of the boroughs of Schöneberg and Friedenau, wondered: "Where did the thousands of people who were abroad in the daytime go at night? In a block of ruined buildings, where it did not seem possible that there was any habitation at all, there might be several hundred people living in cellars, old bunkers, or a room that had somehow been spared. I was becoming accustomed to hearing the term 'ruin dwellers'."

(*Top*) The *Reichstag* and (*bottom*) huge portraits of Stalin and his generals decorating central Berlin, July 1945. The dried remains of flowers from an earlier ceremony can be seen at the base of Stalin's monument.

(*Top*) The Court of Honor in the Chancellery complex near the site where Hitler's burned corpse was found and (*bottom*) the Brandenburg Gate, July 1945.

(*Top*) Anhalter railroad station in operation after extensive cleanup and repair.
(*Bottom*) Wreckage of the Long Bridge and the Koepenick City Hall in the Soviet Sector.

*(Top)* An 88mm antitank gun wrecked during the fighting on Alexander Platz. *(Bottom)* Temporary bridge replacing the Herkulesbrücke over the Landwehr Canal.

(*Top*)Wreckage of the Mühlendamm Bridge. (*Bottom*) St. Hedwigs Cathedral.

(*Top*) Children playing on a destroyed half-track on Savigny Platz. (*Bottom*) Mass inoculations saved Berlin from epidemics during the precarious post-war days.

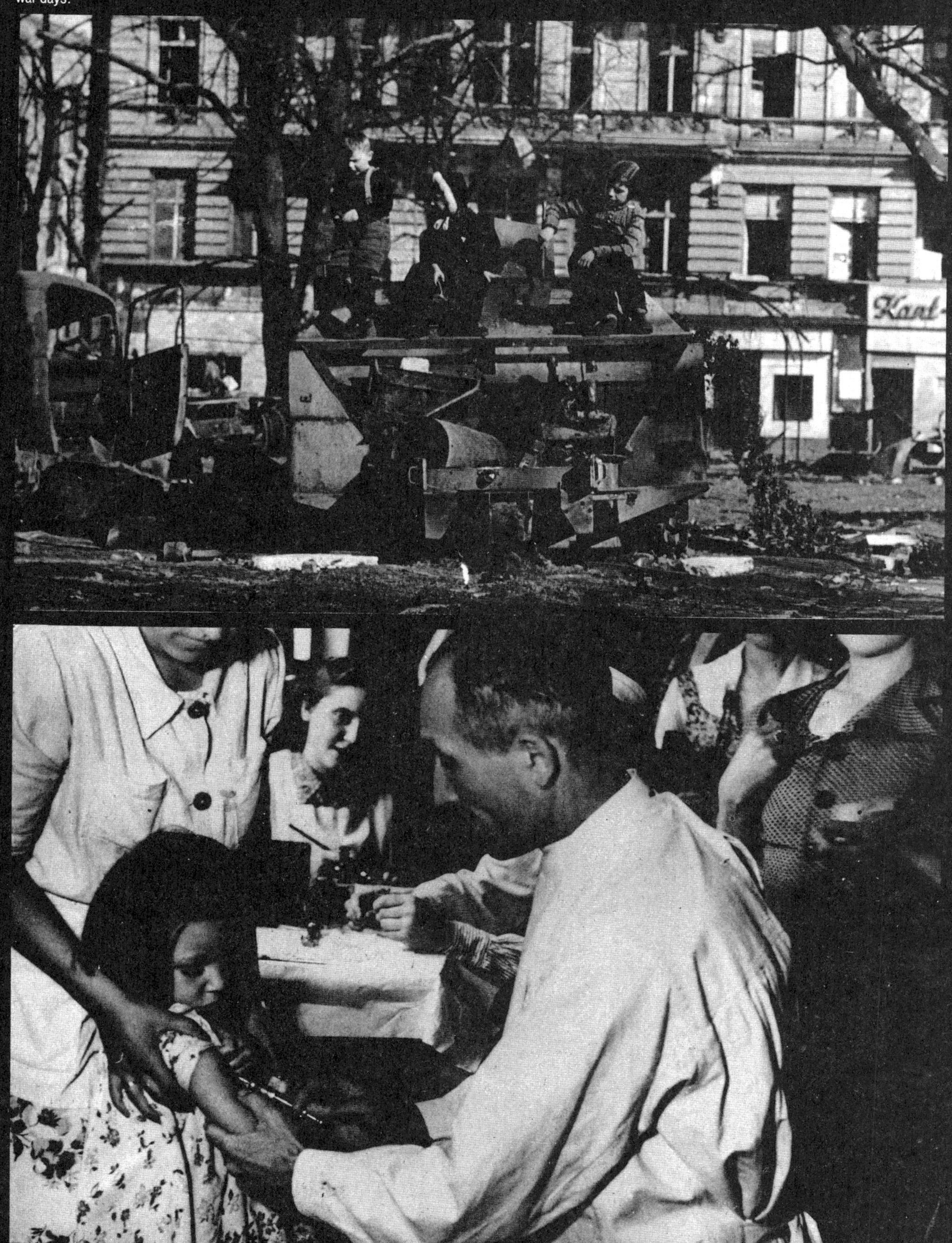

German farm woman cutting potato seeds in half before planting, May 1946.

It appears the Soviets, British, and Americans were willing almost immediately to begin setting up centralized German economic bodies, such as transportation and communication, but the French were adamantly opposed. France had not participated in the Potsdam Conference of July-August 1945, but soon thereafter advised the United States, Great Britain, and the Soviet Union that they could not accept a centralized German administration, German economic unity or readmission of German political parties. In late August 1945, de Gaulle visited Truman in Washington and stated the Rhineland must be separated from Germany and the Ruhr internationalized.[15]

On September 22, 1945, at the Allied Control Council, the British proposed a central statistical agency be established which the French vetoed because "the danger of such an organization as a means of mobilizing." The French also opposed British-US-Soviet plans for a central transportation department to operate the railroads and a central communications department to operate the postal, telephone, and telegraph services. On October 9, 1945, the French objected to a central finance agency and a few weeks later even opposed an all-German federation of trade unions because "trade unions are political structures."[16]

Both the British and US military governors were taken aback by the French positions, and Clay appealed to the State Department to apply political pressure on Paris. However, the State Department feared the weak French government would fall and the Communists, the largest French political party, would come to power. Clay then attempted to get the British and the Soviets to proceed on a tripartite basis without the French, but first the British and then the Soviets turned him down on the basis of the Potsdam Agreements which required agreements for centralized German government agencies must be negotiated for all four zones.

Although the Soviets insinuated on several occasions that the French may have been given the "spoiler" role by the British and the Americans, it became apparent that the Soviets, now aware of the French position, used it to hide their own opposition to British-US centralized economic proposals. This became especially apparent on the currency reform proposals which the French and the British finally agreed to only to have the Soviets delay and stall implementation.

The failure to centralize economic agencies hurt the Soviet Zone the least. Although all four zones were economically unable to support themselves individually, the Soviet Zone came the closest to self-sufficiency, especially in the critical area of food production which was the main concern from 1945 through 1947. By the end of this period, the United States and Great Britain had spent 1.5 billion of

their taxpayer dollars on food costs and had been unable to raise the German food rations in their zones above one-half the recommended diet.[17]

The principal area of dispute between the United States, Great Britain, and the Soviet Union during the first year of occupation arose over reparations. At Yalta, the Soviets had put forward a figure of 20 billion dollars which should be extracted from Germany. Half of this would be going to the Soviet Union. Reparations would be in the form of removal of heavy industry, in-kind payments from German current production, and German labor. The British agreed reparations should be obtained, but categorically refused to be tied to a dollar figure. The United States, acting as arbitrator, finally agreed that a ten billion dollar figure in reparations to the Soviet Union would serve "as a basis for discussions."[18]

At Potsdam, however, Truman emphasized that the United States "could not agree to reparations if parts of Germany are given away" (referring to that portion of Germany given to Poland by the Soviet Union).[19] It was feared

(*Top*) The remains of a synthetic oil and gas plant at Marl overrun by the US 75th Division. (*Bottom*) a reuined half-track factory at Bad Oeynhausen.

Ten mark banknote issued in all four occupation zones and Berlin.

the United States would "finance" the payment of reparations by Germany to the Soviet Union because the United States would be forced to feed and support whatever the German population had left after the Soviets extracted their reparations. The settlement finally worked out at Potsdam called for each power to receive reparations from their respective zone. In addition, the United States and Great Britain agreed to provide 10 percent of industrial equipment "unnecessary for the German peace economy" for transfer to the Soviet Union and an additional 15 percent of such equipment would be supplied in exchange for food, coal, and other commodities.[20] When the United States complained that the Soviets had already dismantled and carried off machinery, industrial plants, and livestock before any inventory could be taken, the Soviets countered that the Americans had taken 10,000 loaded railroad cars from the Soviet Zone before withdrawing in June 1945.[21]

A Level of Industry Committee was established to determine production and consumption ceilings for a German peacetime economy, but the Four Powers could not agree on what these figures should be. US policy required that reparations would not come from current German production until Germany had paid for any imports with exports. Without a centralized export-import agency, reparations from current production were difficult to determine. The Soviet Union, which had suffered the greatest destruction, attempted to extract the largest amount of reparations possible and, therefore, their level of industry figures for Germany were consistently the lowest.

Of the three major powers, the British could least afford to finance the German occupation, and desired to have a higher level of industry so that the German economy could be self-supporting and the least costly to the British taxpayer still reeling from wartime debt. The United States generally supported the British because the US realized it would obtain little, if any, reparations from Germany. It attempted to arbitrate between the low Soviet figures and the high British levels. The Soviets, ever suspicious, accused the British and Americans of deliberately underestimating the value of German exports, especially coal from the Ruhr. Although the French had blocked efforts to establish unified administrative agencies, it was the Soviets who blocked a quadripartite export-import plan on the basis that the question of reparations must first be settled.[22]

When Clay obtained no cooperation on the establishment of a quadripartite export-import program, it became clear that the mission of putting the US Zone on a self-supporting basis was doomed to failure. If the treatment of Germany as an economic whole, as prescribed by the Potsdam Agreement, could not be accomplished, it would particularly effect the US Zone which had no raw materials, and would create a continuing financial liability for the United States.

The unsettled reparation issue, plus the obvious need for a currency reform, provided negative incentives for Germans to produce. On the other hand, the Soviets using

(*Bottom*) The hundreds of informal exchange centers were also hotbeds of black market activity. Note shell craters in the background.

To combat the black market, OMGUS set up, in 1946-47, a barter market system. American personal brought items of value such as food, cigarettes and other goods to an appraising room where the material was appraised by experts in terms of barter units. The Germans, in turn, brought furs, cameras, linens, etc. to another appraising room where this material was similarly appraised. Credit slips issued by appraisers to both Americans and Germans were then taken to a cashier who issued Barter Unit certificates to be exchanged for goods.

much harsher methods made certain their goals in industry and on the farms were met in their zone during the first occupation year.[23] The British had much the same problem as the Americans. It became apparent that the United States and the British urgently needed economic unification, while the Soviets could wait while exploiting their zone. The delay also served the Communists' political goals in Germany.

By comparison, in 1946 the Soviet Zone with an almost self-supporting agricultural base and a smaller population appeared to be doing much better under centralized state operated economic agencies than the British or US Zones. The apparent successes of a planned state-operated economy were constantly publicized by the Communist press in the Soviet Zone.

In May 1946, when several attempts in the Allied Control Council had failed at gaining any progress in treating Germany as an economic unit, Clay ordered a halt in dismantling and began a campaign to merge the US and British Zones.

The problem of a currency reform for Germany became more acute as the occupation progressed and eventually became the issue that effectively split Germany although the strategic and political reasons for division were, in reality, more decisive. The need for a currency reform was evident to American economists even before the war ended, but there was a reluctance to tackle the problem because of interpretations of JCS 1067, the original US directive to the Office of Military Government, United States (OMGUS). This directive instructed Americans not to take responsibility for German affairs, except to the minimum necessary for purely military reasons.[24]

In August 1945, OMGUS reported:

> For the immediate future the two overwhelming dominant factors in the inflationary potential in Germany are the shortage of goods and the heavy excess of purchasing power in the hands of the people. These two factors are a direct result of the Nazi defeat and their wartime policies.
>
> Stability might be achieved and inflation avoided even with a reduced living standard but only if purchasing power were likewise reduced. Yet purchasing power in Germany today vastly exceeds the volume of goods now or foreseeably available for consumption. Germany ended the war with a grossly inflated volume of currency in circulation: at least twice the value of the gross national product available for civilian consumption and several times the value of today's output. In addition, six years of full employment and relatively high level of earnings associated with war production, coupled with severe wartime restrictions on the output of civilian goods, resulted in a great increase of civilian holdings of liquid savings. The swollen national debt, of uncertain value, forms the basis of the assets of most German financial and many industrial institutions.[25]

This critical financial situation was further aggravated by Allied occupation policies. As the war ended, the United States issued Allied Occupation currency and gave a set of the plates to the Soviet Union so that the same currency would be used throughout occupied Germany along with the existing German *Reichsmarks.* The Soviets proceeded to print an unknown large amount of currency to pay their troops, some of whom had not been paid for years, and to buy up consumer goods and equipment. US occupation personnel also became involved in black market activities and it is estimated that US military and civilian occupation personnel sent $200 million to the United States in excess of what they were paid before OMGUS got control of the situation.[26] The currency situation got progressively worse as the occupation continued. Because production and the machinery for production decreased due to wartime destruction and post-war dismantling, more and more currency was chasing fewer and fewer goods. The only things most German civilians could purchase with their *Reichsmarks* were some rationed foodstuffs and, because the civilian population did not trust the currency, anything of value or potential value was hoarded or only used to barter for needed goods and services. What had been "Hitler money" in 1945 gradually became associated with the failure of occupying authorities to improve economic conditions.[27]

By the fall of 1945, Manual Gottlieb, an OMGUS Finance Division economist, developed a rudimentary currency conversion proposal and submitted it to the Allied Control Council for discussion. This was little more than a reevaluation and only intended as a possible interim measure. Early in 1946, the US government sent a group of experts, led by German-born economists Gerhard Colm and Ray Goldsmith, to Germany to develop a more complete plan. Working closely with Joseph M. Dodge, then Clay's financial advisor, a comprehensive currency reform proposal was developed and formally proposed to the Allied Control Council in August 1946 as the Colm-Dodge-Goldsmith Plan.[28]

At first, Four-Power discussion gave promise of rapid agreement. After overcoming initial objections by the British and the French, the early apparent Soviet agreements to currency reform changed to stalling tactics.

> The issue which seemed to cause the greatest difficulty and which eventually led to the collapse of the Four-Power negotiations, was the physical control over the printing of a new currency. Germany's national printing plant, the Staatsdruckerei, was located in the American Sector of Berlin, just over the border from the Soviet Sector. Despite our offer to make it into a neutral area under Four-Power control, the Soviets refused to agree that it should be the sole source of the new currency. They insisted on printing their Zone's share in a plant under their own control in Leipzig.[29]

Because of their earlier experience with the Allied occupation currency plates, OMGUS officials were determined to avoid a similar situation. After the discussions at the Allied Control Council broke off, preparations were made for a separate currency reform. The British, although they had reservations about some of the specifics of the US plan, pushed for a separate Anglo-US currency reform. If the French could be persuaded, they would be included. The United States, recognizing a separate currency reform would split Germany and the onus for the split would fall on the Western powers, hesitated.[30]

Based on rumors and intelligence information that the Soviets were planning a separate currency reform of their own, contingency plans had to be made. In the fall of 1947, an order for the printing of new currency for Germany was placed with the US Treasury Department.[31]

## Cleanup

Only one in five of Berlin's million and a half dwellings remained undamaged. A fantastic amount of rubble was generated by the last two years of war and the Soviet occupation forces put large numbers of Germans, mostly women, to work on clearing the debris. Every woman was compelled to put in one day per week on cleanup operations. If they had any connections to the Nazi Party, the requirement jumped to six days a week.

Little could be done about carting away the mountains of rubble, so the *Trümmerfrauen*, or rubble women would usually either fling the debris into destroyed buildings and shell craters or pile it into unobtrusive, if not entirely out of the way, stacks. The women often found rotting corpses in the smashed buildings, sometimes singly, sometimes in large numbers. Even today, remains are still being recovered. Making matters worse was the fact that Berlin's once lovely canals had become stagnant and polluted with raw sewage making them a breeding ground for literally billions of flies and mosquitoes.

(*Top*) Women removing debris from the Berlinerstrasse and passing it back into the ruins by bucket. (*Bottom*) Clean up work on Preussenstrasse in the Charlottenburg District.

(*Top*) Human chains passing rubble from the street. (*Bottom*) Clean up and salvage work at the Schöneberg City Hall in the US Sector.

(*Top*) Demolition of dangerous ruins on the Karl Marx Strasse. (*Bottom*) A makeshift conveyor belt being used during cleanup on Hagelberger Strasse.

(*Below*) With very little motor transport and almost no horses, workers detailed to repair salvagable buildings must push and pull large wagons of construction materials from site to site. (*Opposite top*) Two of the most commonly seen types of carts on the Hauptstrasse. Note the rows of neatly stacked bricks across the street. (*Opposite bottom*) Huge queues of people patiently waiting for buses was a common site. Here, women and children with carts pass about 350 would-be riders in a block-long line.

# Transport

Soviet forces had confiscated most of the surviving motor vehicles in Berlin and the few that remained in civilian hands received no gasoline unless they performed some function sanctioned by one of the occupying powers such as the transportation of food or coal. Tires, batteries, motor oil, and engine parts were extremely hard to come by. As late as October 1945, the entire US Sector had only 3,748 operable vehicles of which 1,956 (including 200 army trucks released by the US element of the Control Council) were allotted to essential services.* There were, however, an additional 509 vehicles that could be made to run again if engine parts could be found.

Public transportation in Berlin was a shambles. US forces entering the city found that only 37, of what had once been roughly a thousand city buses, were running and the situation hardly improved by year's end. Many streetcar lines were in operation, but it was not unusual to find steam engines pulling the cars as part of the effort to hold down the usage of electricity. The *U-bahn* (subway system) was, and would continue to be, the most efficient means of transportation in the city even though only about one tenth of its cars were usable.

*Swelled by displaced persons and German refugees from the east, the US Sector's population had topped 900,000 in October making an average of roughly one vehicle per 240 people.

(*Below*) A KPD office. (*Opposite top*) Election propaganda for the 20 October 1946 vote, for City Assembly offices, Prenzlauer District, Soviet Sector. Note the Russian language street sign. (*Opposite bottom*) Announcement of election results. District representative Arthur Pieck (son of Wilhelm) is third from left with Lord Mayor Dr. Werner at his left.

As noted earlier, the Soviets permitted political activity almost immediately after the cessation of hostilities, gave the Communist Party a head start and strong support, split the opposition by authorizing two "bourgeois" political parties, and required all political parties in the Soviet Zone to join an "anti-Fascist" bloc led by the Communist KPD. At first, the Communists seemed uncertain about what policy to follow in their relationship with the Socialist SPD—whether to advocate unification of the two worker's parties or not.

The SPD national leaders were still in London awaiting permission to return to Germany when the SPD was permitted to reorganize in the Soviet Zone and Berlin. There were two factions in this newly reorganized SPD; one group favored the formation of a new party based on the principles of the British Labor Party. A second group, headed by Otto Grotewohl, favored organization of a unified worker's party and had contacted the Communist KPD with this proposal. From June 1945 to October 1945, the KPD, while not shutting the door completely to unification with the SPD, retained a reserved wait and see attitude.

Strangely, it was the first post-war elections in neighboring Austria in November 1945, which proved the determining factor. Prior to the Austrian elections, the Austrian Communists had predicted they would win as many seats as the Socialists. However, the election results proved to be a disaster for the Austrian Communists, who like their German comrades had become closely identified with the Soviet Army which had raped, looted, and terrorized the civilian populace. The Austrian Peoples Party won 85 seats, the Social Democrats 76, and the Communists only four. If there had been any doubts in the KPD concerning the necessity for unification with the SPD, they vanished overnight.[32]

From November 1945 until April 1946, when the KPD forced through the merger with the SPD in the Soviet Zone of Germany, the Communists actively campaigned for unification. At first the Communists used propaganda and political pressure. However, when the SPD still hesitated, the Communists resorted to physical pressure in the form of arrests by Soviet military authorities.

In January 1946, an SPD party conference was held in Frankfurt/Main in the US Zone and the party members overwhelmingly rejected unification with the KPD. The SPD complained of Soviet pressure on SPD functionaries in the Soviet Zone, but the decisions of the SPD conference were banned from publication or even oral communication in the Soviet Zone.[33]

On March 31, 1946, a referendum on the merger was held by the SPD rank and file in the three Western sectors of Berlin and the proposed unification of the SPD with the Communist KPD was overwhelmingly defeated. The referendum was banned in the Soviet Sector of Berlin by the Soviet military authorities.

Regardless, on April 21, 1946, the KPD and a renegade faction of the SPD led by Otto Grotewohl merged in the Soviet Zone to form the Socialist Unity Party of Germany (SED). Although nominally the former Social Democrats shared power for a short time, the SED was controlled by the Communists led by Ulbricht and Pieck. The SED became a classical Communist party organization for controlling the state and government which it does today in East Germany.

The SPD expelled Grotewohl and his followers and was

permitted to continue as an independent party in Berlin. Pieck immediately labelled the SPD-Berlin a "sickman's club" and a "joke," but the joke proved to be on Pieck.

During the fall of 1946, the first local elections were held in the Soviet Zone. The SED, in spite of all its support by Soviet military authorities, control of the press and radio, and other incentives, was not able to gain a clear majority. In Berlin, where the SED had to compete with the SPD and other parties in a free election supervised by the four occupying powers, the SED suffered an overwhelming defeat. More than 92 percent of the eligible voters went to the polls with the SPD-Berlin capturing 48.7 percent of the vote, the CDU 22.2 percent, the SED 19.8 percent, and the LDP 9.3 percent. This resulted in the Berlin City Assembly consisting of 130 seats to have the following make-up: SPD 63, CDU 29, SED 26, and LDP 12.

Although the 1946 Berlin election should have resulted in the wholesale replacement of the Communist functionaries installed by the Soviet military authorities before the US, British, and French forces arrived, such was not the case. The Soviets used stalling tactics and their veto power in the Berlin Kommandatura when the City Assembly attempted to make appointments under the new Berlin constitution which had been approved by the four occupying powers prior to the election. Under the Berlin constitution, the City Assembly (legislative body) elects the Lord Mayor and the Magistrat (executive body). However, under Article 36 of the constitution, there was a stipulation that all legislative enactments and instructions of the Magistrat, and the appointment and discharge of leading officials required the sanction (approval by unanimous vote) of the Allied Kommandatura to become effective.

As a result of the October 1946 elections, the Berlin City Assembly elected Otto Ostrowski (SPD) as Lord Mayor

and 17 others to the Magistrat to administer the various departments of city government. After continued delay and stalling by the Soviets, all but two of the Magistrat members finally received Kommandatura approval. However, the Soviets used Article 36 to prevent the new Magistrat members from removing deputies and other leading officials in their departments without Kommandatura approval. This meant that the new department heads were forced to retain many of the Communist officials originally installed by the Soviets in May-June 1945 and, naturally, these officials owed no allegiance to the new city administration.

Ostrowski, recognizing the city administration could not function under these conditions, entered into negotiations in February 1947 with the SED without the approval of SPD-Berlin leaders. When the SPD-Berlin leaders learned of Ostrowski's dealings they brought the matter before the City Assembly which overwhelmingly disavowed Ostrowski and forced him to resign. The City Assembly then elected Ernst Reuter (SPD) as Lord Mayor on June 27, 1947, and Reuter was promptly vetoed by the Soviets because of Reuter's anti-Communist views. Luise Schroeder (SPD), who had been appointed Acting Lord Mayor upon Ostrowski's resignation, then continued on in that capacity until December 1948, when new elections were held. By this time, the city had been split and Reuter was unanimously elected Lord Mayor.

Reuter, who became the spiritual leader of Berlin during the Blockade, had an interesting and unusual past. He had served in the German Army in World War I and had been taken prisoner by the Russians in 1916. He joined the Volga German community after the Bolshevik revolution and returned to Germany a Communist in 1919. He became disgusted with the stark crudities of Communism, joined the SPD, and became mayor of Magdeburg and a member of the pre-1933 German Reichstag. He was arrested by the Nazis in 1933, released in 1934, and immigrated to Turkey where he worked as a school teacher and an official in the Ministry of Economics.

Reuter did not arrive back in Germany and Berlin until January 1947, but almost immediately he was accepted as the outstanding SPD leader in Berlin. This galled Franz Neumann, who until Reuter's arrival, had been the SPD-Berlin leader. It was Neumann who had stood up to the

Communist threats in 1945-46 and had fought for the independence of the SPD when the Communists and the Soviet military had attempted to merge it out of existence. It was Neuman who had secured the backing for the SPD referendum in the three Western Sectors of Berlin on March 31, 1946, which had overwhelmingly demonstrated the opposition of the SPD in Berlin to fusion with the KPD.

Neumann considered himself to be Kurt Schumacher's deputy in Berlin. Schumacher was the acknowledged leader of the SPD in the US and British Zones. However, Neumann's fiery radicalism was offset by the experience and quiet leadership of Reuter, "the little man in the beret." Willy Brandt, then a young disciple of Reuter, described him as "the prototype of a humanist, who, never compromised in the pursuit of his ideals, also never forgets that all human toil is ephemeral."[34] When the City Assembly elected Reuter Lord Mayor of Berlin on June 24, 1947,

Dr. Kurt Schumacher, national SPD leader, in Berlin urging support of SPD candidates in the October 20 elections. (*Top to Bottom*) Franz Neumann, Ferdinand Friedensburg and Konrad Adenauer.

the Soviets vetoed him and claimed he had called the Soveit Union "a nation of slaves" and an "ant-heap of a state."[35]

Political activity in the US and British Zones of Germany started later than in the Soviet Zone and without the sponsorship of any particular party as the Soviets did with the KPD. By September 1945, all applicants had been licensed except former Nazis to form political parties. There was a multitude. However, almost immediately four major parties, the SPD, the Christian Democrats (CDU/CSU), the Communist KDP, and the Liberal Democrats (LDP), later to become the Free Democrats (FDP), became the principal players.

Local elections were followed by *Land* elections and all resulted in either Christian Democrats or SPD victories. Where the Christian Democrats won, their principal opposition was from the SPD, and vice versa. The Communists and Liberal Democrats usually maintained representation, but seldom challenged for leadership. In some instances, other political parties with special interests or local support gained some representation, but never challenged nationally and most gradually died out. Under the basic "nonpolitical" auspices of the US and British authorities, German political parties and behavior, with the exception of the extreme right, gradually reverted to the pre-Nazi era.

Konrad Adenauer, who was later to become the first Chancellor of the Federal Republic of Germany, gradually emerged as the leader of the Christian Democrats. He was the Lord Mayor of Cologne in 1933 when he was forced out by the Nazis. He was arrested in 1944 and barely avoided being sent to the Buchenwald concentration camp by feigning a heart attack. After the German surrender, Adenauer was reinstated as Lord Mayor of Cologne by the Americans.

The leader of the SPD was Schumacher, a former *Reichstag* member, who had constantly attacked the Nazis before Hitler came to power. Arrested in 1933, he spent the entire Third Reich era in Nazi concentration camps. A veteran of World War I where he lost an arm, he disliked the French and the Americans, and hated the Communists whom he called "red-painted Nazis."[36] Although he got along with the British, Schumacher was a German patriot and a dedicated Socialist. His relationship with Clay was often strained. Clay, who never fully understood the German political party system or the SPD relationship with the German labor movement, did not like Schumacher's meddling in local politics and labor disputes. Clay did not understand the control and loyalty Schumacher was able to maintain over local SPD leaders. Brandt described Schumacher as "sincere, courageous, and honest" and as "a dedicated socialist with a real hatred of injustice and privilege."[37]

The French, based on their fears, rivalry, and long history of conflict with Germany, controlled political activity much longer than the other three occupation powers. The French opposition to any form of centralized German administration power carried over to their zone. Political activity remained localized almost until the French agreed to merge their zone, minus the Saar, into the Federal Republic in 1949.

During World War II, Roosevelt followed a policy of "the Grand Alliance" with the determination to get along with the Soviet Union. He was determined to follow this policy after the war and believed the United Nations, one of his pet projects, would maintain the postwar peace.

Robert Murphy, a "personal representative" of Roosevelt during World War II and later the State Department political advisor to Eisenhower and Clay in Germany, reported on what he determined Roosevelt's foreign policy to be at the Teheran Conference in 1943.

> The first of these American policies was established soon after Pearl Harbor, when Roosevelt agreed with General Marshall that international political considerations should defer to military requirements as long as the war lasted. The second policy, emerging in 1943, was that everything possible must be done to win the confidence of Stalin and his associates.[38]

These policies continued throughout the war although there is some evidence Roosevelt began to have some apprehensions at Yalta over Soviet policy in Poland and the other eastern European countries, but Roosevelt maintained he "could handle Stalin." With Roosevelt's death in April 1945, Truman attempted to maintain Roosevelt's policy in getting along with the Soviet Union. However, at the Potsdam Conference in July-August 1945, Truman was exposed to the high-handed demands and intransigence of Stalin.

Unbeknownst to many is the personal affront Stalin imposed rather unknowingly on the American president. One of Truman's pet projects put forward at Potsdam was the internationalization of inland waterways such as the Danube and Rhine Rivers. Truman maintained most wars of the last two centuries had involved access to these and other inland waterways. Although Truman's proposal appeared to be of secondary importance, it became obvious over the course of the conference that it was important to Truman. The British expressed support in general terms, but Stalin refused to consider it. Truman requested the matter be referred to the foreign ministers, but Stalin ignored the request.

On August 1, 1945, the conference began to consider the final communique. Truman stated he regretted that no agreement had been possible on control of inland waterways, but believed the communique should mention the subject had been discussed. The British again agreed, but Stalin objected. Truman then made a personal plea to Stalin, which Stalin rejected outright even before the translation was completed. Truman could not mistake the rebuff and was furious.[39]

American policy toward the Soviet Union did not change immediately, but evolved gradually. Clay, operating on the basis of JCS 1067 and the Potsdam agreements, was determined to get along with the Soviets. His reading of these agreements made clear that his principle mission was the unification of Germany and, therefore, harmonious cooperation with the Soviets seemed a given. Clay told his staff in Berlin:

> We have to make it work. If the four nations cannot work together in Berlin, how can we get together in the United Nations to secure the peace of the world. Obviously, there had to be some give and take and, at the Allied Control Council, this was going to be the American policy.[40]

During the first two years, Clay got along famously with his Soviet counterpart, Sokolovsky. One reporter made the following observation about this relationship.

> There was a great deal of mutual respect and each appeared to recognize that the insults and denunciations that were a standing feature at their meetings had nothing personal in them . . . Sokolovsky, because he had been trained in a school of diplomacy where the calculated insult was a standard weapon, and Clay, because he was alert and adaptable, never stood on their dignity once the fishwives' session was over. Out they would go to the bar, arm in arm, and have a drink.[41]

Later, critics of Clay would comment that he seemed to have blinders on and did not appear to take notice of Soviet actions going on outside Germany. As a military man with a mission, Clay directed all his energy and attention to ac-

Stalin, Truman and Churchill at the Potsdam Conference.

complishing this mission and took too narrow a view of Soviet actions. Because Clay, on his level, had established good working relations with the Soviets, he feared that in the long run the mutual suspicion of the two governments would jeopardize the success of his assignment.

Historians have argued long about when the "Cold War" between the United States and the Soviet Union began. Some cite Churchill's "Iron Curtain" speech at Fulton, Missouri in March 1946. Others cite the decision by the United States to offer "mutual assistance" to Greece and Turkey in 1947 to combat Communist guerrilla forces, while others would state it was the recognition by US policy officials that Communist stated goals had not changed since 1918, only their tactics. Regardless of exactly when the "Cold War" began, in about 1947 the US policy with regards to the Soviet Union changed from cooperation or, at least, attempting to get along with Soviet Communism, to a policy of "containment."

Charles E. Bohlen, who served as translator/interpreter at Teheran, Yalta, and Potsdam and later as US Ambassador to the Soviet Union, has had rare insight into Soviet-American relations. He traces some of the first US misgivings concerning Soviet post-war goals to Yalta and the Soviet handling of the Polish question, followed by the failure of the Soviets to live up to the Declaration of Liberated Europe whereby they systematically installed Communist regimes in the eastern European countries. This was followed by the failure of the Soviets to withdraw their forces from Iran in 1945.

In 1941, the British and the Soviets had jointly occupied Iran to prevent possible enemy occupation. The agreement with the Iranian government provided for withdrawal of

Communist guerrillas captured by the Greek army in the Grammos Mountains. The extensive US military and relief supplies, along with military advisors, sent to Greece were instrumental in helping its government crush the insurgency. (*Inset*) The battleship *Missouri*, sent to Turkey as a gesture of US support for her against Soviet territorial claims. Substantial US aid soon followed.

these troops within six months after hostilities ended. The British withdrew as provided, but the Soviets continued to occupy the northern half of Iran well into 1946 and only yielded after the US brought the issue before the UN Security Council.

This was followed by Communist attempts, supported by the Soviet Union, to take over Greece and Turkey. Great Britain, which had been supporting these two governments, came to the United States in February 1947 and stated they could no longer afford to support this effort. This came as a shock to US foreign policy makers, who, until then, had not realized the extent of Great Britain's decline as a Great Power. Truman, supported by a bipartisan Congress, took up the challenge. Bohlen maintains: "It was in the face of such realization that the United States, in the person of President Truman, made probably the biggest decision for the future of American policy."[42]

The president's message to Congress proposing the Greek-Turkish Act came on the very eve of the Council of Foreign Ministers conference in Moscow which was scheduled to discuss Germany seriously for the first time since Potsdam. The strong anti-Communist text of Truman's

George C. Marshall at Harvard University where he received an honorary degree and delivered a speech outlining his plan for European recovery.

message could not have gone unnoticed by the Soviet leaders.

The Council of Foreign Ministers was established at Potsdam to direct the peacemaking of the World War II belligerents and the members were the same five governments who were permanent members of the UN Security Council—Great Britain, the USSR, the United States, France, and China. Because China had not been involved in the European part of the war, it did not take part in those conferences involving the European belligerents. The council was supposed to meet every three months, but it soon broke down into haggling over protocol and procedure. To separate the massive German peace questions from the other minor Axis partners, it was decided a separate peace conference would first deal with Italy, Hungary, Bulgaria, and Rumania. After much debate, this was finally accomplished in Paris from July to October 1946, but the US Senate did not confirm these peace treaties until June 1947.

In January 1947, Brynes resigned as US Secretary of State and was succeeded by George C. Marshall, the former US Army Chief of Staff during World War II. Marshall had barely taken over when, in March 1947, he was called upon to attend the Council of Foreign Ministers meeting in Moscow which was scheduled to discuss the German peace treaty. The meetings lasted six weeks and the net accomplishment was complete failure.

The failure was due to the stiffening of US attitude toward Soviet actions in eastern Europe and the Soviet Union's attitude that delay would best serve their political purposes. They had consolidated most of their gains in eastern Europe and, by 1947, western Europe was an economic "basket case." The Communist party in France and Italy was the largest of any political party in either country. Although the Communists did not control either government, they and the Communist dominated labor union in both countries could bring down the weak coalition governments on any pretext.

Great Britain had suffered great economic losses as a result of World War II and the British empire was being broken up. India gained its independence in 1947 and the British were deeply involved in the Arab-Jewish problems in Palestine. Food rations in some commodities in Great Britain in 1947 were less than those in defeated Germany. To the Soviets it must have appeared that, if they were patient, the entire European continent would be theirs. The key was to prevent German unification under any terms unfavorable to Communist goals.

Marshall recognized the Soviet tactics and their potential success. Bohlen reported on Marshall's meeting with Stalin at the close of the Moscow conference of the Council of Ministers.

> When General Marshall went to call on Stalin on April 17, 1947, I went along as his interpreter and note-taker. He found Stalin in a very relaxed mood, saying, in effect, what difference does it make if we can't agree now; after all, we can come back in six months and try again, and even if we don't agree then, life will still go on. This attitude impressed General Marshall very much indeed. He talked about it all the way back to the Embassy and all the way back to Washington on the plane. General Marshall felt Stalin was obviously waiting for Europe harassed and torn by war and in virtual ruins, to collapse and fall into the Communist orbit. Stalin, as Marshall saw it, seemed to think that it didn't make any difference to the present situation whether there was much recovery in Europe. By implication, sooner or later the Communist party would take over.[43]

Upon his return to Washington, Marshall immediately established the Policy Planning staff in the State Department, which was headed by George Kennan. The first task assigned was to draw up a plan for economic assistance to Europe. On June 6, 1947, in the low-key forum of the Harvard commencement, Marshall proposed the plan, which was given his name, for the economic recovery of Europe. This plan became one of the great successes of the US postwar diplomacy and a turning point in halting the Communist tide.

The positive reaction by Great Britain and France was immediate. Representatives of sixteen countries met in Paris from July 12 to September 22, 1947, to consider the program. Molotov flew to Paris to represent the Soviet Union and promptly denounced the Marshall Plan as another form of imperialism. He then dramatically rejected the US offer, not only for the Soviet Union, but all eastern European Soviet satellite countries. The western European countries accepted the program, thus dividing Europe more sharply than ever.

Murphy believes Molotov made a tactical blunder in his outright rejection of the Marshall Plan because the US Congress may have balked at economically supporting Communist countries had Molotov agreed for the Soviet Union and the Soviet satellites to participate.[44] When Czechoslovakia accepted the invitation to Paris, Stalin called key members of the Czech government to Moscow and threatened them with severe consequences if they agreed to participate. Under this pressure, the Czechs backed off, but their show of independence in accepting the invitation was evidently too much for Stalin. In February 1948, a Soviet backed coup eliminated the last vestiges of an independent Czechoslovakia and a Communist government was installed.

The last meeting of the Council of Foreign Ministers before the Berlin Blockade took place in London during November and December 1947. Efforts to reach Four Power agreement on Germany went on for four weeks with no important agreement on any subject. It became obvious that the Soviet Union had no intention of permitting unification of Germany. Finally, completely exasperated, Marshall, just before Christmas 1947, proposed the council adjourn indefinitely.

In the meantime, the United States and Great Britain had decided to go forward with plans for the creation of a West German state. Before this should become a reality, they decided, among other things, to implement the long planned currency reform. It was realized that both of these plans would be opposed by the Soviet Union and most likely result in a confrontation. The most likely spot for confrontation was the exposed outpost of Berlin.

YOU ARE LEAV
THE AMERICAN S
ВЫ ВЫЕЗЖАЕТ
АМЕРИКАНСКОЙ
VOUS SORT
SECTEUR AMÉ
MP

US military police at Potsdamer Platz where the US, British and Soviet sectors meet. The square was often the scene of confrontations between Communists and supporters of Western democracy.

# THREE
# Eye of the Storm

*What happens to Berlin, happens to Germany; what happens to Germany, happens to Europe.*—Vyacheslav Molotov

On July 30, 1946, the Americans and British agreed to economically merge their two occupation zones. This bipartite decision was made over French and Russian opposition on the basis that such a fusion was a violation of the Potsdam Agreement. The US and British justification was the French obstruction in the Allied Control Council to the formation of any centralized economic agencies and the need by the United States and Great Britain to reduce the amount of financial support they were being forced to pay to underwrite the feeding and support of their respective zones.

In attempting to justify the new bizone (which rapidly became known as "Bizonia") US Secretary of State James Byrnes, at a Council of Foreign Ministers meeting in Paris on July 11, 1946, invited all occupying powers to merge their zones economically with the US Zone. General Joseph T. McNarncy, then US Military Governor, was instructed to repeat this proposal a few weeks later at the Allied Control Council in Berlin. As foreseen, only the British agreed to the proposal.

Bizonia became operational in January 1947. To manage economic activity in the merged zones, the British and Americans established six boards: Economics, Food and Agriculture, Transport, Communications, Civil Service, and Finance. The British and Americans went to great lengths to avoid French and Soviet charges that they were forming any type of political unification and this resulted in a weak, ineffective organization. To avoid charges they were establishing a West German capital city, the six boards were headquartered in four different cities resulting in poor coordination. To avoid the appearance of a German government organization, the British and Americans maintained strict control over all decisions by establishing an Anglo-American Bipartite Board. This, however, also made it easy for German officials to disclaim responsibility for unpopular decisions.

After the Council of Foreign Ministers meeting in Moscow during March and April 1947, resulted in no agreement on a German peace treaty or German unification, Secretary of State George C. Marshall met with General Lucius Clay in Berlin on April 25, 1947. Clay was instructed "to proceed vigorously with strengthening of the bizonal organization . . . in conjunction with Robertson [British Military Governor], and to expedite the upward revision of the level of bizonal industry to ensure the self-sufficiency of the area."[1]

In response to Marshall's instructions, an elected Economic Council was created consisting of German representatives from each of the *Laender* (states) of Bizonia. The Economic Council was given the responsibility for adopting and promulgating ordinances subject to approval by the Anglo-American Bipartite Board. Although this did not solve all the problems for effective coordination of German agencies, it was an improvement in that the Germans were more responsible for their decisions. The next step was the formation of an executive power or something very close to a government. Before taking this step, it was decided to await the outcome of the Council of Foreign Ministers meeting scheduled for London in November 1947.

In the meantime, the Western European countries had agreed to participate in the proposed Marshall Plan and Clay advocated Bizonia be included. Marshall agreed. On November 18, 1947, just prior to the start of the Council of Foreign Ministers meeting in London, Marshall proclaimed in a speech in Chicago, "The restoration of Europe involves the restoration of Germany. Without revival of Germany's economy there can be no revival of Europe's economy."[2] By tying German recovery to European recovery, Marshall made economic assistance to a recent enemy more palatable to the US Congress and the American people.

After the breakup of the London Conference, Clay reported:

> Shortly after the adjournment of the Council of Foreign Ministers, Secretary Marshall and Mr. Bevin [British Foreign Secretary] met at Ambassador Douglas' residence . . . at a luncheon attended also by Robertson, Frank Roberts of the British Foreign Office, Murphy and me. After luncheon I presented orally, by agreement with Robertson, our joint views on the German problem. We pointed out that currency reform was essential to economic progress and recommended that one more effort be made immediately to obtain quadrapartite approval to put it in effect throughout Germany, failing which we would proceed in western Germany if France would agree, or in the bizonal area if France held back. We further asked for authority to give political character to the bizonal administrative structure without giving it in the name of government. This could be done, we believed, by the direct election in the early summer of 1948 of members of the Economic Council. We proposed to continue to participate in the Allied Control Council unless it was broken up by others. We anticipated difficulties in Berlin and recommended that we stay there regardless of any Soviet pressures. We urged that our governments make it clear to the French Government that it was welcome to join us at any time but that no effort be made to bring any pressure on France.

Before leaving London, Marshall informed Clay that the French were now willing to discuss the possible merger of their occupation zone with Bizonia provided the question of the Ruhr and French security could be settled.[4] However, when Clay and Robertson returned to Germany and were prepared to announce measures to strengthen bizonal powers, the French officially protested and claimed this was a prelude to a powerful centralized government.[5] The French protest was rejected and the new measures were proclaimed during February and March 1948.

When Clay and Robertson informed the Allied Control Council of the measures to strengthen the Bizonal German administration, Soviet General Sokolovsky, in a bitter attack, answered "Under pretense of reorganizing the bizonal economic agency, the U.S. and British authorities . . . have commenced establishing a separatist government."[6]

On January 20, 1948, the United States, Great Britain, and France agreed to hold a conference in London commencing February 23, 1948, to discuss German affairs. The Benelux countries were also invited to participate in those matters effecting them. The Soviet Union sharply protested the meeting maintaining the conference would lead to a divided Germany.[7]

The first sessions of the London Conference ended on March 5, 1948, with the general agreement by the Western powers that western Germany would have a "federal form of government." However, the French still held back from merging their zone with Bizonia. During the conference, on February 25, Communists seized full power in Czechoslovakia. "The coup sent a shock throughout the Western

President Truman with Secretary of State Marshall, Marshall Plan administrator Paul G. Hoffman and Averell Harriman in the oval office of the White House.

# The Marshall Plan

In hindsight, passage of the European Recovery Program of 1948, or Marshall Plan, seems almost a miraculous event. It was launched by the administration of an unelected, "lame duck" president whose loss of the upcoming election appeared to be such a virtual certainty that both press and politicians openly talked about his administration being "scheduled" to leave office in 1949. Indeed, President Harry S Truman's personal popularity was perceived to be so low by his own party that he was actually pressed *not* to assist in the congressional campaign of 1946.

A recovery program of continental dimensions, the Marshall Plan expended more than $12.5 billion (equivalent to roughly $60 billion today) at a time when:

- a worried Pentagon, virtually disarmed by postwar budget cuts, was making a solid case for increasing funding.
- numerous domestic agencies were, with heavy congressional support, clamoring for enlarged welfare programs.
- the US Treasury Department was intent on building upon the existing budget surpluses.
- the president's party did not hold a majority in either house of Congress.

That the Marshall Plan became a reality was due to the energetic efforts of many individuals: the Republican chairman of the Senate Foreign Relations Committee, Arthur H. Vandenberg; British Foreign Secretary Ernest Bevin; eminent Republicans Henry L. Stimson and Robert Patterson who had both become secretaries of war under Roosevelt; Truman himself; and, of course, Secretary of State George C. Marshall, a man venerated by Truman as being "the greatest living American." Curiously, Joseph Stalin was also a key figure behind the passage of the Marshall Plan and Truman once remarked that without his "crazy" moves, "we never would have had our foreign policy . . . we never could have got a thing from Congress."

British soldiers relax in their occupation sector. The Kaiser Wilhelm Memorial Church in the background still sits on the Kurfürstendamm and has been left in its ruined state as a memorial to war.

world. The shock was heightened by the death on March 11 of Jan Masaryk, the Foreign Minister of Czechoslovakia, which was officially presented as a suicide but widely suspected to have been caused by foul play."[8] This was followed by the Soviet breakup of the Allied Control Council in Berlin on March 20, when they walked out charging the Western powers with nullifying any reason for the continued existence of the Allied Control Council by their actions in London.

The Soviet actions made it abundantly clear to the French that they had little choice but to "cast the die" with the United States and Great Britain. They could not go it alone in their zone and the United States kept the pressure on by threatening not to include any Marshall Plan funds for a separate French Zone because standing alone the French Zone would not be a viable economic entity.

Prior to the reconvening of the London Conference for a second session on April 20, 1948, French officials tentatively agreed to merge their zone with the US and British Zones. The memorandum of understanding agreed to by the French called for a constituent assembly to convene not later than September 1, 1948, to prepare a constitution to be submitted to the German Laender for ratification. The constitution was to be approved by the occupying powers.

The Unter den Linden in the Soviet sector looking toward the Brandenburg Gate and British Sector.

This was to be followed by a democratic election and the formation of a government. However, the foreign relations of this government would be handled by the occupying powers pending the signing of a peace treaty. Economically, the French also agreed to the principal of a currency reform prior to the establishment of the German government.[9]

Although the French continued to "drag their feet" on a number of points, a final report, along the lines of the joint memorandum of understanding, was approved and submitted to their respective governments on June 1, 1948. The US and British governments approved the report on June 9, but the French hesitated again before finally approving on June 17, the very eve of the currency reform.

Now, it was the German turn to hesitate. Although many German leaders desired a return to constitutional government, they also realized acceptance of the proposals would result in a divided Germany for an indefinite period. Would they be condemned by the German people for dividing Germany much as their predecessors had been for signing the unpopular Versailles Treaty after World War I?

After considerable deliberation, the German leaders agreed to accept the responsibility after it was agreed to call the group preparing the constitution the "Parliamentary

Council" instead of Constituent Assembly and the document they were to prepare the "Basic Law" (Provisional Constitution) instead of the Constitution.[10] These were efforts to maintain the provisional nature of the proposed government on the outside chance the Soviets might agree to their zone later joining the government.

When the Council of Foreign Ministers meeting in London broke up in December 1947, and the United States and Great Britain decided to proceed with a currency reform for their zones and to establish a provisional West German government, Clay and Robertson realized the Soviets would take counter-action. Because of Berlin's exposed position and its potential as a thorn inside the Soviet sphere, there was little doubt the first challenge to the Western democracies' resolve would come there. Before his return to Berlin, Clay accurately predicted the early end of the Allied Control Council.[11]

Clay and Robertson did not have to wait long to find out what kind of action the Soviets contemplated. In January 1948, Soviet guards stopped a British military train and detached from it two cars carrying German passengers travelling under British auspices. In February, it was the Americans' turn when the Soviets delayed a US military train enroute to Berlin at the Soviet Zone border on a technicality.

Soviet attacks in the Allied Control Council became more abusive and pointed. At the February 11, 1948, Allied Control Council meeting the Western powers protested that the Soviet authorities in Berlin had barred them from a political meeting in the Soviet Sector of Berlin to which they had been invited by Germans. Sokolovsky answered the protest with an attack claiming Berlin was part of the Soviet Zone and accused the Western powers of using "their position to prejudice their right to remain in Berlin."[12] Clay felt the Soviets were attempting to build a record to justify the future blockade.

The attacks were not limited to the Allied Control Council and the Berlin Kommandatura meetings, but continued daily in the German Communist press and radio in Berlin. In January and February 1948, Communist authorities in the Soviet Zone and the Soviet Sector of Berlin began confiscating Western literature in violation of Four Power agreement on free circulation of all literature, other than Fascist literature, within Germany.

Because of their loss of the Berlin elections in 1946 and the obvious preference of a majority of Berliners for Western style democracy over Soviet Communism, the Soviets and their German Communist satraps resorted to various tactics.

> The Soviet response to these political setbacks took the form of a gradually increasing effort to get the Western Allies out of Berlin. Virtually no instrument of intimidation short of actual military force was beneath Soviet use. Planted rumors, press attacks, direct statements, and even Kommandatura conferences were used to spread the idea that the Western powers would leave Berlin.
>
> These efforts, in spite of Western denial and counterclaim, had the effect of shaking the confidence of the Berliners in the West. More importantly, it shook their faith in the democratic institutions the Western Allies in Berlin represented. Many Germans in Berlin hesitated to identify themselves with the West, knowing full well the direction Soviet reprisals would take if in fact the Western Allies did vacate the city.[13]

The March 20, 1948, Allied Control Council meeting proved to be the last one. After the usual arguments about which power had the best interests of the German people at heart, Sokolovsky suddenly demanded to know of all agreements on western Germany reached by the United States, Great Britain, and France in London in February and March. He was informed his request was reasonable and the answers would be forthcoming after their respective governments reviewed and approved the conference report. Sokolovsky hardly waited for the translation before declaring "I see no sense in continuing this meeting, and I declare it adjourned," whereupon the entire Soviet delegation arose and walked out.[14]

Because Sokolovsky was chairman for March and he did not call another meeting, this effectively ended the existence of the Allied Control Council for Germany after almost three years of existence. As Truman was later to observe: "For most of Germany, this act merely formalized what had been an obvious fact for some time, namely, that the four-power control machinery had become unworkable. For the city of Berlin, however, this was the curtain-raiser for a major crisis."[15]

The May 13, 1948 meeting of the Berlin Kommandantura, one of last meetings that the Soviets representatives attended.

Berlin and the Western powers did not have to wait long to find out what the Soviets planned. On March 31, 1948, the Soviets issued an order requiring personnel and baggage on military trains to and from Berlin be checked by their inspectors. They also decreed freight on military trains departing Berlin could not be cleared unless a permit was obtained from the Soviet commander in Berlin. This was in direct violation of Zhukov's oral agreement of June 29, 1945.

Both Clay and Robertson were determined to challenge the Soviet orders, but Clay first cabled General Omar Bradley, the US Army Chief of Staff, concerning his intentions. After considering several courses of action, Clay was authorized to reject the new Soviet regulations and to send US military passenger trains through the Soviet checkpoints. The guards were instructed to prevent Soviet military personnel from entering the trains, but not to fire unless first fired upon. This was basically what Clay had proposed with some modifications. He was not happy with the modifications, though, which did not allow him to increase the train guard. Clay was convinced the Soviets were bluffing and would not risk war, but agreed to proceed as ordered.[16]

On the evening of Monday, March 31, three US military trains entered the Soviet Zone. One train commander evidently lost his nerve and permitted Soviet representatives to board the train. This train was allowed to pass through to Berlin. The other two trains were stopped, but the train commanders denied Soviet entry. The Soviets, however, did not attempt to force access. Since they had complete control of the railroad signals in their zone, they merely had the trains shunted to a siding. The trains remained there

Supplies for the US garrison in Berlin being unloaded from C-47 aircraft at Tempelhof during the emergency air movement later dubbed the "Little Lift," 2 April 1948. (*Inset*) Civilians milling about in Anhalter station on 1 April. The Soviets delayed, but did not completely stop civilian rail traffic during this period.

until morning when they were backed out to the US Zone. Two British military trains were treated similarly to the latter two US trains.[17]

So as not to acquiesce to the Soviet orders, Clay cancelled all US military trains to and from Berlin and laid on an airlift. This became known as the "Little Lift" and lasted only about ten days. The US Air Force Europe (USAFE) flew in about 300 tons of supplies total for the military garrison, but there was no provisions for the civilian populace of Berlin or even a thought of attempting such an operation at that time. The Soviets eased their restrictions on Allied military trains on April 10, but continued to periodically interrupt rail and road traffic during the next 75 days.

Clay, smarting under the humiliation of the "Soviet victory," proposed to Bradley on April 1 to send a military truck convoy through to Berlin to force the issue and determine Soviet intentions. Clay still felt the Soviets were

May Day demonstrations in Berin, 1948. Part of the crowd is turning left to the *Reichstag* rendezvous of anti-communists while others continue to a Soviet demonstration. This photo was taken from the border of the British and Soviet Sectors at a point where the Berlin wall would later be constructed.

bluffing and that they would back down if forcefully confronted. Bradley advised Clay not to proceed with this plan without further consultation.

Clay attempted to enlist Robertson to support his truck convoy plan, but Robertson, just as Bradley, realized a truck convoy could be hindered as easily as a train shunted to a siding by detours, roadblocks, and destroyed bridges. A miscalculation by either side could lead to a "shooting war" or, if unsuccessful in getting through, in being forced to withdraw under further humiliation.

Then on April 5, a major incident occurred when a Soviet fighter plane first buzzed and then collided with a British transport plane approaching the Berlin-Gatow airfield in the British Sector. Both aircraft crashed, killing the Soviet pilot and fourteen passengers and crew, including two Americans. Robertson demanded an inquiry and advised Sokolovsky he had ordered fighter escort for his unarmed planes until Sokolovsky could insure the safety of his aircraft. Although Sokolovsky expressed regret and denied he had directed molestation of British aircraft in the Berlin corridor, he claimed the British plane had violated air safety regulations and was to blame for the accident.

The unfavorable publicity the Soviets received over the incident and the potential for further dangerous confrontations appeared to dissuade the Soviets from further interference in the Berlin air corridors. The Western powers' response indicated they would not tolerate Soviet attempts at intimidation. Just as most Western military leaders seemed to understand the potential of a war situation developing by attempting to force an armed convoy through to Berlin, the Soviet military chiefs appeared to understand the same could be true if they attempted to force the issue in the air over Berlin.

In an April 10, 1948, teleconference, Bradley asked Clay for an estimate of the situation in Berlin. Clay replied:

> I do not believe that we should plan on leaving Berlin short of a Soviet ultimatum to drive us out by force if we do not leave. At that time we must resolve the question as to our reply to such an ultimatum. The exception which could force us out would be the Soviet stoppage of all food supplies to German population in western sectors. I doubt that Soviets will make such a move because it would alienate the Germans almost

Rail and barge traffic begins to stack up as the blockage begins in earnest. Before the currency reform, black-market activity was common throughout Germany. (*Below*) US troops check identification cards and search for unauthorized goods during a "search and seizure" operation.

completely, unless they were prepared to supply food for more (than) two million people.

Clay then went on about his actions in reducing the Berlin garrison before making a prophecy and an emotional appeal.

> You will understand, of course, that our separate currency reform in the near future followed by partial German government in Frankfurt will develop the real crisis. Present show probably designed by Soviets to scare us away from these moves.
>
> Why are we in Europe? We have lost Czechoslovakia. We have lost Finland. Norway is threatened. We retreat from Berlin. We can take it by reducing our personnel with only airlift until we are moved out by force. There is no saving of prestige by setting up at Frankfurt that is not already discounted. After Berlin, will come western Germany and our strength there, relatively, is no greater and our position no more tenable than Berlin.
>
> If we mean that we are to hold Europe against communism, we must not budge. We can take humiliation and pressure short of war in Berlin without losing face. If we move, our position in Europe is threatened. If America does not know this, does not believe the issue is cast now, then it never will and communism will run rampant. I believe the future of democracy requires us to stay here until forced out. God knows this is not heroic pose because there will be nothing heroic in having to take humiliation without retaliation.[18]

A few days later, Clay again proposed to Bradley his armed truck convoy plan, but this time it was enlarged to an entire US infantry division plus a combined Anglo-French division. Bradley let Clay down easily by stating the plan was not desirable at this time.[19]

From April 10 to the announcement of the currency reform on June 18, 1948, the Soviets intermittently interfered with rail, road, and barge traffic. These efforts appeared to be designed to dissuade the Western powers from their plans regarding a provisional west German government and a currency reform by illustrating the vulnerability of Berlin.

When the meeting of the Council of Foreign Ministers in London during November and December 1947, produced no agreement on German economic problems, the Americans and British decided to go forward with plans for the creation of a West German government. Before this should become a reality, they decided that, among other things, a central bank had to be established and a currency reform had to be implemented. In early 1948, the *Bank Deutscher Laender* (which became the *Bundesbank* in 1958) was established to serve as the central bank for the three Western zones. The bank was given authority, among other things, to issue money and control foreign exchange, but it remained temporarily under the supervision of the Allied Bank Commission, consisting of the Financial Advisors of the US, British, and French Military Governors.

Prior to the formation of any West German government, the Western powers decided they would be the implementers of the currency reform. They did not want to saddle a new provisional German government with the potentially unpopular consequences of a currency reform.[20] In any event, only the three military governors had the authority to issue laws valid in more than one *land.*

During the spring of 1948, there were consultations with German economic experts whose input was sought because they would eventually be responsible for developing and uniting the economy after the currency reform. Some of their recommendations were incorporated into the plan, but all the final decisions were made by US, British, and French financial officials. It was also necessary to limit the discussions with the Germans to maintain secrecy on the exact date of implementation.[21]

The forthcoming currency reform was not a surprise to the German population, but to hinder speculation and black marketing, the exact date of implementation was a secret. Rumors of the impending currency reform and preparations by authorities to set up facilities for the exchange of old currency for new appeared in newspapers throughout May and June 1948. In May 1948, British Foreign Secretary Earnest Bevin stated the Western powers were preparing a separate currency reform. On June 16, 1948, the Hamburg Senate announced it had designated 1,500 offices to exchange money and that the exchange would undoubtedly be conducted on a Sunday in the near future.[22]

The possible Soviet reaction to a separate currency reform was also no surprise to the Western powers. In November 1947, Clay stated that the implementation of plans for a unified West German government would be accompanied by an early effort to blockade Berlin and to drive the Western powers out.[23] In answer to Bevin's statement, the

Before the currency reform, black-market activity was common throughout Germany. (*Below*) US troops check identification cards and search for unauthorized goods during a "search and seizure" operation.

official newspaper for the Soviet Military Authority in Germany stated:

> A currency split would mean that one part of Germany irrevocably would become a foreign power for the other. A currency border with strict control would have to be erected . . . as exploitation of exchange rate differences by speculators must be prevented, the borders would be sealed hermetically.[24]

And Edward Tenenbaum, one of the OMGUS currency reform planners, observed:

> We recognized clearly that the date of a bizonal or trizonal currency reform eastern Germany would become a foreign country. The only real link between the four zones — a common currency — would be broken, and the *de facto* absence of economic unity would be turned into a *de jure* state of economic disunity.[25]

During the spring of 1948, the new currency, packed in 23,000 boxes and weighing 1,035 tons was brought secretly to the old *Reichsbank* building in Frankfurt/Main.[26] The banknotes were purposely innocuous: there was no indication of an issuing authority, no signature, nothing promising to redeem the notes. They bore only the denomination and the words "Deutsche Mark" and "Banknote."[27]

With the unsuccessful resolution of German economic problems at the Council of Foreign Ministers in London in 1947, Clay and his advisors urged the currency reform be implemented immediately, but he was instructed by Marshall to make a final attempt to obtain acceptance of a unified new currency for all of Germany. Endeavors were made to obtain quadripartite agreement on currency reform up to and including the last meeting of the Allied Control Council on March 20, 1948, which the Soviets broke up by walking out in protest of the plans by the Western powers to form a provisional West German government.[28]

Clay had originally set June 1, 1948, as the date for the currency reform in the Bizone. At the last moment, the French indicated they would be willing to join the United States and Great Britain by including their zone in the plan for the establishment of a provisional West German government and the currency reform. The date for the currency reform was then reset for Sunday, June 20, 1948, with the official announcement to be made on Friday, June 18 after the banks closed for the weekend. It was also agreed the US, British, and French military governors would notify the Soviet military governor on June 18 by separate identical letters.[29] Between June 1 and June 17, 1948, the French again hesitated and threatened not to join the currency reform, but finally on the very eve, June 17, the French Assembly ratified the London agreements on the future of Germany and the currency reform proceeded with the announcement on June 18. Regarding the implementation, OMGUS reported:

(*Left*) US troops search for contraband at a displaced persons camp near Windsheim. (*Center*) Berlin police round up participants at a black market. (*Right*) US troops arrest a nattily dressed black marketeer in Bad Homburg

The long anticipated currency conversion in the Western Zones of Germany was officially promulgated on 18 June 1948 by the Military Governors of the US, UK, and French Zones. The first law for the reform of the German currency (Military Law No. 61) became effective on 20 June in the three Western Zones of Occupation; it did not apply to the Western Sectors of Berlin which were still considered to be under Four Power rule.

This law established the *Deutsche Mark*, and invalidated the *Reichsmark*, as the basic unit of the new currency. Small notes and coins, however, were to remain in use for the present at one tenth of their nominal value. Every inhabitant was permitted to exchange a per capita quota of RM 60 at a 1 to 1 ratio. Of this sum DM 40 were to be paid out at once and the remaining DM 20 within 60 days. To meet their payrolls, business enterprises were granted advances equal to DM 60 for each employee against the firms' subsequent conversion rights. A moratorium upon all debts until 26 June 1948 became effective immediately. Additional monies held by public, government, and financial institutions were to be converted at a later date. Single persons and family heads were to report all monies and credit balances in their possession. German authorities were also charged with the preparation of laws within a six month period for the equalization of financial burdens (*Lastenausgleichgesetz*). Tax reforms were to become effective as speedily as possible following the financial reform.[30]

As seen from the above, the currency reform was not a simple revaluation, but a comprehensive and complicated set of changes to wages, prices, public and private debt, exchange rates, banking reform, and burden sharing covered by several implementing laws whose full effect took months and years to fully realize. However, the currency reform in the Western zones did not take long to be declared a success. Only a month later, OMGUS stated:

> No event since the capitulation of the German armies has had such an impact upon every sector of German life as did the currency reform in the Western Zones, which became effective on 20 June 1948. Overnight the financial and commercial life of tens of millions of persons was transformed. The foundation, upon which normal ways of life could be reestablished, had been erected.
>
> By the end of July 1948, it was evident that the first phase of currency reform had been successful. Basically the results have been those foretold by proponents of currency reform. The new money has brought out of hiding a relatively large and well assorted supply of goods. Wages and salaries have again acquired genuine purchasing power. Job efficiency has risen and there are indications of increased output in almost all fields of manufacturing.[31]

Upon receipt of the US, British, and French military governors' letters on June 18, 1948, proclaiming the currency reform for the Western zones, Sokolovsky, in a public proclamation to the German people, charged that the agreements under the Potsdam declaration which stipulated that Germany be treated as an economic whole had been violated. Sokolovsky declared the new currency invalid in the Soviet Zone and in greater Berlin and possession of it a criminal offense. He also suspended highway and railway passenger traffic to and from Berlin and reduced freight traffic supposedly to protect the Soviet Zone from an influx of the old devalued currency.

On June 20, Sokolovsky replied to the Western military governors' letters of June 18 by stating the currency reform was illegal, completed the division of Germany and warned if suitable arrangements could not be made it would be necessary to implement a currency reform in the Soviet Zone and Greater Berlin which he considered to be economically integrated with the Soviet Zone. On June 21, Clay replied by letter and denied the implication that Berlin was a part of the Soviet Zone and invited Sokolovsky to a quadrapartite discussion on the currency problem in Berlin to develop a solution which would be satisfactory to all.

The Soviet reaction to the currency reform had been foreseen, but the Western powers were uncertain on what to do about Berlin. Although the British military governor wanted to make a strong protest about the traffic restrictions to and from Berlin, Clay demurred and said the Soviet actions were understandable and that he would have taken similar actions had the Soviets initiated a currency reform before the West. Clay preferred to wait a few days to see how the Berlin situation developed.[32]

As early as April 29, 1948, the Department of the Army, following discussions with the State and Treasury Departments, advised Clay that when the time of the projected Soviet Zone currency conversion was made known, Clay should try to reach immediate agreement on a uniform special currency for Berlin. If that failed, he should point out to the Soviets that the United States was ready to introduce a Western currency into the Western Sectors of Berlin. Clay maintained the establishment of two currencies in Berlin would be most difficult and probably untenable in the long run. When the time came to negotiate, he proposed to negotiate for a monetary union of Berlin with the Soviet Zone , provided the currency was kept under Four Power agreement and control.[33]

The economic planners were not optimistic about Berlin's future. Drawing on the analogies of other such enclave areas as Hong Kong, Luxemburg, Liechtenstein, and

(*Top*) Allied financial experts explain the currency reform at a press briefing at OMGUS headquarters, 18 June 1948. US Deputy Assistant Financial Advisor Jo Fisher Freeman is speaking, British and French advisors are seated to his right and the man at far left against the wall is believed to be Edward Tenenbaum. (*Bottom*) Berliners attempt to decypher the currency reform.

## Currency Control

(*Top*) Berliners line up to exchange currency at a Soviet Sector bank. (*Center*) West Sector residents exchanging *Reichsmarks* for *Deutsche Marks*. (*Bottom*) Clothing store in the British Sector proclaims "New Currency, New Prices!"

The Soviet side of their checkpoint on the autobahn at Helmstedt.

Monaco, they felt the best Berlin could hope for was a similar relationship as a trading center and *entrepôt* for East and West. However, these theories were dependent on Soviet acquiescence.[34]

The economists proposed a separate currency for Berlin under quadripartite control. A Soviet controlled currency was ruled out and a separate Western currency would present problems to maintain a unified city government. If it became necessary to issue a Western currency in the Western Sectors of Berlin, the economists foresaw the possibility of a flood of old devalued *Reichsmarks* and a potential danger to the new *Deutsche Mark* in West Germany. Therefore, to provide control, the new currency distributed in western Berlin would be distinguished from the currency released in western Germany by stamping it with a "B" for Berlin (in the way US dollars issued in the Hawaiian Islands during WW II were overprinted with "Hawaii").[35]

Economists and financial advisors saw other problems for Berlin if a separate Western currency was introduced. The Berlin transportation system depended on a streetcar, subway (*U-Bahn*), and elevated train (*S-Bahn*) network that had been built long before World War II and which travelled freely between sectors and to many outlying suburbs. Large numbers of Western Sector citizens worked in the Soviet Sector and vice versa.

How could the Western Sectors of Berlin exist surrounded by a hostile foreign government? Imagine a city the size of Chicago divided arbitrarily at State and Madison, cut off from its suburbs, with the remainder of Illinois and all of Indiana, Michigan, and Wisconsin being a foreign country, and you get some illustration of the situation confronting the planners in June 1948.

Based on all these factors, the Western powers decided that their policy in Berlin would be defensive. No steps would be taken, other than technical preparations for any eventuality, until the Soviets acted first.[36]

Sokolovsky accepted Clay's June 21 invitation for a meeting of financial experts of all Four Powers to discuss the Berlin currency situation. The meeting was held on June 22 in the ACC building in Berlin. The Soviets refused

(*Top*) *Reichsmark* banknote reissued with a Soviet Zone Monetary Reform coupon at left. (*Bottom*) newly issued Western Zone banknote stamped with a circled B for use in Berlin.

to accept the Western Powers' proposal for a separate Berlin currency and maintained that, because Berlin was closely integrated with the Soviet Zone's economy, Berlin's currency must be the same as the Soviet Zone. As a final fall back position, the Western Powers explored the possibility of allowing Soviet Zone currency to be the sole currency for all of Berlin provided the Four Power Kommandatura of Berlin, or some other agreed upon Four Power agency, could control the issuance and credit policy for Berlin. The Soviets insisted that they alone would control money and credit in Berlin and argued that any separate currency in Berlin would undermine economic stability in the Soviet Zone.

The Western Powers reminded the Soviets that they had no jurisdiction over the Western Sectors of Berlin and that the Western Powers had no intention of surrendering their sovereignty to the Soviets. The meetings continued on until 10 pm without any resolution. Just before adjournment, a Soviet courier arrived to inform the Soviet delegate that a proclamation of a currency reform for the Soviet Zone and all of Berlin was to be released the next day.[57]

On Wednesday, June 23, 1948, the Soviet Military Administration issued SMA Order No. 111 which proclaimed a currency reform for the Soviet Zone and all sectors of Berlin to commence the following day. Although there had been strong indications that the Soviets had been planning a currency reform for some time, their technical preparations were makeshift. Initially, the old currency with a coupon attached was used as the new East Mark.

The US, British, and French commanders immediately declared the Soviet order null and void in their respective sectors and proclaimed a monetary reform in the three Western Sectors of Berlin, effective Friday, June 25, along the general lines of the one previously proclaimed in the Western Zones of Germany. The technical preparations by the Western Powers were somewhat better in that the new West Marks, stamped with a "B," had been flown in secretly beforehand.

The Western Powers, however, hedged their bet by allowing the new East Mark to be circulated in the Western Sectors of Berlin and in making the East Mark acceptable payment for rent, rationed food, taxes, transportation fares, utility bills, and postal services. Shopkeepers dealing in other goods could, at their option, accept East Marks in trade. Soviet Zone postage stamps could also be used when posting mail in the three Western Sectors of Berlin. The Soviets did not reciprocate. Instead, they declared possession of West Marks by Soviet Sector Berliners and Soviet Zone citizens a criminal offense. They returned all mail franked with Western Zone postage stamps originating in the Western Sectors of Berlin precipitating what became known as the "Postal War."

In addition, the restrictions on rail and barge traffic instituted on June 18 to and from Berlin were tightened to include highway and freight traffic. The Berlin Blockade had begun. The Allies countered with the airlift.

Youngsters crowd atop a *Trümmerburge*, or rubble mountain, to get a closer look at aircraft landing at Tempelhof.

# FOUR

# The Airlift Begins

There was a wide divergence of opinion amongst the US, British, and French officials about the feasibility and desirability of remaining in Berlin and almost universal disbelief that the city could be supplied totally by air over an extended time period. Although US and British political and military leaders immediately stated their forces would remain in Berlin, they were not certain they could or, if they could, for how long.

Although Clay had predicted to Bradley on April 10 that the currency reform would develop the "real crisis", the Soviets had taken the action Clay doubted they would risk: that of stopping all food supplies to Berlin because it would "alienate the Germans almost completely."[1] As so often, the Soviets were not worried about alienating any group if they could gain their immediate objective.

Regarding the reasons for remaining in Berlin, Clay summed them up in a cable to Washington on June 13, 1948: "There is no practicability in maintaining our position in Berlin and it must not be evaluated on that basis. . . . We are convinced that our remaining in Berlin is essential to our prestige in Germany and in Europe. Whether for good or bad, it has become a symbol of the American intent."[2]

The British government was in agreement with Clay's views on remaining in Berlin, but the French, while agreeing to accept Western monetary reform in their sector of Berlin, foresaw grave problems and notified Clay: "The French Government is obliged to dissociate itself from all responsibility with regard to these consequences."[3] In spite of this written rebuke, the French government went along with all major decisions made by the US and British governments during the Berlin crisis of 1948-49.

Those who advocated withdrawing from Berlin did so primarily on the basis that Berlin was militarily indefensible and that it would be better to leave voluntarily rather than to suffer the humiliation of being forced out or to admitting they were unable to feed and supply the German population. In June 1948, the US Army and Air Force in Europe,

A light dusting of snow covers surplus US Army vehicles of all types at Wurttemberg in the winter of 1946. The soldiers who operated them had long since returned to the United States.

as elsewhere, were mere skeletons of the mighty well-equipped veteran forces of World War II. The demobilization of 1945-46 and the end of the military draft in 1947 left a volunteer US Army in Europe of approximately 60,000 men consisting of just over 10,000 troops in the understrength 1st Infantry Division and several light armored cavalry units, with the balance consisting of various support and military government units.

The Air Force, which had just become a separate military arm some nine months earlier, had a few tactical fighter squadrons, some weather and other miscellaneous aircraft, and two troop carrier squadrons equipped with C-47s which were used to ferry personnel and supplies. The C-47s were the only aircraft available to US Air Force Europe (USAFE) capable of hauling cargo. The British Royal Air Force was in no better shape and the French had almost no planes at all to offer.

Opposing the Allied forces were some 300,000 to 400,000 Soviet troops supported by a good tactical air force. Had a shooting war broken out, the Soviets would have had a tremendous advantage. One weapon the United States had in 1948 that the Soviet Union did not was the atom bomb. Could the Soviets be certain that, if the US vital interests in Europe were endangered or openly attacked, the United States might not choose to retaliate with the ultimate weapon?

While the decision to remain in Berlin was being debated in Washington, Colonel Frank Howley, US commandant in Berlin, went on the radio on June 24 to quiet the Berliners' apprehension about the Western powers' intentions and stated: "We are not getting out of Berlin, we are going to stay. I don't know the answer to the present problem — not yet — but this much I do know. The American people will not stand by and allow the German people to starve."[4] Later, the same day, Clay proclaimed in Heidelberg that "they [the Soviets] cannot drive us out by an action short of war as far as we are concerned."[5]

Government officials in Washington were not overjoyed by these statements from the field and Clay was instructed by Kenneth C. Royall, US Secretary of the Army, in a telephone conference on Friday, June 25 to explain the "by anything short of war" statement. Clay said he believed he had been quoted out of context and that he had no intention of provoking an armed conflict. Royall, evidently not realizing that western currency had already been introduced into Berlin, asked about the feasibility of holding up on this issuance while Washington analyzed the decision.

After Clay explained that this was no longer feasible, Royall asked Clay for an analysis of the Berlin situation. Clay again expressed his opinion that remaining in Berlin involved US prestige in Germany and Europe and that the currency issue was being used by the Soviets as an excuse to provoke the crisis. Royall then advised Clay that the Army

A miniature city is used to instruct military police in Germany on the situations likely to arise in various parts of a city, September 1946. After the war, Western forces were geared toward support and civil control.

was considering the desirability of asking the Air Force to provide additional air transport if Clay had urgent needs to fill his requirements. Clay's answer clearly indicates that he had not, as yet, seriously considered a full scale airlift because he told Royall that he had sufficient planes to meet his needs, that he would check with General Curtis LeMay, USAFE commander, and then report back. Clay, meanwhile, cabled Army Under Secretary William Draper.[6]

> I am still convinced that a determined movement of convoys with troop protection would reach Berlin and that such a showing might well prevent rather than build up Soviet pressures which could lead to war. Nevertheless, I realize fully the inherent dangers in this proposal since once committed we could not withdraw.[7]

The telephone conference with Royall made it clear that the possibility of such a potentially dangerous course of action would not be considered at this time. Soon after this telephone conference, General Robertson visited Clay and advised him the British government would not consider the armed convoy plan. Robertson then suggested to Clay that he consider the possibility of supplying Berlin by air and that Robertson had already secured agreement of the Royal Air Force to start supplying the Berlin garrison. The British government was also considering supplying the civilian population by air.[8]

Clay was not certain a city of two million people could be totally supplied by air. While mulling over his alternatives, Clay called in Ernst Reuter, the Mayor-elect of Berlin, who was accompanied by his aide, Willy Brandt. Also present was Robert Murphy, Clay's political advisor. Clay indicated for the first time that he was seriously considering an airlift operation. Clay told Reuter: "Look, I am ready to try an airlift. I can't guarantee it will work. I am sure that even at its best, people are going to be cold and people are going to be hungry. And if the people of Berlin won't stand that, it will fail. And I don't want to go into this unless I have your assurance that the people will be heavily in approval."[9] Reuter, although skeptical, assured Clay that Berlin would make all the necessary sacrifices and that the Berliners would support his actions.

Although we cannot be absolutely certain of Clay's thought processes on June 25, it would seem most likely that he weighed his options carefully. While Clay is on record to favoring an armed truck convoy, this had been vetoed, at least temporarily, by Washington. His only other option, other than an airlift, was some type of compromise or "surrender" to the Soviets on the currency issue and the possibility of opening up the entire German question, including the provisional government, which he was determined not to do. Therefore, by process of elimination, Clay was forced to choose the only option open to him — the airlift. He already had the support of the British through Robertson and the Berliners through Reuter on this course of action.

Clay then made his decision. He telephoned LeMay in Wiesbaden and ordered him to drop all other uses of transport planes and to begin flying supplies for Berlin. He also telephoned his deputy army commander in Frankfurt and ordered the movement of supplies to the airfields at Rhein-Main and Wiesbaden. The first planes began arriving in

Generals Albert Wedemeyer (*left*) and Curtis LeMay.

Berlin on Saturday, June 26.

Even with this decision, Clay was only thinking of a temporary solution to a problem that he believed would have to be solved by diplomatic or other more permanent methods. Clay estimated the maximum that could be expected was 700 tons a day and he knew from his planners this was far short of the minimum to sustain the population of the Western Sectors of Berlin with even bare sustenance. No-one, including Clay or any of his advisors, were thinking, at this time, of an airlift operation lasting more than a few weeks.

On June 26, Clay's decision to initiate an airlift was supported by Truman at a cabinet meeting and against the advice of some of his counselors. Truman ordered the airlift be put on a full-scale organized basis and that every plane in the European Command be pressed into service. It is evident that Truman was also thinking of a temporary measure because after making this decision, he stated, "In this way we hoped that we might be able to feed Berlin until the diplomatic deadlock could be broken."[10]

Clay's decision was also supported by two other important players, William Draper and General Albert Wedemeyer, the Army Chief of Plans and Operations. Draper and Wedemeyer were in Europe on an inspection tour when the Berlin blockade began. Draper had been Clay's economic advisor in Berlin prior to becoming Army Under Secretary and was familiar with the amount of food and other supplies necessary to sustain Berlin. Wedemeyer had been US Army theater commander in China during World War II and had been supplied by air "over the hump" from India by Army transport planes. (This operation had been commanded by General William Tunner, who was later

# From Milk

**A**irlift supplies from the United States came primarily by ship to Bremerhaven, then by railroad to a railhead near the airfield, and then by truck to the airplanes. Supplies from sources in Europe were transported primarily by train or barge to the railhead. The Quartermaster Corps and the Bizone Control Office procured the supplies; the Transportation Corps operated the ships, trains, and truck companies to deliver the supplies to the planes; and the Ordnance Division provided the maintenance to keep the trucks operating. Most of the labor to load the planes was provided by Labor Service Companies consisting of displaced Poles, Estonians, Letts, Lithuanians, and other Eastern Europeans.

(*Opposite*) Jewish Passover food arriving in Berlin. (*Top*) protecting coal against the weight increasing effects of rain, German loading crews prepare to truck this airlift cargo from train to plane at Fassberg. (*Center*) Berlin-bound cargo arrives on a Danish ship at the port of Bremerhaven. (*Bottom*) Fresh milk being loaded on a C-47. Shipments of whole milk soon were dropped in favor of more weight efficient condensed milk.

# to Matzos

Some of the airfields used in the airlift had convenient access to railheads while others did not. This presented a varying problem in trucking. To keep the supplies flowing at a constant pace, a three-day supply was warehoused at each railhead. Large ten ton trailers, roughly corresponding to the carrying capacity of a C-54, were pulled up to the freight railcars and loaded in accordance with how the cargo was to be placed in the aircraft. The cargo was then trucked to the airfield control point where it was met by an Air Force airlift representative and a Transportation Corps representative. An airplane returning from Berlin would be given instructions before landing on which hardstand number to

C-47 transport aircraft, containing 190 sacks of flour each, arrive at Tempelhof, 2 July 1948. A pair of B-17 weather aircraft can be seen at the far side of the airfield along with a lone C-54 at extreme right. (*Bottom*) Young Berliners unload coal packed into GI duffel bags.

pull up to and the trailer would be there to meet the incoming plane. The loading would be supervised by the airlift representative in accordance with loading requirements to make sure the weight was properly distributed on the plane for safety in flight. Upon its arrival in Berlin, the plane would be met by a crew of German workers and immediately off-loaded.

From June 26, 1948 to September 30, 1949 more than 2,325,000 tons of food and supplies were flown to Berlin on some 277,500 flights. Of this total the most carried cargo was coal with more than 1,500,000 tons and then food with more than 500,000 tons. Other cargo items included liquid fuel, raw materials, industrial supplies, construction equipment, mail, newsprint, vehicles, medical supplies, and people.

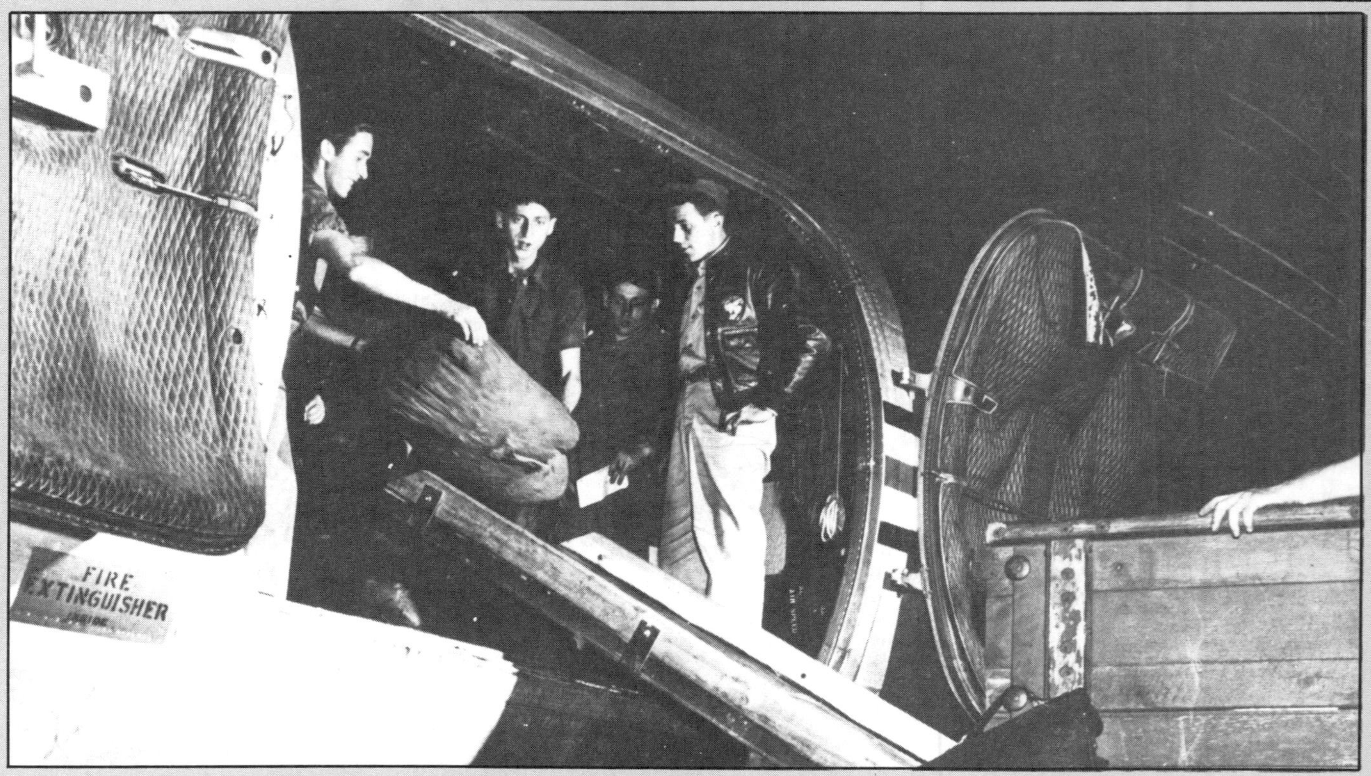

named to head the Berlin Airlift operation.) Both Draper and Wedemeyer recommended that supplying Berlin by air be attempted and Draper telephoned Royall on June 24 to recommend the Air Force be requested to immediately move additional air transport to the European Command.[11]

From June 25 to June 30, 1948, there was a flurry of activity in Washington, London, and Paris. Although Clay and Murphy had sent numerous warnings over a period of months on possible Soviet actions against Berlin, no contingency plans had been developed. The Western powers contemplated sending a protest note to Moscow, supported a temporary airlift, and made plans to send several B-29 bomber groups to Germany and England to display to the Soviets their determination to meet force with force. However, many US military and government officials expressed the belief that sooner or later the Western powers would be forced to withdraw from Berlin.

British Foreign Secretary Ernst Bevin, who was a strong advocate for remaining in Berlin, indicated Parliament would support the basing of B-29s in England, and advocated the airlift be built up immediately to 2,000 tons a day. Clay was informed of the British support by Robertson and Clay cabled Draper on June 27 proposing the airlift be stepped up.

> I have already arranged for our maximum airlift to start on Monday [June 28]. For a sustained effort, we can use seventy Dakotas [C-47s]. The number which the British can make available is not yet known, although General Robertson is somewhat doubtful of their ability to make this number available. Our two Berlin airports can handle in the neighborhood of fifty additional airplanes per day. These would have to be C-47's, C-54's, or planes with similar landing characteristics as our airports cannot take larger planes. LeMay is urging two C-54 groups. With this airlift, we should be able to bring in 600 or 700 tons a day. While 2,000 tons a day is required in normal foods, 600 tons a day (utilizing dried foods to the maximum extent) will substantially increase the morale of the German people and will unquestionably seriously disturb the Soviet blockade. To accomplish this, it is urgent that we be given approximately 50 additional transport planes to arrive in Germany at the earliest practicable date, and each day's delay will of course decrease our ability to sustain our position in Berlin. Crews would be needed to permit maximum operation of these planes.[12]

Also on June 27, a Sunday, an emergency meeting was going on in the Pentagon to discuss three possible courses of action: 1) to decide to withdraw from Berlin at some appropriate time, 2) to decide to defend the US position by all possible means, including supplying Berlin by truck convoy or using force in some other manner, and 3) to maintain the unprovocative but firm stand in Berlin by every local means and later diplomatic means while postponing the ultimate decision.[13]

No concrete decisions were arrived at during this meeting, but the following day Truman made a momentous decision. According to Secretary of Defense James Forrestal, when the question arose of whether or not the United States was going to stay in Berlin, Truman interrupted to say, "there was no discussion on that point, we are going to stay — period."[14]

Although this was not a final decision as Truman so indicated, it set the course for the immediate future. On June 29, Truman approved a British request for joint military planning and a joint Anglo-American military meeting was held the following day. It was determined that the airlift could deliver 2,000 tons a day at the present level of operations. Both countries agreed that the proposal of forcing armed truck convoys through the Soviet Zone to Berlin was too dangerous and impractical.

On June 30, Bevin announced to the House of Commons that Great Britain and the Western Allies would maintain their position in Berlin because there is "no alternative between that and surrender, and none of us can accept surrender."[15] Marshall, in Washington the same day proclaimed, "We are in Berlin as a result of agreements between the governments on the areas of occupation in Germany and we intend to stay."[16] The French are not on record for any public statements, but they had indicated through diplomatic channels that they would support the British and Americans by maintaining their position in Berlin.

Probably at no time in post-World War II history, with the exception of the Cuban Missile crisis of 1962, has the world ever been closer to World War III than it was during the period from June 25 through late July, 1948.

July 3: Clay, Robertson, and French General Roger Noiret meet with Sokolovsky in Potsdam at Sokolovsky's headquarters to urge him to lift the blockade. Sokolovsky makes it clear there will be no change in the traffic restrictions until the Western powers are willing to discuss the results of the London Conference concerning Germany. Sokolovsky does not mention the currency problem which is the supposed reason for initiating the blockade. It is clear the Soviets want to reopen the entire German question which the Western powers are unwilling to do.

July 6: The three Western powers deliver almost identical protest notes to the Soviet Union. The notes emphasize that the Soviet blockade is a violation of Four Power agreements concerning the administration of Berlin and that the Western powers will not be induced by threats, pressure, or other actions to abandon their rights. They express their willingness to negotiate, on the condition the blockade be lifted prior to any discussions.

July 10: Clay again recommends to Washington that, if the blockade is not lifted by a specific date, his plan for an armed convoy to Berlin be considered and that the Soviet government be advised in advance of this planned movement. Again, Washington, after obtaining specifics of Clay's plan which included infantry, tank destroyers, and engineers with bridge equipment, decides not to approve Clay's armed convoy plan at this time.

July 14: The Soviet Union replies to the Western powers' protest notes of July 6 and blames the Western powers for the Berlin situation by initiating a currency reform in their zones, by introducing a separate currency in the Western Sectors of Berlin, and by planning to form a separate German government. The Soviet Union goes on to say it is not adverse to negotiations, but the Soviet government cannot accept any preliminary conditions and that the discussions must include Four Power control of Germany and not just the administration of Berlin.[17]

July 15: The National Security Council approves the Dispatch of B-29 bombers to England after the British government agrees to receive and base them. The B-29s are widely known to be capable of delivering the atomic bomb and the implication of dispatching B-29s to where Moscow would be in their range cannot be missed by the Soviet Union. Unbeknownst to most, these B-29s do not carry atomic bombs, but there was wide speculation they do and the action emphasizes the Anglo-American commitment not to bow to Soviet threats.

July 17: While visiting Berlin, William Donovan, the former head of the Office of Strategic Services during World War II, holds a press conference and declares: "The place to make a stand against the Russians is right here in Berlin." Donovan, a civilian, holds no official government position at this time, but his statements are broadcast immediately in Berlin and receives wide coverage in the United States. Also this day, Bradley, after weighing all possible courses of action, including Clay's armed convoy plan, recommends the Air Force provide as many C-54s as the Berlin airfields could handle.

July 18: *The New York Herald Tribune* equates the Berlin crisis with the Munich crisis of ten years earlier.

July 19: Truman meets with his top military and diplomatic officials. Many proposals and options are discussed and Truman decides the United States would maintain its position in Berlin and and will take all necessary measures to insure its rights even at the risk of war.

July 21: Marshall holds a press conference and, in an answer to a question about the possibility of war over Berlin, he states:

> I can merely say at this time that our position I think is well understood. We will not be coerced or intimidated in any way in our procedures under the rights and responsibilities that we have in Berlin and generally in Germany. At the same time we will proceed to invoke every possible resource of negotiation and diplomatic procedure to reach an acceptable solution to avoid the tragedy of war for the world. But, I repeat again, we are not going to be coerced.[18]

July 22: Finally, after almost a month of crisis and "brinksmanship," the decision is made to fully commit to building an airbridge to Berlin. The occasion for this decision is a meeting Truman had with the National Security Council and others, including Clay and Murphy who had been ordered back to Washington for this conference. Clay and Murphy, supported by some State Department officials, still advocate the armed convoy plan, but this is unanimously opposed by the Joints Chiefs of Staff. Clay also reports the airlift had far exceeded his expectations and is now averaging about 2,500 tons daily which is adequate to handle food requirements, but inadequate to include the necessary amount of coal. Clay estimates 4,500 tons was the minimum to sustain Berlin without extreme hardship, although 3,500 tons per day might suffice in summer. Clay

The first C-54 cargo planes arrive at Rhein-Main airbase from the United States, July 1948. (*Below*) US air traffic controllers at the Berlin Air Safety Center check and post flight progress strips indicating movement of American aircraft in and out of Tempelhof. The Soviet panel for their airfield at Schönefeld is at right and a corner of the British panel for Gatow airfield can be seen at left.

estimates an additional 75 C-47s will enable him to reach 3,500 tons daily.

Air Force Chief of Staff, General Hoyt Vandenberg opposed the sending of additional planes on the grounds that such a commitment would disrupt other operations. He also argued that another major Berlin airfield was needed to support the proper use of additional planes and, in the event of hostilities, a large number of planes might be destroyed. This would adversely affect the US ability to wage strategic warfare.

Truman, after analyzing the input, decided the question was how to remain in Berlin without risking war?[19] He summed up the situation by stating, "the airlift involves less risks than armed convoys," and directed the Air Force to furnish the fullest support possible to the problem of supplying Berlin. The National Security Council then formally reiterated American determination to stay in Berlin. To support this determination it approved the construction of a new airfield in Berlin and approved the dispatch of approximately 75 C-54s to Europe to support the airlift. It also recommended that a diplomatic approach be made to Stalin personally.[20]

On his return to Germany on July 23, Clay told reporters he was confident that the airbridge could supply Berlin indefinitely and there was an excellent chance for a peaceful settlement of the Berlin crisis.[21] Clay, ever the realist, had shifted gears. Recognizing the opposition to his pet armed convoy plan could not be overcome, he decided to give his full support to making the airlift work.

Although the Western powers had only the verbal agreements with Zhukov from June 1945 for rail and road access to Berlin, the necessity for air safety had led to some important written agreements concerning air traffic by the Allied Control Council in November 1945 and October 1946.

In November 1945, the Western powers proposed, and Zhukov agreed to, three 20 mile-wide air corridors connecting Berlin with Hamburg, Frankfurt/Main, and Hannover-Bueckeburg.[22] From this came a set of flight rules published by the Allied Control Authority Air Directorate on October 22, 1946, which proved to be crucial.

The rules not only further defined the air corridors, but also established the Berlin Control Zone which permitted airplanes landing and taking off from Berlin airfields to fly within a 20 mile (32 kilometer) radius of Berlin. This permitted Allied aircraft to overfly the Soviet Sector of Berlin and the Soviet Zone on their approaches and departures. The three air corridors were formally specified as Frankfurt-Berlin, Bueckeburg-Berlin, and Hamburg-Berlin, each 20

The limited load capacity of the C-47 aircraft necessitated that the much larger C-54s be added to the airlift as quickly as possible. A single C-54 was capable of carrying as much cargo as four of its older cousins.

English miles wide. The agreement did not specify altitude, but by practice and custom Allied aircraft have been constrained by a 10,000 foot ceiling although the right to fly higher had never been yielded in principle.[23]

These agreements in 1945-46 also established the Berlin Air Safety Center to control flights to and from Berlin. The center was staffed by air traffic controllers of all four occupying powers. Although the Soviets walked out of the Allied Control Council and the Berlin Kommandatura, they continued to staff the Berlin Air Safety Center located in the Allied Control Authority building in the US Sector throughout the duration of the Berlin crisis of 1948-49. According to rules agreed to in 1945-46, each power was required to post each flight in the air corridors and notify the other powers' representatives.

During the Berlin Airlift the Berlin Air Safety Center served as the initial contact for air traffic control before the information was passed to the Approach Control Centers at the Berlin airfields. It also served as the clearing house for the rescue operations of downed aircraft in the corridors. The Soviet controllers took the last known information on the aircraft and arranged by telephone to get Soviet troops to the crash site. The Berlin Air Safety Center was and still is one area where cooperation has continued over the years.

After receiving Clay's telephone call on Friday, June 25, LeMay immediately gave orders to the 60th and 61st Troop Carrier Groups headquarters at Rhein-Main and Wiesbaden Air Bases to start flying in food and supplies to Berlin. On Saturday, June 26, these two groups with their C-47s were able to fly in 80 tons of supplies. The British, who had initiated their effort on June 25 independently flew about six long tons that first day. LeMay appointed Brigadier General Joseph Smith of his staff as project officer for the US component of the airlift and the call went out immediately for every available cargo aircraft in Europe.

All military operations must have a code name and how the Berlin Airlift came to be called "Operation Vittles" has several versions. Supposedly, at Smith's headquarters in Wiesbaden, several potential names got kicked around. One officer suggested "Operation Lifeline," but that was considered too dramatic and someone suggested "Operation Airlane." "Hells fire," said General Smith, "we're hauling grub, I understood. Call it Vittles if you have to have a name." And Vittles it became. The British dubbed their airlift operation appropriately "Operation Plain Fare."[24]

When the airlift began, organization was makeshift, but enthusiastic. Colonel Arthur Eve, Jr. (then a Captain) was the Chief of Personnel Operations for the 7100 Support Wing, 7120 Air Base Group, Wiesbaden Military Post and recalled: "When the Airlift started, pilots assigned to staff jobs at USAFE Headquarters, Wiesbaden Military Post, European Air Transport Service, augmented the two troop carrier wings to provide around the clock flights. My assignment was to furnish German nationals as loading crews. It was Saturday, June 26th, the day after the blockade started. Fortunately, the standard work week for German nationals was six days, so it didn't take long to round up enough people to start."

The C-47s had a load capacity of only two and a half tons and their relatively low cruising speed made them poorly suited for the airlift operation, but they valiantly held the line until larger aircraft could be obtained. The orders went out around the world for C-54s, the only Air Force plane available in suitable quantities to fulfill the mission. The C-54s had a load capacity of approximately ten tons. The giant C-74 Globemasters, with a load capacity of 25 tons, would have been ideal for this type of operation, but in 1948 only twelve such aircraft had been built.[25]

When the calls went out in late June 1948 for C-54s, the first units called on to supply aircraft were: the 20th Troop Carrier Squadron, Panama Canal Zone; the 54th Troop Carrier Squadron, Anchorage, Alaska; the 19th Troop Carrier Squadron, Hawaii; and the 17th Air Transport Squadron, Great Falls, Montana. Other C-54s came from Bergstrom AFB, Fairfield Suisun AFB, California, and Brookley AFB, Alabama. By July 10 some 54 C-54s had ar-

"Peasants" chatting over a brief lunch at Tempelhof.

# The Pilots

The references by the newspapers to Berlin's 20 mile wide air corridors as "narrow and dangerous" infuriated the airlift pilots, who often referred to themselves as "peasants" because they were hauling coal and potatoes. In height, they pointed out, they literally had infinity, although the scrupulous exactitude at which they flew assigned altitudes, limited them even more than the 20 miles did horizontally. But 20 miles, except in the foulest weather, was neither narrow or dangerous. After all, as one said after the term "peasant" caught hold: "Us peasants ought to stay in a twenty-mile lane unless we were crocked, and I don't want to be up there with any crocked peasants."

To relieve the routine and tension even while in the air, pilots were not above having some fun with newcomers. Guy Dunn reported overhearing the following transmission on a run back from Berlin:

"BW 17 over Braunschweig at 05 at 7,000 feet upside down in a thunderstorm. What do I do now—over?" A new voice came on. "Now listen closely son. Over

(*Left*) Fueled by doughnuts, hamburgers and coffee, these pilots at Rhein-Main flew four round trips per day. (*Right*) Parachutes in hand, Berlin-bound pilots take a quick look at the morning paper before heading for their plane.

your head there is a little switch marked 'Inverter.' Take your right hand off the wheel and reach up and move that switch to the rear position and when the red light next to that switch goes out, you will be flying right side up and then you go to Rhein-Main—out."

Sometimes the pilots had to overcome adversity on the ground too. Jeff Warren advised that he and his crew often got back to their billeting area near Rhein-Main in the wee hours of the morning after twelve hours of duty. They would just get to sleep when at 6:00am a cannon would go off to announce reveille for the Army troops billeted on the same base. Entreaties to the post commander were to no avail until one night the crew decided to take affirmative action. Using ropes and block and tackle they hauled the offending cannon to the top of a four-story barracks. Their message seemed to get through and reveille was no longer announced with a 6:00am cannon shot during the airlift.

(*Top*) Sunderland flying boat zooms past the Gatow control tower toward the *Havel See*. (*Center*) Berliners head for shore with a newly arrived load of salt while others watch and snap photos.

rived to supplement the C-47s.

Lt. Colonel Guy B. Dunn, Jr. (then a 1st Lt.) was assigned to the 1703rd Air Transport Group at Brookley AFB, Alabama and recalled:

> The Saturday morning in early 1948 that we got the call to provide the first four C-54s from MATS (Military Air Transport Service) to the "Lift," I was enroute to the golf course when Colonel Cassidy (George S. Cassidy, CO of the 1703rd) stopped me and said let's go to work. We were to provide four aircraft, three crews per aircraft, and 62 maintenance people to start a squadron to be assigned to the 61st T.C.W. They, the 61st had four squadrons, but needed more aircraft. MATS mission at the time would not allow the movement of a complete squadron from one unit. So, Lt. Colonel Jim Haun, the Commander of the 17th (Air Transport Squadron) set up and organized a complete squadron from people from Travis AFB, California; Great Falls ABF, Montana; and Brookley AFB. We did this while in the air between Westover and Rhein-Main. When we landed at Rhein-Main, ten of the twelve aircraft were in up status so with some of the dead heading crews we had all ten aircraft enroute to Berlin within one hour."

The French had most of their limited amount of transport planes tied up in operations in Indo-China, but the British did their part. On June 27, the RAF dispatched 16 C-47s, (which the British called Dakotas) to Wunsdorf Airfield near Hannover. These were soon joined by 42 more C-47s and 40 British Avro Yorks. However, the most dramatic aircraft to fly into Berlin proved to be the Sunderland flying boats of the British Coastal Command. Taking off from *Finkenwerder* on the Elbe River near Hamburg they landed on the *Havel See* in Berlin with nine tons of cargo to be met by Berliners paddling out in boats with flowers like some scene from a South Pacific travelogue film. Crews for the British planes came not only from the United Kingdom, but also from India, Australia, New Zealand, and South Africa.

When the airlift began, there were only two airfields in Berlin; Tempelhof with one runway in the US sector and Gatow with one runway in the British sector. In 1945, when the Americans arrived in Berlin, Tempelhof's lone runway was sodded and had been used only for small aircraft and fighters during the latter stages of World War II. It was beautifully equipped with hangars and a large terminal building, but it was surrounded by high apartment buildings which required a 500 foot ceiling in thick weather. Be-

Early morning airlift operations at Tempelhof, 22 August 1948. Note the trio of aircraft parked beneath the overhang of the airport structure.

# Tempelhof

fore June 1948, US Army engineers had built a 12 foot thick rubber base runway and covered it with steel landing mats which was adequate for US military needs before the airlift. However, under the continuous pounding of heavy, loaded aircraft the steel landing mats started to break. Depressions in the runway began to form and soon a force of 225 men was kept busy working on the runway between plane landings in attempting to keep the field operational. In early July 1948, construction on a new runway at Tempelhof began without interrupting airlift traffic and during the same period the old runway was being constantly repaired. In late 1948, construction began on a third Tempelhof runway.[26]

Gatow, the other available airfield in West Berlin in June 1948, was located in the far southwest corner of Berlin and on the west side of Wannsee. In late June 1948, con-

Pierced steel planking for a new runway at Tempelhof arrives aboard a C-47. (*Inset*) Work crews of Berliners laboring to keep the Tempelhof runways in order despite the continual pounding of daily flight operations.

struction began at Gatow to lengthen and improve the one existing runway, and, on July 16, 1948, the new 1,800 meter concrete runway was opened for service. Plans were also made to construct a second runway at Gatow, but it became obvious that, if the airlift continued to expand, a third West Berlin airfield site must be found.

On July 5, the first British Sunderland flying boat participating in the airlift landed on the Havel Lake in Berlin. Soon ten of these planes from the Royal Air Force Coastal Command were shuttling between Hamburg and Berlin. On July 7, the first twenty C-54s to carry coal to Berlin landed at Tempelhof. By July 15, the US effort numbered 54 C-54s and 104 C-47s making runs to Berlin. The combined US-British tonnage being flown into Berlin was averaging around 2,500 tons in over 600 daily flights. It was still short of the 4,500 tons established by the planners as the

A pilot's eyeview of Tempelhof shortly before the blockade. Many of the large buildings surrounding the airport were destroyed by Allied bombing during the war. Unfortunately for the air crew who later ran the blockade, the leveled buildings were not on the flight paths to the runways.

daily minimum requirement to feed and support the Allied military and Berlin civilian population, but a marvelous achievement in such a short period of time.

During the first month of the airlift, enthusiasm was high, but confusion often reigned. Many pilots and air crews who had been desk bound for months and even years were pressed into service while others were making their way to Europe. It was a great adventure at first to report to Flight Operations, get a plane on the spur of the moment, and take off for a four hour round trip flight to Berlin. However, the tedium and danger soon became apparent. Pilots and crews were asked to make two and more round trips a day, seven days a week, in all kinds of weather, in World War II airplanes—often in need of repairs—poorly suited

A C-54 flys over a graveyard and perilously close to some apartments buildings while making its landing approach at Tempelhof.

for cargo duty, and landing on makeshift runways.

Ground operations were also uncoordinated during the first month. Planes often sat at airfields in Berlin for an hour or longer before unloading began. Air traffic control units were understaffed and operating under out-dated procedures which required 25 minutes separation between take-offs. Other operating procedures, not suited to an emergency airlift operation, requiring the utmost in use and efficiency, also died hard. These included one which required each pilot to visit the airfield weather office and sign a clearance form before take-off. Because the Airlift Task Force—which would later prioritize cargos according to absolute needs of the Berlin civilian and military population—was just getting organized, planes sometimes carried some frivolous and unnecessary cargo into Berlin.

There also remained some very real differences of opinion on whether the Allies could maintain their position in Berlin and on what course of action should be taken. Walter Lippmann, the most prominent columnist on foreign affairs at the time, believed the Allies should negotiate the German peace treaty because ". . . to supply the Allies sectors of Berlin by air is obviously only a spectacular and temporary answer to the ground blockade. . . The operation can only be carried on for a while in the summer months. But in the long run, especially in the fog and the rain of a Berlin winter, the cost in lives of the pilots and crews of planes which would have to be replaced, and of the money, would be exorbitant."[27] On the same day, Churchill proclaimed that if the Western powers yield to the Russian attempts to squeeze them out of Berlin they would "destroy the best chance which is now open to us of escaping a third World War."[28]

In the *Time, International Edition* of July 12, 1948, Harold MacMillan, at that time leader of the British Conservative Party and the opposition to the ruling Labour Party, was quoted on the situation in Berlin: "We must . . . face the risk of war. . . . The alternative policy—to shrink from the issue—involves not merely the risk but almost the certainty of war." And U.S. Secretary of State Marshall was quoted as saying: "We intend to stay." But *Time* also editorized by stating that ". . . it was obvious that Operation Vittles could not be carried on at the summer rate when winter comes. . . ."

As it became more apparent that the Soviets had no intention of lifting the blockade and that the airlift was going to last more than a few weeks, it became clear that the airlift would have to be expanded and that operations at all levels would have to become more efficient. The romanticism would have to be sacrificed for standard procedures if the airlift was to have any chance for success through the fall and winter months.

Survivors of a crash in the Soviet Zone, March 1949.

## The Ultimate Sacrifice

There was danger in the air to and from Berlin. The sheer number of flights in fatigued aircraft with overworked crews was bound to result in some casualties. On July 30, 1948, *The Berlin Observer* reported: "The third accident and the second fatal crash of the 7,231 flights logged in "Operation Vittles" occurred early Sunday morning when a C-47 piloted by Lieutenant Charles H. King of Britton, South Dakota, and Lieutenant Robert W. Stuber of Arlinton, California, crashed into the street in front of an apartment building in the Berlin-Friedenau district. Both the pilot and co-pilot were killed instantly."

On September 21, *Der Telegraf* reported "Shortly after taking off for Berlin, a four-engined "York" plane crashed at the Wuns-

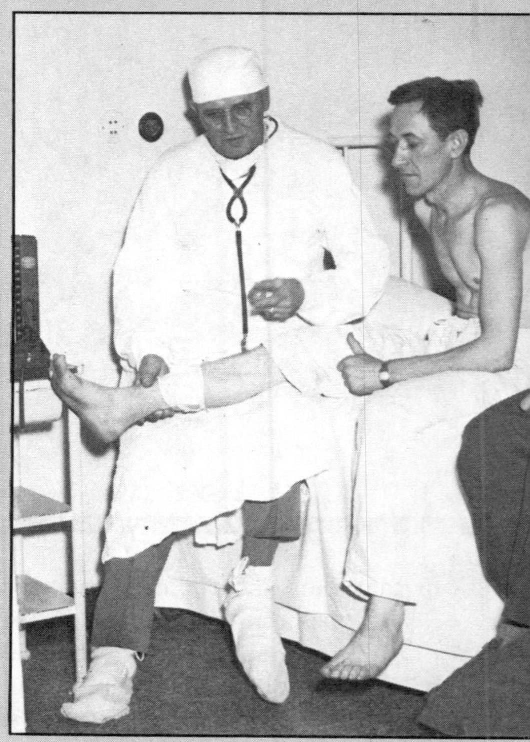

A tire rupture caused the crash of this C-82A in December of 1948 (*top*) while brake failure almost led the C-54 to smash into apartment buildings at the end of the runway in August.

Remains of a Navy C-54 after a crash landing on the night of November 15, 1948.

dorf airfield. The plane burned completely and the crew of five lost their lives."

On December 6, DPD reported "A U.S. Skymaster carrying coal to Berlin crashed at a distance of three kilometers from the Fassberg airfield, killing three members of the crew."

Not all crashes were fatal. On September 14, Captain Kenneth W. Slaker of Lincoln, Nebraska, and Lieutenant Clarence Steber of Mobile, Alabama, were enroute from Wiesbaden to Berlin in a C-47. Just after entering the Soviet Zone both motors quit and the two men bailed out. Steber was picked up by the Soviet military and turned over to US military authorities in Berlin a day later. Slaker, with the help of some friendly German civilians, simply walked back through the Iron Curtain to West Germany. Such things were possible in 1948.

In all, 31 Americans, 41 British (including an Australian and a South African), and 5 German civilians lost their lives in airlift operations.

There were many tributes to these peacetime heroes. The Air Force named the streets of a dependent housing community in Wiesbaden for the fallen Americans. A more lasting tribute was provided by the city of Berlin. The Berlin Scholarship Foundation was established to provide education scholarships for all the children of the British and Americans who gave their lives for the citizens of Berlin. In addition, the names of the fallen American and British airmen are engraved in the airlift monument built in front of Tempelhof and the square in which the monument sits was renamed "Platz der Luftbruecke" (Airlift Plaza).

Lieutenant Donald W. Measley of Hampton, New Jersey is presented with a bouquet of flowers by nine-year-old Suzanna Joks of Berlin.

The first month of the Soviet blockade and the Allied airlift brought anxiety and change to the lives of Berliners residing in the three Western Sectors. Although they had become accustomed to spending most of their waking hours seeking food and shelter, they now had to cope with the possible loss of their freedom if they identified too closely with the Western powers and the Western powers decided to pull out.

Although Clay, Robertson, and the Western political leaders publicly stated the Western powers would remain in Berlin, the Soviet and German Communist press and radio constantly printed and broadcast reports and rumors of the eminent Allied departure. There were also not-too-veiled threats that those Berliners who openly supported Allied policies would be harshly dealt with when the Allies left. Who was telling the truth? Would the Soviets lift the blockade after a few weeks as they had previously in April? If not, could the airlift possibly supply Berlin over an extended period? Would there be war? These were the questions uppermost in the minds of Berliners in June and July 1948.

As Ernst Reuter had predicted, the Berliners were prepared to make sacrifices for their political freedom. They demonstrated their determination throughout the 11 month ordeal in spite of Communist intimidation and harassment which eventually led to the split of their city.

All of this determination was not immediately apparent during June and July 1948. What was apparent to the Berliners was their former foes were not willing to sacrifice Berlin on a matter of principle, and the Berliners responded by pitching in and supporting the airlift. Although the position of the Western powers for remaining in Berlin was based on international power politics rather than any altruism, there became a shared comradeship between the Allied personnel and the West Berliners. Although the sacrifices by Allied personnel were minor compared to those of the Berliners, the occupied and the occupiers began to identify with each other for the first time since the war ended.

Many Allied personnel who were in Berlin during the blockade and the airlift have commented on this change of their attitude towards the civilian population. And the Berliners who were old enough to have experienced the blockade and airlift have demonstrated over and over again

by word and deed their support for the continued presence of the Western powers. Undergoing a common ordeal brought about a cooperation, support, and understanding that was not previously evident.

> . . . On a street corner in Lankwitz, Sergeant Major Jim Madison of the 18th Constabulary squadron was as moved as his wife—"standing there with forty Berliners . . . we were just one person as the planes went over." Secretary of the Air Force Stuart Symington, at Tempelhof on an inspection trip, felt a lump rise in his throat as he watched little girls in pigtails, wearing white puff-sleeved blouses and velvet bodices, pressing nosegays of flowers on the pilots as they piled from their planes. The wife of Berlin's American Overseas Airline chief, Barbara Parsons, summed up the mood that the armada evoked: "It was no longer 'them' and 'us' — it was 'us'."[29]

During the first weeks, the Berliners had to learn how to cope with dehydrated potatoes, powdered milk for infants, a lack of fresh fruit, vegetables, and meat, a dual currency system, reduced electrical power requiring severe rationing, and loss of jobs because of restricted power which forced many factories and offices to close. They also had to deal with the subways, elevated trains, buses and streetcars operating on reduced schedules because of gas and electric rationing. In short, every phase of what they had become accustomed to as normal daily routine was disrupted. They were forced to adapt to survive.

Fortunately, the average Berliner had grown accustomed to rationing and shortages during six years of war and three years of occupation. The ordeal of the blockade was an additional burden, but it may have been more difficult to overcome had the Berliners not been accustomed to hardships.

As stated earlier, certain essential services and rationed food could by law be paid for with either East or West marks in the US, British, and French Sectors of Berlin. In addition, no person employed in the Western Sectors could demand more than 25 percent of his wages in West Marks.

The strict controls on the amount of West Marks circulating in Berlin plus the population's awareness of Communist hostility to private capital caused a flight to the West Mark. Initially pegged at par, the West Mark quickly rose against the East Mark in black market trading. By July 1948 it was two East Marks to one West Mark; in August, 3 to 1; and by October 1948, 4 to 1. The exchange rate then fluc-

Pilots landing on the 100th day of the airlift (October 1, 1948) exited their planes to find large crowds of Berliners with specially made gifts for the occasion.

## Grateful Berliners

Just three years earlier many airlift pilots had been bombing the then-capital of Nazi Germany and the citizens of Berlin had run for their air raid shelters and cellars when the drone of airplane motors was heard. Now these same pilots were risking their lives to feed and supply Berlin and the Berliners welcomed the noise of the airplanes roaring over their city day and night to preserve their freedom.

In 1948, the Berliners did not have much in material goods to offer, but to show their gratitude they offered what little they had. Captain Earl Overholser, a native of Washington state, had been stationed at Tempelhof for more than two years before the airlift began. Because of a

(*Top*) A British pilot is greeted with flowers at Gatow airfield. (*Center*) Berlin school children present ornate beer mugs to pilots at Tempelhof, Winter 1948.

shortage of ground officers, he held nine different duties, including Public Information Officer, during the early months of the airlift. Overholser recounted at the time, "One of my jobs . . . is to handle all the grateful Berlin citizens who show up. Seems to me I've met every German in Berlin. They come down here, clutching extremely valuable heirlooms against their breasts, and want to make a little ceremony of giving the stuff to the pilots. Or some child will show up with flowers or a valued picture book. It's no act either. An old man so thin you could see through him showed up a few days ago with a watch that would have fed him for months on the black market. He insisted on giving it to an American. He called it 'a little token from an old and grateful heart'."

The gifts were not all valuable heirlooms. They knitted scarfs and sweaters. One lady presented two young boxer puppies to pilot Captain Robert G. Livesay. A particularly thoughtful gift was received by Overholser in a cardboard box addressed to "Lt Keller, Greenfield, Iowa" in early August 1948. The sender had read a story about Keller in the previous Sunday edition of *Der Tagespiegel*, a Berlin newspaper, which had mentioned Keller had two small children back in Iowa. The box contained two homemade rag dolls for Keller's children.

(*Top*) Berliners line up to exchange East and West Marks at daily posted official rates at a British Sector Exchange office. (*Bottom*) An Exchange Office in the Charlottenburg district, British Sector.

(*Top*) A crowd of Berliners gather to purchase stolen East Zone coupons to place on their devalued *Reichsmarks*. (*Bottom*) A black market in stolen East Zone coupons in the US Sector.

tuated between three to four East marks for one West Mark for the remainder of 1948 and early 1949. In July 1948 the first official exchange offices were established in the Western Sectors by the Berlin Finance Office in an attempt to gain some control over exchange rates and to facilitate legal currency transactions.

The exchange ratio between East and West currency also caused certain government agencies to run up large deficits. A prime example of this was the Berlin postal department which was required to sell postage stamps and other services for East Marks if offered in payment. It was also required, as all Berlin employers, to pay their employees 25 percent of their salaries in West Marks.

In July 1948, the Soviets froze the Berlin Magistrate's funds then on deposit in a bank in the Soviet Sector. Almost overnight the city administration was bankrupt and unable to pay city employees. Even after this crisis was overcome, city employees and contractors were often paid late due to continuing city fund shortages causing dissatisfaction and morale problems.

One of the most severe problems faced by the Berliners was the lack of sufficient electrical power sources in the

Knitting by candle light during an electrical cut-off.

Western Sectors. Upon commencement of the blockade, this required immediate and strict rationing for homes, factories, offices, and transportation services. Family home life soon became regulated around when electric power was available. For most, this was two hours a day and staggered over the 24 hour period. Schedules were printed and, depending on district of residence, some Berliners were forced to get up at 2 am to accomplish tasks, such as cooking requiring electrical power. Lack of electrical power caused many factories to close, increasing the unemployment rolls. Even when goods could be manufactured they could not be exported because of the blockade.

In spite of these hardships, the Berliners demonstrated their political independence by continual challenge to Soviet pressure. The Berlin City Council passed a resolution on June 30, requesting the United Nations mediate the dispute between the occupying powers. On July 11, at the Schoeneberg District Hall in the US Sector, Reuter condemned the Soviet blockade and reiterated the unshakeable will of the Berliners to resist an attempt to starve them into political submission. On Thursday, July 29, the City Council, meeting at its regular location in the Soviet Sector, courageously passed a resolution demanding the blockade be lifted. Its instigators were charged with a "crime against humanity."

In July, the inevitable split of the Berlin city government began. Because of repeated insubordination, Paul Markgraf, the Communist appointed city police president, was

The rationing of electrical power meant that this mother had to iron at night when power was briefly available in her area.

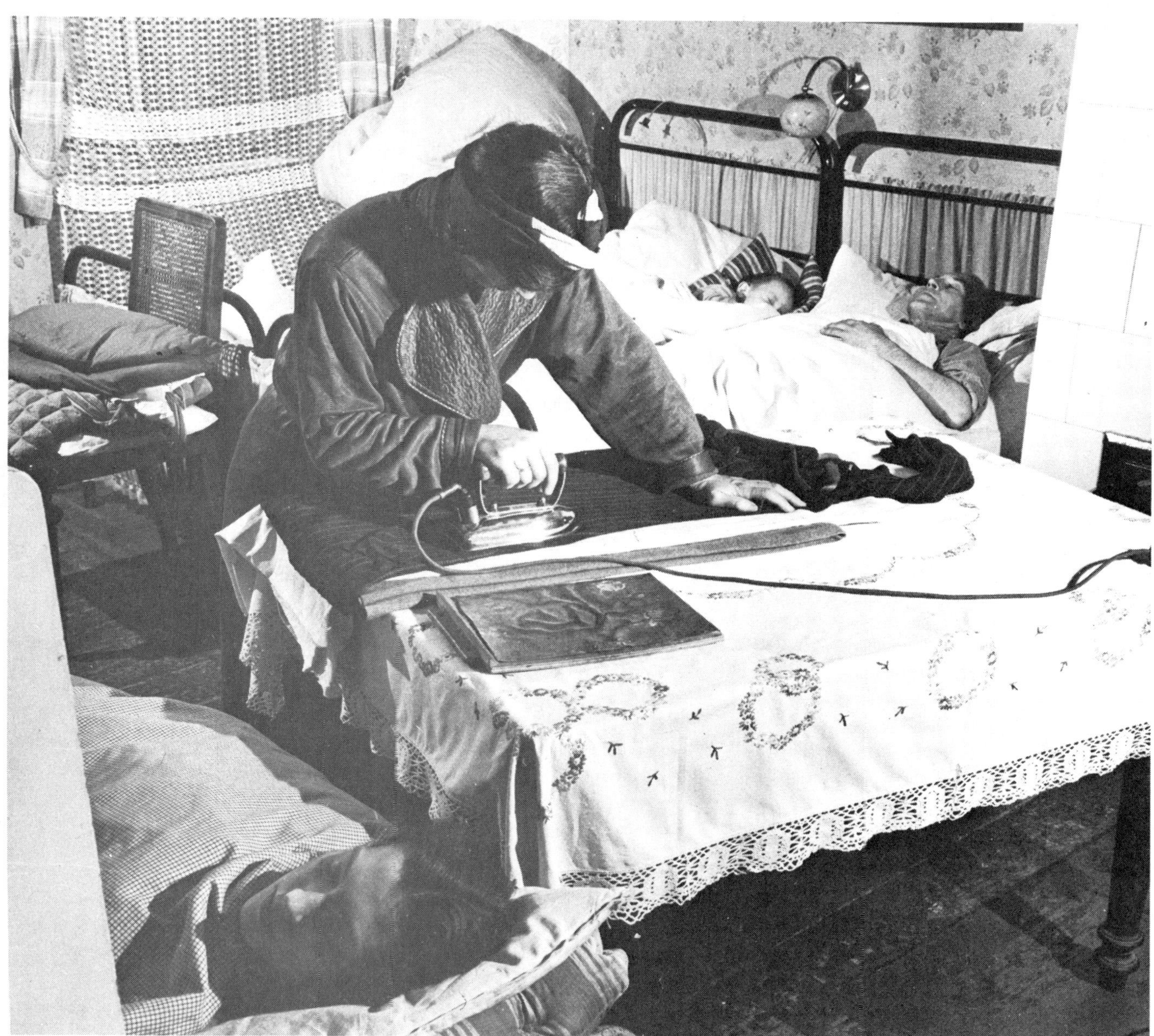

suspended on July 26 by the Magistrate. Dr. Johannes Stumm was appointed Acting Police President. The Soviets refused to recognize Markgraf's suspension and, because the Berlin police headquarters was then located in the Soviet Sector, Stumm and the Magistrate were forced to make a decision. Stumm set up an alternate police headquarters in the US Sector and called for all police to report to the new headquarters on Wednesday, August 4. Approximately 1,500 of the 2,000 personnel reported to the new police headquarters while the remainder stayed with Markgraf.

Thus, the Berlin police department became the first city department to split.

# The Lighter Side

**A** fitting successor to Bill Mauldin's World War II cartoons was found in the pen of Staff Sergeant Jake Schuffert. Almost daily in *The Task Force Times,* the airlift newspaper, a Schuffert cartoon was featured which captured the foibles and ironies of life on the airbridge. His darts at the VIPs and high brass were loved by the pilots and crewmen. Later, Schuffert's cartoons were published in book form as *Air Lift Laffs.* This volume is treasured by many airlift veterans. Another example of written airlift humor is the famous *Fassberg Diary.* Unpublished, by an anonymous author, typewritten reproduced copies still survive today of this tribute to the Americans assigned to the British base at Fassberg. The author claims these Americans were sent there by "Emperor or Uncle Tumbler, Commander of the Airwick Task Force," ands forgotten until a journalist stumbled in during the year 3200 as they were still awaiting their replacements. The *Diary* begins:

And so it came to pass, that after the one-hundred-and-eightieth day of his durance, a Voice from afar spoke unto him, saying:

"Dost desire PCS*?"

And he made swift reply in this wise saying:

"Hell, no!"

And so it came in time to pass that His orders were extended for an additional one-hundred-and-eighty days. . . ."

The *Diary* continues on in a similar vein for another 18 pages.

* Permanent Change of Station

"Seems to me I've seen him somewhere before . . ."

"The comments you have just heard on 'Airlift Rotation' do not necessarily reflect the opinions of this station!"

"YEAH, THAT PLANE IS FROM TEXAS, WHY??"

"—WELL, IF YOU'RE NOT A REPLACEMENT, WHO THE HELL ARE YOU??"

"You don't take this Airlift very serious, do you, Grady?"

"I THOUGHT WE LANDED AT RHEIN MAIN TO PICK UP PASSENGERS!!"

"OH, OH, I FORGOT TO WAKE SGT. HOGAN BEFORE WE TOOK OFF!!"

"YUP SONNY, AN THEM THAR LAST TWO I GOT FOR THE AIRLIFT BACK IN 1948-!!"

ERSHEY'S
ERSHEY'S

A young Berliner smiles after capturing Hershey bars dropped by an airlift pilot.

# FIVE

# "Vittles" Gets Organized

After President Truman made the decision to commit to the airlift and furnish an additional 75 C-54s, the US Air Force decided to better organize airlift operations. General Curtis LeMay had appointed General Joseph Smith in June to manage the airlift, but this had been a temporary assignment. Smith and his British counterpart had done a remarkable job in getting the airlift started and up to 2,500 tons delivered daily by July 20. However, if the airlift was going to increase this tonnage, it not only required more planes, but better organization. The romanticism would have to be sacrificed for a standardized precision operation.

In July 1948, the US Air Force had one of the best possible men available sitting in Washington, D.C. as deputy commander for operations of the Military Air Transport Service (MATS). He was General William H. Tunner. Tunner, the son of Austrian emigrant parents, had graduated from West Point in 1928 and had picked the then fledgling Army Air Corps. In 1941, Tunner helped organize the Army Air Corps Ferrying Command which delivered airplanes to England under the Lend-Lease Program.

In 1941, the Army Air Corps had no capability to transport materials and had very few transport planes of any type. By June 1944, Ferrying Command had grown into the Air Transport Command with the Ferrying Division as its major component. Tunner had advanced to commanding general of the Ferrying Division with 50,000 military and civilian personnel under his authority. It had delivered more than 21,000 airplanes to foreign designations and made more than 291,000 domestic ferrying movements. It had regular routes to all parts of the world including Africa, the Soviet Union, Europe, Asia, and the Pacific.

In the summer of 1944, Tunner was selected to take over the Air Transport Command airlift in the China-Burma-India (CBI) Theater, which was commonly referred to as the "Hump" operation because the airlift was over the Himalaya Mountains from India to China. The Hump had begun in April 1942 as a makeshift operation under the US Tenth Air Force, a combat command. In December 1942 it was decided to turn the job over to the Air Transport Command.

Although ATC had managed to raise the monthly tonnage to 23,000 tons by the time Tunner took over, this was not sufficient to meet the needs of the China Theater, under command of General Albert Wedemeyer. In addition, the accident rate was high, morale low, and the airlift command had been a graveyard for several previous commanders. By July 1945, Tunner had upped the monthly tonnage to more than 71,000 tons, lowered the accident rate, and raised morale.

General William H. Tunner.

The CBI Theater did not receive the media attention of the European or Pacific Theaters and, therefore, Tunner's efforts were not well-known at the time. However, Wedemeyer, who had directly benefited from the Hump was well aware of Tunner and the potential of airlift operations.

Prior to returning from his inspection trip to Europe in June-July 1948, Wedemeyer sent a recommendation to General Hoyt S. Vandenberg, chief of staff of the Air Force,* that Vandenberg appoint Tunner to run the Berlin Airlift. Although General Lucius Clay felt he had suitable personnel operating the airlift, Wedemeyer felt the job should be entrusted to the one person who had successfully operated an airlift.[1]

There was no immediate action on Wedemeyer's recommendation. Clay was happy because tonnage was increasing. LeMay and Smith, both Air Force combat commanders, were doing a good job. There was a lot of good publicity and the run to Berlin had been humorously dubbed "LeMay's Coal and Feed Company." However, LeMay realized the Berlin Airlift was not going to be a short-term operation: "That was when we yelled for Bill Tunner to come over and take the chore. He was the transportation expert to end transportation experts. He had run those ferries over the Hump in the CBI and he had headed Ferrying Command for a while . . . it was rather like appointing John Ringling to get the circus on the road."[2]

When Wedemeyer returned to Washington, he visited Vandenberg and again recommended Tunner be given the job. After the July 22 National Security Council meeting and the decision by Truman to commit to the airlift, Vandenberg finally decided to name his best man for the job. Tunner gathered up some selected staff and reported to LeMay in Wiesbaden on July 29, 1948. LeMay told Tunner simply, "I expect you to produce." Tunner answered, "I intend to."[3]

Tunner and his staff spent the next few days inspecting and reviewing airlift operations. As he had anticipated, Tunner was confronted with a "cowboy" operation. Flight crews and ground crews did not have any schedules, maintenance was haphazard, loading and unloading were not well coordinated, everything was temporary, and confusion reigned.[4] In spite of these shortcomings, the airlift had been a success up until the end of July, but tonnage had reached a plateau and the operation required better organization if it was to keep increasing the tonnage.

Tunner and his staff began almost immediately to tighten procedures. After noting crews lounging around Tempelhof in snack bars, frequent departure delays, and schedules not being met, Tunner initiated his first unpopular order on July 31, only three days after his arrival. No American crew member was to leave the site of his airplane at Tempelhof or Gatow in Berlin. Upon taxiing to the unloading ramp, the plane was met by a large truck with an unloading crew.

An operations officer met the plane with a clearance slip and passed along any problems anticipated on the return trip. A weather officer provided information on weather conditions and a mobile snack bar provided coffee, doughnuts, and sandwiches. Although plane crews were unhappy at first about these regimenting procedures, they soon came to like the idea because the mobile snack bars were manned by very pretty Berlin girls hired by the German Red Cross. Turn around time in Berlin was reduced to 30 minutes.

Tunner noted on his first trip to Berlin that the southern air corridor used by US planes departing Wiesbaden and Rhein-Main was the longest. It required an altitude of 5,000 feet to get over the Harz Mountains while the central corridor from the British Zone was the shortest and over flat terrain all the way. An airplane using the central corridor could make three trips for every two trips by planes using the southern corridor. Tunner decided he would request permission from the British to station US planes at British airfields so that better use could be made of the short central air corridor. The British agreed and during August the Air Force moved three transport groups to the British air base at Fassberg which was used primarily to fly critical coal from the Ruhr to Berlin.

Tunner also found that his operational problems were completely different than he had experienced in the Hump

*General Vandenberg was also the nephew of Senator Arthur H. Vandenberg, one of the principal backers of the Marshall Plan.

Vittles aircrews at Tempelhof's mobile snack bar which rolled up to aircraft as soon as they taxied to a halt.

airlift. In India he had 13 bases feeding airplanes into six bases in China, all of Southeast Asia to maneuver in, and little interference from the enemy. The Berlin Airlift had or could have had sufficient bases to feed planes into Berlin, but there were only two Berlin airfields available to accept planes that had to fly in restricted air corridors over or near Soviet airfields. If planes could not land, they had only a 20 mile radius to circle in, and that almost directly over the two Berlin airfields.

This latter problem became readily apparent to him on Friday, August 13, 1948, known as "Black Friday." Tunner was in the air over Berlin. The ceiling sank early and fast that day on Tempelhof.

> The clouds dropped to the tops of the apartment buildings surrounding the field, and then they suddenly gave way in a cloudburst that obscured the runway from the tower. The radar could not penetrate the sheets of rain. Apparently both tower operators and ground-control approach operators lost control of the situation. One C-54 overshot the runway, crashed into a ditch at the end of the field, and caught fire; the crew got out alive. Another big Skymaster [C-54] coming in with a maximum load of coal, landed too far down the runway. To avoid piling into the fire ahead, the pilot had to brake with all he had; both tires blew. Another pilot, coming in over the housetops, saw what seemed to be a runway and let down. Too late he discovered that he'd picked an auxiliary runway that was still under construction, and he slithered and slipped in the rubber base for several precarious moments, then groundlooped.
>
> With all that confusion on the ground, the traffic control people began stacking up the planes coming in—and they were coming in at three-minute intervals. By the time we came in, the stack was packed from three thousand to twelve

The C-54 which almost skidded into the street beyond Tempelhof's runway on "Black Friday," 13 August 1948.

thousand feet. A space was saved for my plane at eight thousand feet, and we flew right into it. Planes behind us, however, had to climb to the top of the stack—God knows why there were no collisions. As their planes bucked around like gray monsters in the murk, the pilot filled the air with chatter, calling in constantly in near panic to find out what was going on. On the ground, a traffic jam was building up as planes came off the unloading line to climb on the homeward-bound three minute conveyor belt, but were refused permission to take off for fear of collision with the planes milling around overhead.[5]

To avert a disaster, Tunner took the unusual action of ordering the Tempelhof tower to send every plane in the stack back to their home base. As a result of this experience, Tunner ordered an unusual and, for the time, revolutionary procedure. Thereafter, any plane arriving over Berlin would have only one pass at landing. If for any reason, the pilot could not bring his plane in, the pilot was ordered to return to his home base in West Germany. This avoided "stacking" planes over the small 20 mile radius over Berlin. With planes landing and taking off every three minutes this reduced accidents. Thereafter, the system truly worked like a conveyor belt.

Another procedure introduced by Tunner was that all US planes in the Berlin corridors would fly under instrument flight rules, at all times, regardless of weather. Tunner initiated this policy because of the constantly changing weather conditions in the Berlin air corridors. The choice was between visual or instrumental flight rules and the need to standardize. A pilot can fly visually or on instruments in

C-54 transport aircraft were already beginning to crowd out the smaller, twin-engine C-47s when the photo below was taken at Rhein-Main Air Base, outside Frankfurt, on 26 July 1948.

clear weather, but only under instruments in poor weather. Therefore, the choice of instrument flight rules was logical.

Other standard procedures were instituted to make the maximum number of flights per day. Planes were to take off every three minutes, hit certain check points at certain altitudes and air speeds, descend and land at approximately three minute intervals between planes. Pilots and crews normally flew two roundtrips to Berlin per day and then turned the plane over to the next crew.

Major Jeff Warren (then a 2nd Lieutenant) was assigned to the 22nd Air Transport Squadron, Fairfield-Suisun, California, when his orders came down and he departed for Rhein-Main on July 30, 1948. Within hours after landing, he was in the air as a co-pilot in a C-54 on his first trip to Berlin. Between August 1948 and February 1949, Warren made 145 trips to Berlin and only twice was he forced to return to Rhein-Main without dropping his load in Berlin. Once, because visibility was less than 100 feet at Tempelhof and the other time because a plane was off the runway and burning. He recalls only one short layover in Berlin of a couple of hours due to weather.

It was determined by a planning committee in Berlin that the city needed 4,500 tons per day to support the civilian and military population with the bare minimum needed to feed, heat, and furnish some electrical power. Tunner and his staff calculated they needed 225 C-54s to fulfill these tonnage requirements. They did not have that number to begin with, so the C-54s had to be supplemented by the smaller and slower C-47s plus other available aircraft types. The British used every military transport they could scrape up and contracted with every European civilian transport company willing to participate.

Orders went out and by mid-August 81 more C-54s had been added or were en route. The planes and crews came from the 11th and 12th Air Transport Squadrons, Westover AFB, Massachusetts; the 8th and 9th Air Transport Squadrons, Kelly Field, Texas; the 22nd and 23rd Air Transport Squadrons, Fairfield, California; the 3rd Air Transport Squadron, Tokyo, Japan; and the 1st Air Squadron, Hickam Field, Hawaii. In the fall of 1948, 73 additional C-54s including all 24 available R5D's, the Navy version of the C-54, from the Navy VR-6 and VR-8 Squadrons joined the airlift.

The need for an additional airport in Berlin was appar-

(*Top*) German cement workers laying Tegel Airfield's runway, 17 August 1948. (*Left*) Tractor being unloaded from one of the five C-82 aircraft taking part in the airlift. (*Right*) Grading a future taxiway to an adjoining apron, 28 September.

# Tegel Construction

ent. The feasibility of further expanding Tempelhof and Gatow was limited. A search for the best available site led to a tract of land in the Tegel area of the French Sector of Berlin, once used as a training area for the German *Wehrmacht*. The French were consulted and it was agreed the United States would construct the field and operate it, while the French would maintain it and provide manpower to unload the aircraft. Construction began on August 5, 1948 with a target completion date of January 1, 1949.

The obstacles to overcome to build a modern airport in blockaded Berlin appeared insurmountable. There was little heavy equipment, no raw materials, and no skilled laborers. The only way to get the needed large construction equipment in was to cut it up with acetylene torches at Rhein-Main, load it into large C-74s and C-82s for the trip to Berlin, and then weld it together again in Berlin. The raw material problem was solved by using rock and brick rubble from the bombed out streets and buildings of Berlin.

Empty asphalt barrels line the area adjacent to the 5500-foot runway at Tegel Airfield in the French Sector. The barrels pictured are part of the 10,000 barrels flown in by "Vittles" aircraft.

The labor problem was solved by using thousands of volunteer Berliners who pitched in with a renewed spirit to save their city. Men, women, and children, mostly unskilled, worked around the clock with US Army engineers to complete the Tegel airfield in three months, almost two months ahead of schedule. The first C-54 landed at Tegel on November 5 and the airfield went into full operation on December 15.[6]

By the end of August 1948, the combined US-British airlift was averaging more than 4,000 tons to Berlin each day. By the end of September they were approaching the 5,000 ton mark. On September 18, 1948, US Air Force Day was celebrated by demonstrating the potential of the airlift with 900 trips to Berlin by US and British aircraft carrying almost 7,000 tons of food and supplies. On September 30, General Tunner phased out the C-47s on regular US airlift runs to Berlin because there were now sufficient C-54s in Germany to handle the lift.

(*Bottom*) Thousands of tires, checked constantly for deterioration, were kept in a state of readiness at Rhein-Main Air Base for use on the Skymasters flying round-the-clock into blockaded Berlin. (*Right*) The line of maintenance docks during night crew operations at the Oberpfaffenhofen Air Force Depot.

## 24-Hour Maintenance

During the height of airlift operations the Air Force had 354 C-54 aircraft allocated to the operation, but the average daily number of C-54s available (in commission) was only 128. In other words, on any average day there were only 128 C-54s actually carrying supplies to Berlin. Where were the other 196 C-54s allocated to the airlift? They were down for maintenance or spare parts.

The average airlift C-54 "in commission" was flying eight to ten hours each day. This was actual "flying time" and not counting loading or unloading or time for crew changes. These aircraft were making four to five trips a day to and from Berlin. The C-54 was a passenger plane that had to be modified for cargo hauling. The aircraft was carrying heavier loads than it was designed for, making numerous take-offs and landings at glide angles that caused hard landings. There was excessive ground idling time while aircraft waited in line for take offs. All of these factors and others, including the cargo hauled such as coal, not usual in normal C-54 operations, caused abnormal maintenance problems.

The Air Force required that 50 hour

83

The Wash Dock installation at Oberpfaffenhofen Air Force Depot, 7 September 1949. The Wash Docks were used in the first stages of 200 hour inspection of C-54s engaged in the airlift.

maintenance checks be performed at the airfield from which the aircraft operated and work went on at these bases 24 hours a day, seven days a week. When the aircraft had gone through three intermediate 50 hour maintenance inspections and was getting ready for a fourth, and more detailed one, it would be flown to Burtonwood, England, where the Air Force had established a maintenance depot early in the airlift operation. After four such cycles and due for a fifth, the aircraft was flown back to the US to contractor facilities in New York, Texas, or California for a complete 1,000 hour inspection. When one realizes that this was the cycle of regularly scheduled maintenance and did not account for engine failures, crashes, and other unscheduled maintenance and repairs, it becomes more apparent why it took 354 aircraft to keep an average of 128 in daily operations.

Hundreds of miles from the nearest western airlift terminal, aviation fuel for Air Force planes flows through tubes from a Navy tanker at the Army-run port of Bremerhaven.

# It Takes A Lot of Gas

Prior to the airlift, the USAFE average monthly consumption of aviation fuel was 30,000 barrels. In July 1948, the first full month of airlift operations, consumption jumped to 82,500 barrels. By January 1949 it had climbed to 191,000 barrels and then peaked in July 1949 at 291,000 barrels. More than 100,000,000 gallons of aviation fuel was consumed during the airlift. This fuel was brought over on US Navy tanker ships to Bremerhaven and then piped or shipped by rail to the airfields. The planning and execution of such a logistical operation is another example of the type of problem that had to be met and overcome daily.

After Truman decided to commit to the airlift versus withdrawal from Berlin or the more provocative armed convoy plan, the Berlin crisis entered a phase where diplomatic negotiations took center stage. During the summer of 1948, Truman, apparently a lame duck president, turned over the day-to-day management of the Berlin problem to Secretary of State George C. Marshall as he hit the campaign trail in one of the most amazing comebacks in American political history to defeat Thomas Dewey in November.

While initial success of the Berlin Airlift relieved some of the pressure for more overt action to break the blockade, Berlin had become a symbol of Western resolve making concessions to the Soviets or withdrawal much more difficult. The heroic actions of the pilots, air crews, ground support, and the evident resolve of the Berliners to endure was front page news in the daily newspapers across Western Europe and the United States resulting in a groundswell of support and a propaganda coup for the Western Powers.

The diplomatic efforts of August and September 1948 to resolve the Berlin crisis included the relatively little known fact that the Western Powers were willing to withdraw the West Mark from Berlin circulation in favor of the East Mark. This depended on whether proper Four Power controls over currency and trade could be agreed upon and the Soviet Union lifted the Berlin blockade and agreed to provide for adequate transportation access to and from Berlin.

These diplomatic maneuvers began on Monday, August 2, 1948, when the US, British, and French ambassadors to the Soviet Union met directly with Stalin in Moscow to determine if there was any solution to the Berlin crisis. Stalin proposed the simultaneous introduction of the East Mark in place of the West Mark in the western sectors of Berlin together with removal of Soviet traffic restrictions to and from Berlin. He stated that it was the "insistent wish" of the Soviet government that the London agreement (formation of a provisional West German government) be suspended.

On August 3, Marshall conditionally accepted substitution of the West Mark with the East Mark provided there was control on issuance and credit. Marshall chose to ignore Stalin's "insistent wish" regarding the formation of a West German government.

From 6 to 23 August, 1948, the Western ambassadors in Moscow met with Molotov and Stalin five times to see if the two proposals could be reconciled. Stalin finally agreed to make the Soviet Zone bank that printed and issued East Marks subject to Four Power control as to its authority in Berlin. He also deferred the question of a provisional West German government pending the next meeting of the Council of Foreign Ministers.

Marshall cabled Walter Bedell Smith, US Ambassador to the Soviet Union, on August 25 that the Soviet proposal was unacceptable. Marshall advised "our basic requirements for agreement" were: insistence on co-equal rights to be in Berlin; no abandonment of our position with respect to Western Germany; unequivocal lifting of the blockade on communications, transport and commerce for goods and persons; and adequate quadripartite control of issue and continued use in Berlin of the East Mark.

The US position was unacceptable to the Soviets and, as an alternative, the Berlin problem was referred back to the Military Governors in Berlin. They were instructed, within seven days, to work out detailed agreements for the simultaneous lifting of the blockade and the introduction of the East Mark into all of Berlin under Four-Power supervision.

During the first seven days of September 1948, Clay, Robertson, Koenig, and Sokolovsky met in Berlin with the wary Berliners watching the negotiations with considerable apprehension. The hardened positions of the two opposing power blocks could not be changed and no agreement could be reached. The meetings and the negotiations broke off with each representative reporting back to his government. At the same time these meetings were going on, the Soviet-backed German Communists caused the *de facto* split of the Berlin city government.

Not only did the Soviets not give any ground, but they also attempted to introduce air traffic restrictions in the Berlin air corridors. In addition, they announced periodic air maneuvers and anti-aircraft gun practices in the air corridors in an attempt to disrupt airlift traffic.

When the Soviets were unsuccessful in stopping or delaying the start of the work of the German Constituent Assembly on September 1 in Bonn under Konrad Adenauer, they appeared to lose interest in any settlement of the Berlin crisis. During the last 20 days of September 1948, after the break off of Four Power negotiations, the threat of war again loomed. Truman was pressed by the Secretary of Defense and other senior administrators about conditions

Berlin children on their way to a British Sunderland Flying Boat which will take them to western Germany, 17 August 1948. Over 68,000 Berliners, mostly children and the elderly, were evacuated from Berlin during the Soviet blockade.

under which he would authorize the use of the atom bomb in the event of war with the Soviet Union.[7]

In August, the Americans had approached the British again about planning for armed convoys to supply Berlin. The Americans were already working on a unilateral plan under the code name "Task Force Truculent."[8] The British replied on August 27 that they were still of the opinion that any attempt to force armed convoys into Berlin was militarily and politically unsound because the Soviets, without resorting to force, could interpose sufficient technical obstacles to obstruct such convoys.[9]

When the Americans approached the British in September about the possibility of assembling atom bombs on English soil in the event of war and the use of English soil to launch planes carrying atom bombs, Attlee and other British leaders supported these proposals.[10] But the British still favored negotiations as long as there was any possibility of a solution. Clay had earlier approved the transfer of the B-29 group stationed in Germany to England, but requested for political reasons that one squadron remain in Germany on rotation.[11] Clay obviously desired to keep the B-29s visible to Soviet intelligence and on display as one of the few trump cards available to him.

Faced with alternatives of withdrawal from Berlin—which was unacceptable—or war—which was undesirable unless extreme provocation occurred—the Western Powers reluctantly decided to refer the Berlin problem to the United Nations. Although they had little hope the United Nations could resolve the issue satisfactorily, referral won time without surrendering principles. Clay reported the airlift had progressed to the point that he believed Berlin could be sufficiently supplied during the winter months providing additional C-54s were allocated. The economic and political revival of Western Germany since the currency control of the previous June was exceeding all expectations.

On September 29, 1948, the United States, Great Britain and France formally submitted a complaint to the secretary general of the United Nations charging the "illegal" blockade of Berlin made further negotiations impossible. This and other coercive measures taken by the Soviet Union constituted a threat to international peace and security.

(*Top*) Lights from Wiesbaden Air Base's round-the-clock operation silhouettes C-47s being loaded with food for blockaded Berlin.

# Night Operations

(*Top*) C-54s at Tempelhof. (*Bottom*) Searchlights over the busy airlift Base at Fassberg in the British Occupation Zone of Germany served a dual purpose by illuminating the parking ramp and serving as a navigational aid for pilots on the return trip from Berlin.

Workers delineating the line between the British and Soviet sectors in Potsdamer Platz, 24 August 1948.

With the split of the Berlin police force in July and August 1948, the situation of the Berlin City Council and Magistrate to govern all four sectors of the city became more precarious with each passing day. The seat of the City Council was in the Soviet Sector and technically the City Council was still answerable to the four occupying powers.

Almost every day City Council members and the Magistrate were called before the Soviet commander in Berlin or one of his staff officers. They were ordered to institute Soviet rules and regulations in all of Berlin. Often these orders carried the implied threat of arrest for failure to comply. These orders were routinely countermanded by the Western Powers as they pertained to the three Western Sectors of Berlin. The Berlin City officials were in a "Catch 22" situation.

The Soviets accused the officials of collusion with the Western Powers when they failed to institute orders and regulations proclaimed by the Soviet commander. The Western commanders were sympathetic to the plight of these officials, but they could do little to protect them. Many Berlin political officials and outspoken anti-Communists disappeared. Although the Western Powers accused the Soviets of kidnapping, the Soviets denied it outright when there was no evidence or claimed the individuals arrested had committed criminal offenses when there were witnesses. Many of those who disappeared were never heard from again while others did not return for many years after serving in forced labor camps in the Soviet Union.

It took admirable courage to be an outspoken anti-Communist in Berlin during 1948-49 and in late July, Clay addressed a long standing request from the Department of the Army to designate those Berliners who would be evacuated in the event of a Western Power withdrawal. Clay estimated a maximum of 20,000 Berliners would be so designated, but doubted seriously if that number would actually request evacuation in the event this step proved necessary.[12]

In August 1948, after Soviet military police had continually invaded the Western Sectors to arrest Berliners and had ignored Western Power protests, the Western Powers began erecting barricades in some areas of the city to distinguish where sector boundaries ended.[13] In a city where literally hundreds of streets intersected at unmarked sector boundaries these barricades served as both warnings and advice.

(*Top*) Vehicle barrier being erected in Potsdamer Platz, 24 August 1948. (*Bottom*) US and Soviet military police at the corner of Stresemann Strasse and Nieder Kirchener Strasse, 13 August.

(*Top*) Lord Mayor Louise Schroeder requesting that demonstrators leave the 23 June 1948 City Council meeting. This was the first of many occasions that communist demonstrators disrupted council proceedings. City Council Chairman, Otto Suhr is at Schroeder's left and representatives of the occupation forces are seated along the wall. (*Bottom*) The breakup of the 26 August City Council meeting.

The success of the airbridge and the failure of the Western Powers to withdraw from Berlin as predicted by the Soviets and their German Communist allies seemed to incite the Soviets to take more drastic action. Using the German Communists, they initiated actions to disrupt City Council meetings in the Soviet Sector. They attempted to intimidate the non-Communist members in a classic Communist maneuver, *ala* Petrograd, November 1917. If they could force the non-Communist majority to withdraw or resign, the Communists could quickly elect a mayor, select a Magistrate, and declare themselves the legitimate government for all of Berlin.

Even if this tactic was unsuccessful, their actions might incite the democratic Berlin majority to rise up in anger, causing disturbances and anti-Soviet actions beyond the ability of the small Allied garrisons in Berlin to control. The Soviets would then be able to claim they had been forced to take control of the city to restore order. Both scenarios were played out in Berlin during August and September 1948; however, neither resulted in what the Communists' hoped for.

Because elected mayor Ernst Reuter (SPD) had been unable to assume his post because of Soviet opposition, Louise Schroeder (SPD) had served since 1947 as Acting Mayor. Schroeder, a frail woman, had been an ardent Socialist since the Weimar Republic era. She was quiet, unassuming, completely dedicated to democratic government, and refused to be intimidated by the Communists. Affectionately called "Tante Louise" (Aunt Louise) by Berliners, her health broke down in mid-August 1948 and she was forced to take a leave of absence to recuperate. She was succeeded by Deputy Mayor Ferdinand Friedensburg, a Christian Democrat. Under the Berlin provisional constitution, if Friedensburg was forced out, his replacement would be the next deputy in seniority who happened to be a Communist SED official.

The Soviets wasted no time in putting the pressure on Friedensburg. On Wednesday, August 25, 1948, Communist newspapers in Berlin called for a "popularly elected" Magistrate and "direct action" to change Berlin city government. The following day, the Berlin City Council was scheduled to meet in the City Hall in the Soviet Sector when they were confronted by some 5,000 of the SED's

Communist demonstrators in front of the New City Hall in the Soviet Sector of the city, 26 August 1948. The demonstrator's signs demand a uniform currency and administration, the withdrawal of occupation forces from Berlin and Germany, the end of the "bankrupt Magistrate," and a unified Germany.

Free German Youth and Communist union members who had been transported to the meeting place by Soviet licensed trucks. Carrying banners and shouting Communist slogans, they broke into the assembly chamber and disrupted the meeting which had to be adjourned. The Berlin Soviet Sector police stood idly by and made no effort to restore order.

On Friday, August 27, Otto Suhr (SPD), Chairman of the City Council, wrote a letter to General Kotikov, the Soviet Berlin commandant, requesting adequate protection for City Council meetings, but Kotikov's reply was evasive and non-comittal. A scheduled City Council meeting set for Tuesday, August 31, had to be called off when Communist demonstrators again gathered at Citv Hall.

In an effort to continue an all-city government, the City Council scheduled another meeting for Monday, September 6 and took along approximately 50 Western Sector policemen in civilian clothes to maintain order. Each of the four powers maintained an office in the Soviet Sector City Hall which was used by accredited US, British, French, and Soviet liaison officers representing the four city commanders.

Again the Communists disrupted the meeting and, when the Western Sector police attempted to restore or-

Communist demonstrators force their way into the New City Hall, 6 September 1948.

der, uniformed Soviet Sector police under direct command of a Soviet Army officer started to arrest the Western Sector police. The Western Sector police took refuge in the offices of the three Western Powers liaison offices. Soviet Sector police broke into the US liaison office late that evening, leading off 20 of the Western Sector police,[14] and, breaking an agreement made with French officials, arrested 26 more the following evening as they were leaving the Soviet Sector.[15]

The Berlin City Council was forced to adjourn to a new meeting place in the Berlin Technical University in the British Sector. The SED Communist faction members refused to participate, claimed the City Council was proscribed by law to meet in the City Hall, and the *de facto* split of the city began. A formal protest by Clay through Howley, the US Commander in Berlin, to General Kotikov, the Soviet Berlin Commander was basically rejected.[16]

Reuter, Neumann, and other non-Communist Berlin political leaders called for a protest demonstration on Thursday, September 9, near the *Reichstag* and the Brandenburg Gate in the British Sector, but bordering the Soviet Sector. The avowed purpose was to demonstrate to the Soviets and the world the Berliners support for democratic government in their city. Although Clay had reservations about the demonstration because it would be provocative, Robertson, in whose sector the demonstration was to be held, decided to authorize it.[17] General Herbert, the British Berlin commander, decided to deploy some 500 troops in the ruins of the *Reichstag* in the event the Berliners decided to storm the Soviet Sector.

At 5:00 pm, a crowd of some 200,000 to 300,000—much larger than any of the organizers had predicted—massed in the *Platz der Republik* outside the *Reichstag* under the watchful eyes of Soviet officers with binoculars observing from the Soviet side of the Brandenburg Gate. Speaker after speaker came to the platform to address the crowd and

The City Council meeting at the Berlin Technical University in the British Sector, 6 September 1948. Carl Hubert Schwennicke of the LPD is at the podium, Otto Suhr is seated at the center of the table to his right. Ernst Reuter is sitting at the far right in a light grey suit and bow tie with Ferdinand Friedensburg at his right. (*Inset*) Otto Suhr at a special meeting of the Magistrate, 8 September.

Ernst Reuter addressing up to 300,000 Berliners outside the *Reichstag* after the repeated disruption of City Council meetings in the Soviet Sector, 9 September 1948. Franz Neumann (Partially obscured) and Otto Suhr are standing behind Reuter.

Enlarged newspaper photograph from the 12 September 1948 edition of *Der Tagesspiegel* of a Soviet jeep near the Brandenburg Gate being stoned by a crowd of Berliners after the demonstration.

castigate the Communists and the Soviets for attempting to subjugate them and destroy their city government. The final speaker was Ernst Reuter, the elected Lord Mayor who had been unable to assume his position because of Russian opposition.

According to newspaper reports of the time, the crowd was relatively peaceful, but there was a current of electricity in the air. Reuter could have incited the crowd to do just about anything, but perhaps realizing the danger and futility, plus his responsibility, Reuter chose to appeal to the conscience of world opinion. Reuter stated: ". . . this demonstration gives Allied statesmen an opportunity to find out what the Berlin people really stand for. We cannot be bartered, we cannot be negotiated, we cannot be sold. All political discussions in Berlin are backed by the will of the people determined to maintain its freedom. Whoever would surrender this city, whoever would surrender the people of Berlin, would surrender a world, more, he would surrender himself. . . . People of the world. Look upon this city! You cannot, you must not, forsake us! There is only one possibility for all of us: to stand jointly together until this fight has been won."[18]

After thunderous applause, the meeting began to break up peacefully. However, some youths became unruly and shouted epitaphs at a truck carrying Soviet soldiers.

They also confronted the Soviet guard detail proceeding

View of the 9 September demonstration from the steps of the *Reichstag*. The Soviet War Memorial is at center left.

to the Soviet War Memorial near the Brandenburg Gate just inside the British Sector. This potentially flammable situation was defused by a British Army officer. However, a group of youths then scaled the Brandenburg Gate and tore down and burned the Red flag that had flown over Berlin since May 1945. Shooting broke out in another location where youths had stoned Soviet Sector police, resulting in the fatal wounding of a young 16-year-old Berliner. Finally, the crowd drifted away as more police arrived. Five Berliners, four of them teenagers, arrested at the scene were promptly tried by a Soviet Military court on September 13 and each was sentenced to 25 years imprisonment for "Assault on the Occupation Forces" and "Injuries to Public Order."[19]

On Sunday, September 12, the Communists staged a counter-demonstration in the Soviet Sector. The danger of this situation was summed up by Clay in a cable to Draper:

> The anti-Communist demonstration held in the British sector is being matched tomorrow by a Communist demonstration in the Soviet sector and we are in the midst of a dan-

gerous game. Obviously, western military governments had nothing to do with the anti-Communist demonstration except that the British military government issued a permit. The huge attendance was I am sure a great surprise even to the Germans and led the German political leaders into inflammatory speeches. However, careful documentation of charges indicates some advance planning to this end.

It was difficult if not impossible for the British to refuse the permit in view of the planned Communist mob actions, but to my mind we are playing with dynamite. Mass meetings directed against Soviet military government can easily turn into mass meetings against other occupying powers and can develop into the type of mob government which Hitler played so well to get in power.[20]

Under the provisional Berlin Constitution of 1946 approved by the Four Powers, a City Council election was required during the Fall of 1948. During September 1948, the City Council, now meeting in the British Sector, petitioned the occupying powers to call the required election.

A new R-2000 engine, called "wasps" by the maintenance crews, being swung into position on a waiting C-54 at Rhein-Main Air Base.

# Globemasters to the Rescue

The constant need for spare parts and spare R-2000 engines for the C-54s was critical. Without a constant supply of extra engines, the ability of the maintenance crews to keep C-54s "in commission" would have been impossible. The mission of ferrying these C-54 engines was given to 6th Air Transport Squadron flying C-74 Globemasters out of Brookley Air Force Base, Alabama. There were only 12 C-74s in operation when the airlift began. One was sent over to Rhein-Main in August 1948 for test purposes and completed its 100 hour cycle on September 18, 1948, Air Force Day, when it flew eight 40 ton loads of coal into Berlin to help the US Air Force set a then one-day record for tonnage delivered. But according to Lieutenant Colonel Guy B. Dunn, Jr.:

"The big job done by the C-74 squadron out of Brookley that played a major role in the success of the "Lift" was not the one C-74 that flew the Lift, but the ten aircraft that flew R-2000 engines into and out of Rhein-Main from Kelly Air Force Base, Texas. The unit flew one flight a day from Kelly to Rhein-Main and return hauling 14 engines per trip. Without these overhauled engines the Lift would have broken down due to engine shortages in January 1949.

"When the Lift first started engines were shipped to Westover in their heavy metal cans and then airlifted by Slick Airway (a private commercial contract airline) to Rhein-Main two at a time. As the requirement increased that method could not supply adequate spare engines. Out of the can, we could get 14 engines on the C-74 and leave the cans at Kelly."

(*Top*) Readying an R-2000 engine for its exit at Rhein-Main Air Base. (*Bottom*) A giant C-74 unloading at Gatow Airfield becomes an attraction for sightseers.

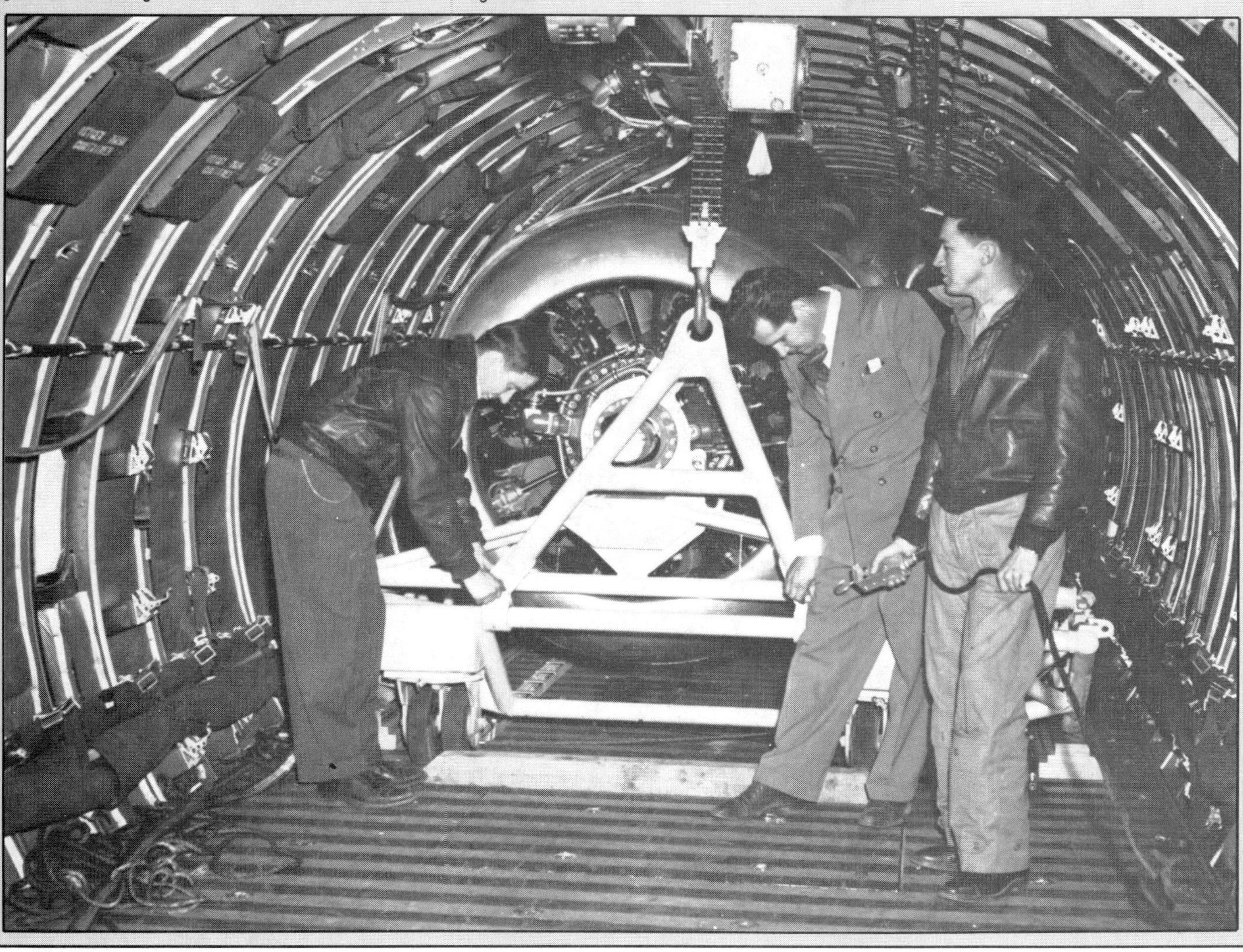

A group of Berlin children try to express their appreciation to Lieutenant Gail S. Halvorsen, the originator of "Operation Little Vittles," for the thousands of packages of gum and candy he and his friends dropped over Berlin in tiny parachutes.

# The Chocolate Flyer

The airlift pilots and crews were especially captivated by the children who waved to them on their final approach into Tempelhof. The most celebrated pilot of the airlift became Lieutenant Gail S. Halvorsen, "the Chocolate Flyer." Halvorsen had been assigned to 17th Air Transport Squadron, Mobile, Alabama, when

(*Top*) Miniature parachutes can be seen dropping from Halvorsen's C-54 as he brings the plane in for a landing at Tempelhof. (*Bottom*) Berlin children scramble for Halvorsen's tiny presents.

he got his airlift orders so suddenly he only had time to park his car under a tree in Mobile and hide the keys. After flying the "Vittles" run for two weeks in July 1948, Halvorsen got permission to make a personal trip to Berlin.

Halvorsen, a veteran of the North African and Italian campaigns of World war II, had experienced the children of these wartorn countries begging for candy, gum, and cigarettes. When he met a group of Berlin children, he was taken aback by their reserve and recalled at the time. . . . "I got in the middle of these kids, and what do you think happened? None of them jerked at my pants. . . . They wanted to hold a polite conversation and try out their English on me. Their English is about as bad as my German. After about one hour, in which I gained considerable stature as an airlift pilot, I noticed something was missing. I couldn't put my finger on it, but it nagged me. And finally I realized what it was. Those kids hadn't begged for a single thing. . . . it wasn't lack of candy-hunger that held them back; they just lacked the brass other kids have. So I told them to be down at the end of the runway next day and I'd drop them some gum and candy. That night I tied up some candy bars and gum in handkerchiefs and had my chief sling them out on a signal from me next day. Day by day the crowd of kids waiting for the drop got bigger, and day by day my supply of handkerchiefs, old shirts, GI sheets, and old shorts, all of which I use for parachutes, gets smaller."

Halverson's philanthropy was picked up by the Berlin press and then the American newspapers. He became so famous he was sent back to the United States where he was interviewed by radio, newspaper, and magazines. Halvorsen was followed by a series of "chocolate fliers," who served as some of the best good-will ambassadors the US Air Force ever had.

Halvorsen's bunk becomes a factory for miniature parachutes weighted with Lyons chocolate bars.

(*Left*) Captain Eugene T. Williams dropping sweets during the landing approach to Tempelhof. (*Bottom*) Captain Lawrence Caskey loading boxes of candy onto his C-54 at Wiesbaden Air Base. Before Caskey took over "Operation Little Vittles," he had flown 134 wartime trips over the "Hump" between India and China and made flights into the jungles of Brazil supplying a *National Geographic* expedition in 1947. (*Right*) A young girl with one of the estimated 150,000 *Schokoladenflieger* gifts dropped over Berlin.

UNITED STATES AIR FORCE

Airlift C-54s being unloaded at Tempelhof after the heaviest snowfall of the winter blanketed the airport in white on 1 March 1949. High winds, poor visibility, and icing conditions near ground level forced a temporary cessation of operations during the night, but clearing skies the following day brought tonnages to the near normal level.

# SIX

# The Winter Campaign

During October 1948, the 100th day of the airlift was celebrated with speeches, statements, and a special Berlin postal cancellation on mail. The initial stage of the airlift had been very successful, but the Soviets showed no signs of ending the blockade and the big test of winter was approaching. Would the Western Powers be able to continue the pace during the normal bad weather of late fall and winter in northern Europe? Would the Berliners continue to support the Western Powers if food and coal ran out? The Soviets were still betting the airlift could be not sustained during the winter and continually publicized the forthcoming withdrawal of the Western Powers from Berlin.

One of the problems still existing which thwarted maximum airlift efficiency was divided command. General William H. Tunner headed up the American effort which had been designated the 1st Airlift Task Force with headquarters in Wiesbaden under the USAFE commanded by General Curtis LeMay. The British effort was headed by Air Commodore J.W.F. Merer, commanding the No. 46 Group, under Air Marshal Sir Arthur P.M. Saunders, commander in chief of the British Air Forces of Occupation (BAFO). Some aspects of the airlift were coordinated, but if schedules could be consolidated at all participating airfields, smoother and more efficient operations could result. Tunner had already sent C-54s to the British airfield at

Awaiting their turn to take off for Berlin, US Air Force C-54s will land at Gatow in the British Sector of Berlin just one hour from their British Zone airlift terminat at Fassberg.

Fassberg in August and desired to send more to take advantage of the short central air corridor.

At Tunner's suggestion, LeMay approached Saunders about establishing combined US-British airlift operations. The British, realizing the Americans would get the top post because the US airlift effort was much larger than theirs, were reluctant, but finally in the interest of a more efficient operation, the British agreed. On October 15, the British and Americans announced the establishment of the Combined Air Lift Task Force (CALTF) with Tunner commanding and Merer as deputy commander.

The central and northern Berlin air corridors into the British Zone of Germany were not only shorter, but over flatter terrain than the southern corridor leading into the US Zone. By October the airlift was utilizing six British

(*Top*) A British armored car guards a string of Fassberg-based C-54s being unloaded at Gatow Airfield in the early morning haze. Even the residue from the unloading of coal is not wasted. Swept into neat piles, it is rebagged and added to the beleagured city's supplies. (*Bottom*) British and American personnel at Fassberg's traffic control center.

Zone airfields—Fassberg, Wunsdorf, Bueckeberg, Fuhlsbuettel, Luebeck, and Schleswig-Land—with a seventh nearing completion near Celle plus the seaplane base at Finkenwerder. Only Wiesbaden and Rhein-Main from the US Zone were being used.

The British, who had a very mixed fleet of military and civilian contract planes, could not fully use their better situated airfields. The Americans, who had by October 1 standardized their fleet with the larger C-54s, capable of delivering a ten ton load per plane, were supplying more than 3,000 tons per day versus the 1,500 tons per day by the British. It made sense to station even more C-54s at the British fields where two planes could do the work of three from Wiesbaden or Rhein-Main and Tunner moved additional C-54s there when Celle was completed in December.

It also made sense to use the large C-54s for the basics, such as coal and foodstuffs, and use the British mixed fleet for more specialized cargos. Liquid fuels were supplied largely by a British civilian tanker fleet operating out of Wunsdorf. Prior to the arrival of the British tankers, liquid fuel had been hauled into Berlin in 55 gallon drums which were clumsy, space consuming, and had to be steam-cleaned in Berlin and lifted back out.

Another difficult commodity was salt and Berlin required 38 tons per day. Salt is difficult to transport because it eats through alloys and cables causing severe damage to airplane control systems. At first, the British Sunderland flying boats, which were treated to resist the corrosive action of salt water, were used. They operated out of the

A British Army enlisted man directs the parking of a coal truck as German laborers prepare to load a shipment of coal aboard a C-54 at Fassberg.

Finkenwerder seaplane base near Hamburg and landed on the Havel Lake in Berlin. However, when winter came and ice formed on the lake, the use of the Sunderlands had to be terminated. Thereafter, the British assigned Halifax bombers to haul salt. The salt was carried in special basket-like containers slung in the bomb-bay section.[1]

To build the new airfield at Tegel in Berlin, heavy construction equipment was necessary. In addition to the US C-82s and one C-74 Globemaster available to transport such heavy equipment, the British Bristol freighters were used for these awkward loads. Luebeck airfield became the receiving station for some 68,000 persons, mainly children and elder persons, evacuated from Berlin while Bueckeburg airfield operated a passenger shuttle system to and from the city.

The establishment of CALTF also changed the concept of the airbridge. Previously, the airlift's mission was to assure the minimum daily required tonnage arrived in Berlin. Thereafter, the effort would be to increase tonnage from daily quotas to unlimited tonnage. In other words, if there was congestion in the Berlin air corridors and operations had to be slowed down, a US C-54 with ten tons of cargo took precedence over a Royal Air Force Dakota with three tons.

Of all the difficulties facing the airlift, one of the greatest single problems was weather. Low clouds, fog, freezing

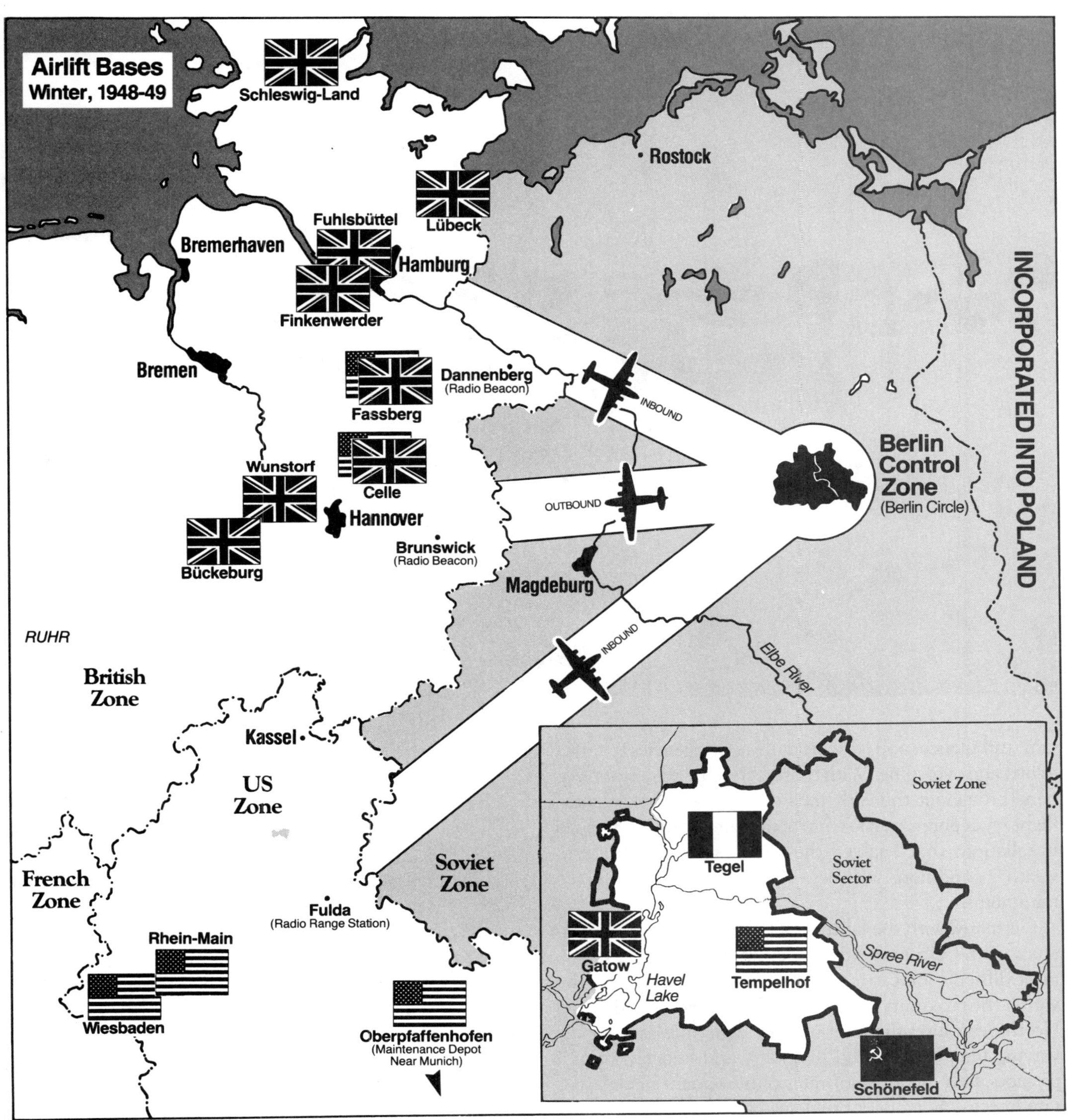
Airlift Bases
Winter, 1948-49
Schleswig-Land
Rostock
Lübeck
Fuhlsbüttel
Bremerhaven
Hamburg
Finkenwerder
INCORPORATED INTO POLAND
Bremen
Dannenberg
(Radio Beacon)
INBOUND
Fassberg
Berlin
Control
Zone
(Berlin Circle)
Wunstorf
Celle
OUTBOUND
Hannover
Brunswick
(Radio Beacon)
Bückeburg
Magdeburg
RUHR
INBOUND
Elbe River
British
Zone
Kassel
US
Zone
Soviet Zone
Tegel
Soviet
Sector
French
Zone
Soviet
Zone
Fulda
(Radio Range Station)
Rhein-Main
Gatow
Havel
Lake
Tempelhof
Spree River
Wiesbaden
Oberpfaffenhofen
(Maintenance Depot
Near Munich)
Schönefeld

(*Opposite and below*) A sample of the kind of weather that plagued flight operations throughout the airlift.

rain, turbulence, and ice were daily contingencies that had to met and overcome. With these facts in mind, airlift planners throughout the early days of the operation prepared flight procedures, traffic control measures, and landing aid installations that enabled the airlift crews to operate in weather conditions well below the established Air Force minimums.

Germany, with the latitude of Labrador and the temperature of the US mid-Atlantic coast, presents one of the most difficult forecasting areas in the world. During the winter the proximity of the warm Gulf Stream and the cold North Sea causes the inter-mixture of air masses of widely varying temperatures and humidity, and frequent frontal passages with inconsistent rates of movement made accurate forecasting a major problem. Newspaper reports such as these were not uncommon in November and December 1948:

Berlin, November 3, 1948, *Der Kurier*: "Although rain and fog during the last 24 hours greatly hampered operations, 412 US and British flights moved more than 4,000 tons of supplies to Berlin." Berlin, November 4, 1948, *Der Kurier*: "During the past 24 hours, 315 US and British flights carried more than 3,000 tons of supplies to Berlin. Due to unfavorable weather conditions, flying operations at the Gatow airfield had to be interrupted for ten hours. . . ." Berlin, November 8, 1948, (AP): "During the night to Monday, a dense fog over Frankfurt and Wiesbaden greatly obstructed airlift operations." Berlin, November 18, 1948, *Der Kurier*: "Due to overcast conditions prevailing in Western Germany, only 25 airplanes were able to

take off from Frankfurt. All of the crews had reported for duty voluntarily. . . ."

By the end of October 1948, the airlift operational techniques were established. The necessary planes and personnel were in place. However, the question remained: Could the Airlift Task Force supply a city of more than two million people totally by air during the poor flying weather season from November through January? Many historians have wondered what the outcome of the Berlin Airlift would have been had the Soviets instituted the blockade in October instead of June.

The minimum conditions for the airlift airfields were 200 feet ceiling and one-half mile visibility, except Tempelhof (because of the apartment buildings) which was 400 feet ceiling and one mile visibility. The US Air Force, which before the airlift had a single weather squadron in Europe, did everything it could to beef up its weather forecasting. A B-29 squadron in England was assigned to conduct weather observation. A squadron of B-17s was operated out of Wiesbaden on weather observation missions. Airlift pilot reports were used extensively, but a change of 1 degree in temperature or a few knots change in wind force could mean a variation of visibility and ceiling that could mean the difference between a successful landing or a pass over and return to base without landing the necessary supplies for Berlin.

Pilot Jeff Warren recalls several landings at Tempelhof when his altimeter read 100 feet and he could not see the landing strip. As Warren stated it would have been easy to refuse landing under such conditions and turn around for

(*Top*) Radio operators on the B-17 weather patrols of the airlift corridors reported on flight conditions every 20 minutes from pre-determined check points. (*Center*) Airlift pilots receiving weather information from a briefing jeep at Tempelhof. (*Bottom*) A weather officer at Oberpfaffenhofen Air Force Depot briefs the crew of a B-17 before its six-hour patrol of the corridors.

home. Why did pilots, who had three years earlier been bombing this same city, now risk their lives to feed and support it? Several pilots have stated it was a simple matter of pride. They had a mission to accomplish and they set out to prove to everybody and anybody they could fulfill that mission under any condition.

From July to October 1948, the tonnage delivered to Berlin increased each month. In July, 69,000 tons were delivered; in August, 119,002; in September, 139,623; and in October, 147,581. In November, the first month of the bad weather period, the tonnage delivered declined to 113,588. What would happen in December, January, and February?

Several events occurred in November and December 1948 which turned things around for the airlift. The new Tegel airfield in Berlin and another new airport in the British Zone at Celle-Wietzenruch became operational. The US Air Force increased the total number of C-54s assigned to the airlift to 225. The number of British Royal Air Force planes was also increased and the number of chartered planes from private airlines increased.

The significance of the two airfields in the British Zone at Fassberg and Celle was immense. Because of their close location in two of the three air corridors, flying time between these two airports and Berlin was only about half that of Rhein-Main and Wiesbaden to Berlin. Celle and Fassberg were also close to the Ruhr which supplied coal, the most important and most carried commodity into Berlin. In December 1948, delivered tonnage to Berlin dramatically increased to 141,468 on 16,487 flights. This was 2,300 fewer flights than were required to carry almost the same tonnage in September when the C-47s were still being used. In January 1949, a new record monthly tonnage of 171,959 was delivered.

The initial minimum requirement to feed and maintain Berlin was set at 4,500 tons daily, but during the fall of 1948 this was revised upwards to a minimum comfort level of 5,620 tons per day. After January 1949, this minimum comfort level was exceeded every day and the excess went for stockpiling. To demonstrate this success to the Soviets, the world, and especially to the people of Berlin, East and West, in January the daily food ration for West Berliners was raised from 1,600 to 1,880 calories a day.[2]

(*Top*) Air Installations personnel clear taxiways at Tempelhof after a 19 March snowstorm. (*Bottom*) C-54s at Wiesbaden stand out against a background of snow, 2 March 1949.

(*Opposite left*) The first C-54 to arrive at Tegel Airfield lands during a light rain, 5 November 1948. (*Opposite right*) The Radio Berlin broadcast tower which obstructed the air approaches to Tegel Airfield. (*Opposite bottom*) The dedication of Tegel Airfield, 1 December 1948. General Jean Ganeval, who ordered the demolition of Radio Berlin's broadcast tower, is saluting at front row left.

The French, because of a lack of transport planes, were unable to do much to support the airlift, but, in December 1948, they demonstrated they too could contribute. The new Tegel airport in Berlin, located in the French sector, was completed on Friday, November 5, almost two months ahead of schedule and test flights began immediately. Before the new airfield could become fully operational, however, something had to be done about a large 200 foot radio tower sticking up in the approach path. The tower was owned by the Soviet controlled Radio Berlin and numerous French requests to the Soviets to move it or dismantle it had been ignored.

Finally, in December when Tegel was to become fully operational and the tower still stood presenting an obvious danger to aircraft, the French attached explosives to its base and blew it down. The next day, Kotikov, the Soviet Berlin Commander, stormed into French General Jean Ganeval's headquarters protesting and threatening dire consequences for the French. Ganeval politely, but firmly, told Kotikov that the Soviets had had ample time to solve the problem, had ignored his requests, and, therefore, he had had no other alternative to insure planes and lives were not threatened.

This courageous action by the French commander won the support of his British and American colleagues and the admiration and praise of the Berliners. A few days later, the French further endeared themselves to the Berlin populace when General Pierre Koenig, the French military governor, made his private plane available to transport Christmas gifts for Berlin children.

By the end of January 1949, the airlift had proven that it could supply Berlin indefinitely in any kind of weather. It became obvious, even to the Soviets, that, short of war, the blockade had been broken. The Western Powers had demonstrated their continued will to remain in Berlin. The propaganda defeat suffered by the Soviets was inescapable. News media coverage described the daily successes of the airlift and "world opinion," as demonstrated by the United Nations resolutions, was massively on the side of the West Berliners and the Western Powers. In addition, a counter-blockade begun in mid-1948 was beginning to have an adverse economic effect on the Soviet Zone. The only question left was how long did the Soviet Union want to continue this failed operation, but the Western Powers would have to be alert to any Soviet signal and permit some graceful way out.

## Airlift Intrigue
### or
### How Records Are Broken

In an attempt to raise morale and give recognition to outstanding efforts, General Tunner set up competition between units by establishing a "Howgoesit" board at each installation. Each day every unit was given a quota and at the end of the 24 hour period the results were posted on the boards and published in the *Task Force Times*, a daily newspaper established by Tunner specifically for airlift task force units. The daily competition soon set off intense rivalry between units and bases even spilling over to loading and unloading crews.

(*Top*) While waiting for their "block," pilots relax in the pilots' lounge at Wiesbaden. (*Bottom*) During yet another monotonous flight to Berlin, the radio operator aboard a C-54 describes interference he's receiving as the engineer (seated behind the pilots) wonders aloud about a light outside the right window.

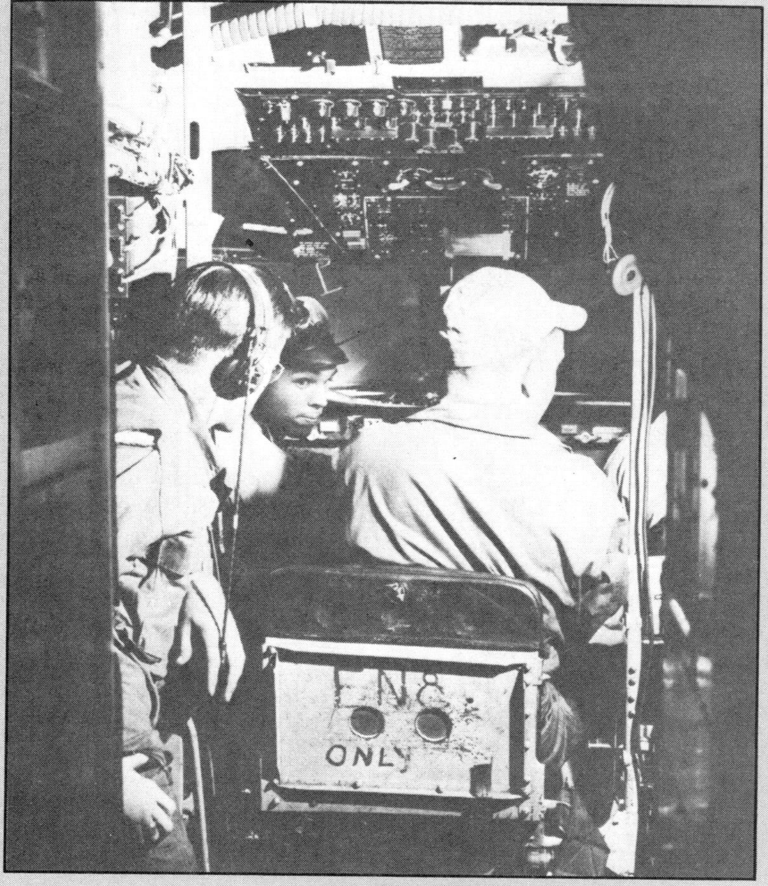


# Dull Routine

The pilots and crewmen who flew the airlift came from all over the world on short notice. They were uprooted from their families and placed on temporary duty for 45 to 90 days. For some it seemed like a lark to get away from peacetime routines and take part in a mission that made headlines almost every day in the newspapers of America and Europe. However, as the airlift dragged on with no end in sight and the temporary duty orders were extended, involuntarily in many cases, for another 90 or 180 days, many men and their families experienced hardships. Many arrived without personnel or financial records. Records were sometimes lost which resulted in financial problems for their families in such far off places as Alaska, Japan, Hawaii, and the Canal Zone. As these difficulties were overcome, the dull routine of 12 to 16 hour days, seven days a week, set in.

(*Top*) Project Sleighbells brought Christmas gifts from dependents of Vittles fliers from all parts of the world to Germany. In the foreground are some of the mail bags to be loaded and to the extreme left can be seen some of the C-74 crew members. At the extreme right are crew members of a plane which had just arrived from Alaska bringing in gifts for the project. The women and children are dependents of Vittles personnel from Brookley Air Force Base and Mobile, Alabama. (*Bottom*) Air Force personnel from Fassberg RAF Station are shown aboard the "Rotation Special" which will take them to the Bremerhaven Port of Embarkation. This was the first group to be returned to the United States under the 6-month Airlift rotation plan.

The office complex of Soviet controled Radio Berlin.

The Berlin City Council originally set the date of November 14, 1948, for the city-wide elections, but the three Western Sector commanders, meeting on October 5 to approve the election regulations, moved the date to Sunday, December 5. The question then became: Would the Russians permit the Soviet Sector to participate in the face of a certain rejection of the Communist SED in proportions more overwhelming than their 1946 defeat? If not, what excuse would be used? On October 20, 1948, the Soviet Sector commander replied to the City Council request for city-wide elections by declaring the Soviet Sector would not participate because of "terrorism, political persecution, and Fascist war propaganda" in the three Western Sectors.[3]

In the face of these absurd charges, the election laws were amended to suspend the election in the Soviet Sector. However, to provide for Soviet Sector continued representation, the City Council agreed to hold over the 32 members (16 SPD, 11 SED, and 5 CSU) chosen in the Soviet Sector in the 1946 elections. This measure adopted by the City Council was an obvious effort to maintain the semblance of a city-wide government after the December elections.

The Communist SED recognized it could not realistically face the Berlin electorate because it had supported the blockade. It refused to permit the party's name to appear on the ballot. In an attempt to dissuade and intimidate Berliners from the three Western Sectors from going to the polls, the Communists press and radio engaged in a bitter campaign against the elected city leaders and the legal city government. The Communists resorted to constant reports of the eminent Western Power withdrawal from Berlin and rumors that polling lists of participating voters would then fall in Soviet hands. The implication was that reprisals would follow.

One of the leading instruments of the Communist propaganda campaign was Radio Berlin (*Berliner Rundfunk*) which had been controlled by the Communists since June 1945, before the Western Powers arrived in Berin. All efforts by the Western Powers to gain a voice in the direction of Radio Berlin, one of the most powerful radio signals in Europe, had been thwarted by the Soviets and their German Communist allies. Frustrated and with no other choice than to surrender the air waves to the Communists, the Americans had licensed RIAS (Radio In America Sector) in September 1946, and provided it with a 1,000 watt transmitter. In early 1947, this was increased to 2,500 watts and on July 1 1947, a 20,000 watt station went on the air with a radius of 75 kilometers.

At first, RIAS only operated a few hours a day and its listening audience was limited because of its weak signal. In February 1948, Clay gave RIAS permission to answer

Communist anti-Western propaganda, installed an American director to bear the brunt of any Soviet criticism for the RIAS German staff, and increased its air time to 13 hours daily. When the Berlin blockade began, RIAS immediately began to broadcast 24 hours a day and provided all types of emergency information for Berliners regarding daily power allocations and availability of rationed items. Because newsprint was scarce in the early months of the blockade, RIAS sent out mobile trucks with loudspeakers to various neighborhoods to get needed information and news to Berliners without newspapers and radios. At the request of the Air Force, RIAS also provided a homing beacon for airlift pilots en route to Berlin.[4]

RIAS became the voice and spirit of Berliners determined to fight the attempted Communist takeover of their

During an electrical cut-off, a RIAS announcer reads the news over a loudspeaker to Berliners at the corner of Hardenberg Strasse and Joachimstaler Strasse.

(*Top*) RIAS announcer doing a remote broadcast from Potsdamer Platz, 28 August 1948. (*Bottom*) RIAS announcer reading the news during one of numerous electrical cut-offs in the Western Sectors. The loud speaker is the barrel shaped object mounted on the vehicle's right fender.

city. Top-notch German commentators were recruited to cover all news events. Forums and round table discussions were conducted on all political questions. But the most popular programs were the political satire programs featuring noted Berlin comedians and satirists poking fun at the Communists, the Western Powers, and the Berliners themselves.

The most popular of these political satire programs was *Die Insulaner* (The Islanders) with a cast of characters of "typical" Berliners such as housewives, workers, teachers, and Communist party functionaries explaining the latest news. With truth and ridicule, they made the Berliners laugh with lines like: "To insure a warm Christmas, the date was to be shifted to July 25." And to poke fun at the dehydrated American foods they were forced to use: "Decorations for Christmas would be no problem, the Allies would fly in powdered Christmas trees that could be reconstituted with water." The warmed-over toast they ate became "Stalin cutlets," and one of the best jokes was: "We are in luck. Just imagine if the Americans were blocking Berlin and the Russians were running the airlift." Clay was later to state, "Next to the airlift, RIAS was the strongest weapon in the Cold War."[5]

The Berliners responded to the alternative of the fair, truthful broadcasting of RIAS as opposed to the slanted Communist propaganda of Radio Berlin. Independent surveys showed RIAS' listening audience in Berlin increased from 34 percent in early 1948 to 80 percent by October 1948.

Without the participation of the Communist SED in the Berlin election campaign, except in the negative sense of attempting to discourage participation, the Socialists (SPD), Christian Democrats (CDU), and the Liberal Democrats (LDP) parties concentrated on getting the vote out and making the election a referendum for Berlin's support for democracy versus totalitarianism. Their purpose was not only to demonstrate to the Soviets and their German Communist allies that they could not be intimidated, but also to show the world their determination and desire for freedom.

The Western Powers expected the Soviets to take some action after the December 5 elections to formalize the *de facto* split of the city which had begun in June with the cur-

(*Left*) Communist Free German Youth demonstrators, 1 December 1948. (*Right*) Ernst Reuter casts his ballot during the city elections, 5 December.

rency reform and had become more aggravated in the following months when the City Council and other city agencies had been forced out of the Soviet Sector. The Communists decided to move the time table up. On Tuesday, November 30, 1948, just five days before the election, the SED and the "Democratic Bloc" staged a meeting in the Soviet Sector of Berlin; elected a "provisional" democratic Magistrate for Greater Berlin; and "unanimously" elected Friedrich Ebert Jr., son of the first president of the Weimar Republic, as Lord Mayor of Berlin. This sham puppet city government promptly claimed to be the only "legal" government for all of Berlin and was immediately recognized by the Soviet military governor as such.

Why the Soviets acted before December 5 when they could have blamed the Western Powers for splitting the city by acting after the elections, is unknown. Perhaps, it was a further step at intimidation and an additional measure to discourage Berliners from the three Western Sectors from going to the polls. Regardless, it is easy to see what the fate of Berlin would have been without the presence of the Western Powers—a classic Communist *coupe d'état*. What likely would have occurred in the Western Sectors of Berlin would have been a replay of what had happened earlier that year in Czechoslovakia when elected non-Communist leaders attempted to demonstrate a measure of independence.

It is interesting to note that November 30 was the worst day of the worst month of the airlift. Because of extremely poor flying weather conditions, only one US C-54 carrying ten tons of supplies was able to land in Berlin. The British were able to land a few planes, but the total tonnage delivered was only 72 tons, a fraction of the minimum 4,500 daily tonnage required. The first few days of December 1948 were not much better. This was on the very eve of the election.

The Soviets kept up their barrage of propaganda and false rumors. On December 4, the official Soviet Military Authority German language newspaper, *Taegliche Rundschau*, printed a banner headline, "The Western Powers Will Leave Berlin in January."[6] To demonstrate their opposition to this election, the Communist SED exhorted its followers to cast spoiled ballots as evidence of their displeasure with the democratic parties and the election itself.

What would be the reaction of the Berliners? Here was a city and a population which had had very limited exposure to democratic government and, what little they had from 1919 to 1933, had not been successful. Before that was a

West Berliner reading a newspaper by candle light during an electrical cut-off, July 1948.

monarchy. Then a totalitarian state dominated by a dictator's single political party led to six years of war ending in bombings, pillaging, and total defeat. Their city over 60 percent destroyed and under occupation by two opposing political ideologies, they were being asked to make a choice while undergoing a blockade and severe economic hardships.

If one looked at it through the eyes of a Berliner in 1948, who could have blamed them for surrendering to what looked like the inevitable? Which power block was the stronger? All they had to do was look around. The Soviet Union had already swallowed up eastern Europe. France and Italy were tottering on the brink of succumbing to Communism. Great Britain was a shell of a once-great power. Only the United States appeared to be capable of challenging the Soviet Union. But the United States was far away and the Soviet Union was on their doorstep. Plus, the United States always seemed to vacillate with its democratic form of government breathing hot and cold on whether to become involved in "foreign entanglements." There was no hesitation on the part of the Soviet Union. It spoke as one voice for world Communism and its determination to destroy capitalism.

The Berliner is known to have a quick mouth and a self-deprecating cynical view of the world, but Berliners had also become very politically sophisticated having been wooed by the experts in propaganda. They had learned to look behind the banners and slogans to see if the deeds and actions matched the words. Although political realities might have convinced them they had little future with the West, the deeds and actions of the Soviet Union and the German Communists in destroying the unity of their city required their protests be heard. The one way available to them in December 1948, was the ballot.

On Sunday, December 5, 1948, Berliners demonstrated to the Soviet Union and the world they would not be intimidated. They went to the polls in overwhelming numbers to show their support for democratic government. More than 86 percent of all eligible voters cast ballots with the SPD getting 65 percent, the CDU 19 percent, and the LDP 16 percent. Of the eligible 1,586,461 voters in the three Western Sectors, 1,369,492 cast ballots and less than 1 percent were deliberately spoiled as advocated by the Communists. In spite of Communist threats to create disorder at polling places, the election went off peacefully with only a few minor incidents.

The political events of November 30 and December 5, finalized the split of city government and administrative agencies. Although some cooperation continued in certain limited areas, Berlin has been politically, socially, and economically two cities since December 1948.

On December 7, the old City Council met and again elected Ernst Reuter as Lord Mayor and, with no potential of a Soviet veto, Reuter assumed his rightful post denied him since 1947. This action was reconfirmed on January 14, 1949, when the new City Council reelected Reuter, his two deputy mayors, Louise Schroeder and Dr. Friedensburg, and a new Magistrate. Although Reuter rightfully proclaimed his government was the legal government for all of Berlin, reality then and now is that his authority was

Free University students, 1949.

limited to the 12 western boroughs of Berlin. Reuter became the first mayor of what is now West Berlin.

Another significant event occurred during the first week of December 1948, when on December 4, the Free University in West Berlin was formally opened in an official ceremony at the Titania Palast. The need for an alternative to once world famous Humboldt University, located in the Soviet Sector of Berlin, became evident in early 1948 when the Communists began ousting professors and students who did not conform to the ideology proclaimed by the Communists. In April 1948 an informal arrangement began with US assistance in the Dahlem district around a nucleus of buildings formerly housing the Kaiser Wilhelm Academy. Professors and students first came from Humboldt University and became the nucleus for, what is today, a symbol of academic freedom with an international student body. In 1950, the Ford Foundation contributed funds for classrooms, an auditorium, and a library.

With the city now more or less officially divided, there was a pressing need to begin establishing a sound economic foundation in West Berlin. To attain this, one of the first orders of business had to be to establish the West Mark as the sole legal currency for West Berlin and the city fathers began pressing the Western Powers to initiate the necessary measures. Since June 1948, the Western Sectors had operated under a dual currency system. Because the Western Powers had been negotiating with the Soviet Union through mid-September 1948 on the basis of withdrawing the West Mark and making the East Mark the only legal currency for all of Berlin, the Western Powers had deliberately restricted the amounts of West Marks in circulation in Berlin. This, and other factors, had caused the West Mark to appreciate against the East Mark.

During late 1948 and early 1949, one West Mark bought

A Currency Exchange Office in the British Sector. The sign in the window gives the exchange rate for that day.

three and one-half to four East marks. Because East Marks could be used to buy most goods and services furnished by the Berlin city government, government agencies took in East Marks almost exclusively. However, by law they were required to pay their employees 25 percent of their salaries in West Marks. This caused every city agency to operate at a deficit which had to underwritten by the Western Powers, plus additional support was needed from the Western Zones of Germany.

Still the Western Powers hesitated. In September 1948, they had put the currency question before the United Nations and they were reluctant to take action pending the UN decision. However, after the city split in December, delay became unnecessary. The possibility of a solution that would reunite the city became remote and the need to set the Western Sectors on a firmer economic foundation became overriding.

Beginning in late December 1948, certain telecommunications services and postal fees could only be paid for with West Marks in the Western Sectors of Berlin and the first

## Coal and Liquid Fuel

Coal, which represented two-thirds of all tonnage airlifted to Berlin, presented some unique transportation problems. The coal dust would sift out from the sacks and seep into the inner fuselage, wings, and even the engines. At first coal was sacked into Army duffel bags, but later cloth and paper bags were developed. Dust control was attempted by laying a tarpaulin on the aircraft floor and by dampening the cloth bags or by doubling the paper bags, but the dust problem persisted throughout the airlift. Commander Herman Krol recalled flying a Navy R5D back to the United States in March 1949 for its 1,000 hour maintenance check. Upon dropping off the plane, he was informed it was almost 1,000 pounds overweight. Later, he learned this was coal dust which had seeped into the fuselage.

Liquid fuel hauling presented a different problem. At first, 55 gallon metal drums were used, but proved unsatisfactory because of the material tonnage lost in the drums' weight, the necessity of steam cleaning the empty containers, and outlifting them from Berlin. Then the British contracted for the services of a fleet of commercial tanker aircraft capable of delivering 550 tons a day of liquid fuel. Because the tanker method of fuel transport proved by far the most efficient, the airlift of all liquid fuels was assigned to this fleet.

British bases were used, with approximately half of the total fuel airlifted originating at Wunsdorf, where a unique loading system was installed. This consisted of rail sidings which permitted rail tank cars to deliver directly to underground storage pools from which the various fuels were pumped to twelve distributing points at aircraft parking positions. To load an aircraft, the desired quantity was selected on the

(*Top left*) Coal being unloaded at Tempelhof. (*Top right*) Aircraft of the Gatow-Fassberg coal run. Note the spilled coal at left which will eventually be rebagged. (*Bottom*) Much of the coal flown into Berlin was unloaded into barges on the Havel River. When filled, the barges carried coal to Kladow or Westhafen area for distribution to industries and homes in the blockaded city. The barges carried an average of 500 to 700 tons of "vittles" coal daily. (*Bottom right*) A resident of the Neukoeln District receiving her weekly coal ration.

regulator dial; and electric pumps provided a flow of 100 gallons a minute and stopped automatically when the pre-set tonnage was reached. Tankers then flew into Gatow and Tegel, where pipes to underground storage tanks enabled unloading by gravity flow directly from the aircraft at a rate of $8^1/_2$ tons in 18 minutes.

(*Left*) Elderly Berliners taking advantage of one of the many warming centers established in the Western Sectors during the winter of 1948-1949 because of the coal and electrical rationing. (*Right*) Children stealing coal from a delivery truck to warm their homes against the long, cold nights.

steps toward making the West Mark the sole legal tender in West Berlin began.

This question was first raised by Clay on September 28, 1948, in a cable to Army Under Secretary William Draper. Over the next six months, the subject came up at least 18 times in cable traffic between Clay and Washington. After Clay finally won over Washington objections about disturbing the status quo while the UN commission of experts was studying the question, the French continued to throw up roadblocks. Even after the Communist action of setting up a rump city government in the Soviet Sector and the elections in the Western Sectors had effectively split the city, the French continued to object. Ever fearful of possible German resurgence, the French did not want any ties between West Berlin and the proposed West German government.

On December 22, the United Nations committee of experts, formed in November to study the Berlin currency issue, made a preliminary draft of its findings. The experts, ignoring the division of the city earlier in December, recommended the West Mark be withdrawn from circulation and the East Mark be made the only currency for all of Berlin. Clay immediately made his objections known and the United States government rejected the draft report as unworkable because it was based on a unified Berlin which no longer existed.

This rejection caused the British, who had heretofore supported the US position on making the West Mark the sole legal tender in the West Sectors, to back off because the US rejection shut off any discussions or possible agreement with the Soviets. Discussions on the Berlin currency issue continued in Geneva between technical specialists representing the Four Powers and the UN committee through January and early February 1949, but finally ceased on February 11 when the UN committee reported they had been unable to recommend a plan acceptable to all four powers. At one time during January 1949, because of continued British and French opposition, the US delegation in Geneva proposed unilateral action by the US to make the West Mark the sole legal tender in the US Sector of Berlin, but Clay rejected this proposal as unworkable.[8]

After the Western Powers submitted their official complaint to the United Nations on September 29, they seemed to lose interest in a negotiated settlement. Even with winter approaching, the Western Powers, and especially the United States, seemed to believe that time

Harry S Truman, happy (and unexpected) winner of the 1948 US presidential election.

was on their side.

On October 3, 1948, the Soviet Union disputed the competence of the United Nations Security Council to deal with the Berlin crisis and proposed, instead, a meeting of the Council of Foreign Ministers to discuss Berlin and Germany as a whole. The Western Powers declined a Council of Foreign Ministers meeting as long as the Soviets were blockading Berlin, but agreed to such a meeting if the Soviets would first lift the blockade. The Soviets, still not convinced that the airlift could succeed through the Berlin winter, were not willing to lift the blockade without a concession and a chance to stop the formation of the West German state. The Western Powers, and especially the United States, were determined not to permit the question of the provisional West German government to be raised. The German Constituent Assembly was working on the draft of the Basic Law (or provisional constitution) and slow progress was being made. Over the objections of the Soviet Union, the Berlin question was put on the UN Security Council agenda and the Soviet Union promptly announced it would not participate in the Security Council discussion.

During October, the US presidential election was coming to a climax with Truman still appearing to be a certain loser. In light of the tension of a potential war and the desire for peace discerned by Truman during his campaign, he allowed some of his political advisors to persuade him to propose sending US Supreme Court Chief Justice Fred Vinson to Moscow on a "peace mission." To Truman's credit, he withdrew this obvious political ploy after meeting determined opposition from Secretary of State Marshall who had not been consulted on this proposal. Marshall's objections were that such a unilateral action would undercut the US position at the United Nations and that it would be misunderstood by its British and French allies.

Truman rebounded later the same month with another firm decision for continued support for the airlift. On October 22, he approved a National Security Council recommendation that 66 additional C-54s be allocated to the airlift and that adequate steps should be taken to insure availability of aviation fuel, personnel, and financial support. Clay and Murphy had again been brought back to Washington for this important National Security Council meeting and Clay stated later, "that Truman had impressed him as a man of great courage and one who did not hesitate to make his own decisions."[7] With this decision, a reaffirmation of the July 22, 1948, decision to commit to an airlift versus war or withdrawal, Truman put the airbridge on a sound foundation for the winter and thereafter.

In October, the UN Security Council presented a resolution calling for the lifting of all restrictions on traffic and commerce; resumption of quadripartite talks on the currency problem; and a reconvening of the Council of Foreign Ministers to consider the entire German question. The three Western Powers voted to accept the resolution on October 25, but the Soviet Union vetoed it. Stymied, the Western Powers proposed that the United Nations select a commission of experts to study the Berlin currency problem, which, as noted earlier, the UN agreed to do. However, the UN also advocated direct negotiations between the Soviet Union and the Western Powers to resolve the Berlin dispute. On November 13, the UN secretary general

An East Sector truck driver's papers are checked during the counter blockade.

and the president of the UN General Assembly addressed a letter to the Four Powers advocating this step. The Soviet Union basically agreed to the proposal on November 16.

Truman and Marshall, though, would have none of this as long as the Soviet Union continued the blockade of Berlin. Having confounded the political experts by defeating Dewey on November 2, Truman held his first post-election press conference on November 17. When asked about the UN proposal for direct negotiations with the Soviet Union, Truman emphatically stated he would not go to Moscow to see Stalin and that the United States would not negotiate with the Soviet Union over the German situation until the blockade of Berlin was lifted.

By late January 1949, it was apparent that the airbridge had succeeded in breaking the back of the blockade. This technical achievement had enhanced the standing of the United States and Great Britain in the eyes of Germany and all of Western Europe. The Berliners had survived the worst months of winter and, although they had been cold and hungry at times, had been forced to chop down some of their beloved trees for firewood and had seen their city split, their food rations had actually been increased and genuine hope now existed that the Western Powers would not sacrifice their interests and freedom. The currency reform in Western Germany had awakened the economy and Marshall Plan funds were beginning to flow into Western European countries. The Italians and the French had, at least temporarily, withstood the challenge of the Communists. It was too early to proclaim victory, but the Western democracies led by the United States and Great Britain had demonstrated the will to challenge Soviet Communism on the European continent.

In addition, the counterblockade initiated by the Western Powers in mid-1948 was beginning to have a profound effect on the Soviet Union and its Eastern European satellites. Although loosely applied at first as a countermove to the blockade of Berlin, the counter blockade had been expanded and tightened to cut off steel, chemicals, and manufactured goods from Western Germany and Western Europe. Moreover, goods and raw materials transiting the Soviet Zone could no longer pass through Berlin's western sectors with rail and barge traffic suffering severe dislocations.

On January 20, 1949, Truman was inaugurated for his second (first full) term as President of the United States. He named Dean Acheson as his Secretary of State to replace the ailing Marshall. Almost immediately after assuming his post, Acheson was presented with an opening to solve the Berlin crisis.

On January 31, Stalin replied to a question posed by Kingsbury Smith of the International News Service on whether the Soviet Union would be prepared to remove the restrictions on access to Berlin if the Western Powers agreed to postpone the establishment of a separate West German state pending the meeting of the Council of Foreign Ministers. He answered that Soviet restrictions could be removed, provided that the transport and trade restrictions introduced by the Western Powers were removed simultaneously.

No mention had been made of the currency question or other preconditions for lifting the blockade. Acheson, Charles Bohlen, and other State Department officials were determined to ascertain if these omissions had been intentional or not.

(*Top*) A student pilot receiving radar instructions for his simulated flight down an airlift corridor. (*Bottom*) A synthetic trainer, once used to train bombardiers during World War II, was adapted to instruct pilots in navigating to Berlin in all kinds of weather.

## Vittles Training in Montana

By the late summer of 1948 it became apparent to the airlift planners that it would be best if pilots, crews, and maintenance men had some basic training in their unique operation before arriving in Germany. To accomplish this, the Air Force moved the Military Air Transport Service school from Fairfield-Suisun Air Force Base (now Travis AFB), California, to Great Falls Air Force Base, Montana, in September 1948 to establish the "Vittles" training operation. Hundreds of pilots and crewmen, many of whom were recalled to active service, were checked out on the C-54 aircraft and on flight procedures to and from Berlin by practicing ground and flight procedures on mock-up duplicates of facilities at Rhein-Main, Wiesbaden, and Berlin.

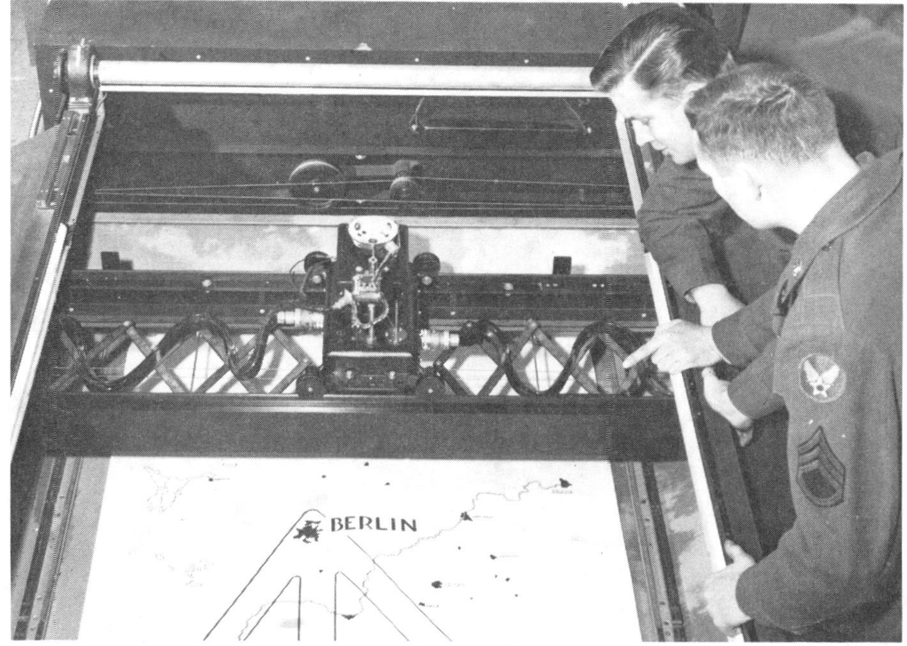

(*Top*) Crews unload flour from rail cars and prepare to truck this airlift cargo from train to nearby plane-side at Wiesbaden Air Base. (*Bottom*) Using a fork lift, crews load bags of flour onto a C-54 at Rhein-Main Air Base.

(*Below*) Aircrew checking the load distribution of Berlin-bound flour. (*Right*) Unloading flour at Tempelhof.

# Flour for Berlin

Bread baked from airlifted flour.

A four-year old girl who lives in one of Berin's Western Sectors, totes her family's weekly bread ration from a bakery near her home. The bread was baked from American flour and is wrapped in a Soviet-licensed newspaper which carries a banner headline reading: "AIRLIFT USELESS."

US NAVY
114
BLOCKADE ENDS
"AIR LIFT"-WINS!

Rhein-Main Air Base, Frankfurt, Germany, 12 May 1949. Base personnel greet a returning aircraft with the news that the nearly year-long blockade was over. (*Below*) Berliners and British aircrew at Gatow Airfield celebrate the 1,000,000th ton of freight being delivered to Berlin, 18 February 1949.

# SEVEN
# Blockade Lifted

With the weather problem solved, the airlift continued unabated through February, March, and April 1949, and average tonnage set new records each month. In February average tonnage was 5,437 tons per day (152,240* tons for 28 days); in March it increased to 6,328 tons per day (196,160* tons for 31 days); and in April it climbed to 7,845 tons per day (235,364* tons for 30 days).

More tonnage was now traveling over the airbridge than had been delivered to Berlin by truck, rail, and barge prior to March 1948.

General Tunner's "conveyor belt" had been honed and refined to the point that the airlift could be carried on indefinitely short of some major Soviet disruption of the Berlin air corridors. The Western Powers had made it clear that such a Soviet action would be considered a hostile act and a possible cause for war.

To demonstrate the airlift's potential to the Soviets and the world, Tunner put on a spectacular show over the 24-hour period ending at noon, Easter Sunday, April 16, 1949, dubbed the "Easter Parade." During this period, 1,398 flights delivered almost 13,000 tons of coal to Berlin. This not only demonstrated the load capacity, but also the ability of the system to handle an unprecedented density of air traffic with almost 2,800 incoming and outgoing flights at the three West Berlin airports located in less than a 20 mile radius of each other. The airbridge had, on a single day, handled the equivalent of 600 rail cars of coal without injury or accident.[1]

The blockade of Berlin had become inconsequential in the ability of the city to survive. However, General Clay

*Monthly tonnage figures vary slightly in several sources. Above figures are from *Berlin Airlift, a USAFE Summary*, prepared by the US Air Forces in Europe.

saw a potential danger and stated the airbridge would add to the prestige of the Western Powers as long as diplomatic avenues to gain a settlement continued. If, however, they were to exhaust all peaceful means, and then rely only on an airlift to remain in Berlin, they would begin to lose prestige.[2] Evidently, Dean Acheson and the State Department agreed with this assessment, but for security reasons Clay was not advised of State Department initiatives.

Joseph Stalin's answer to Kingsbury Smith's question about the possibility of lifting the Berlin blockade was discussed at the State Department and by Acheson with President Truman on February 1. There was uncertainty about whether Stalin was, in fact, sending a signal and, if so, what the price would be. It was decided that Acheson, at his regular weekly press conference, would downplay Stalin's references to the Berlin blockade while indicating diplomatically the signal had been received and a private channel should be used for further communication. This was accomplished in such a manner that it was not apparent to most of those present. It was also decided that any negotiations resulting from these signals would be tightly compartmentalized in case of failure. Only Truman, Acheson, and a few State Department officials were involved. Neither the British nor the French were informed, nor was Clay in Berlin.

As the private channel, Acheson selected Philip Jessup, the deputy chief of the United States Mission to the United Nations in New York, rather than the US Embassy in Moscow. Jessup was instructed to discreetly ask Jacob Malik, the Soviet Union representative to the UN, if Stalin's omission of the Berlin currency problem in his answer to Smith was significant. This conversation took place on February 15 and a month later, Malik told Jessup the omission was "not accidental." This was followed by discreet inquiries and discussions between Jessup and Malik about conditions for lifting the blockade. The Soviet Union agreed to lift the blockade if a definite date could be set for a Council of Foreign Ministers meeting to discuss the entire German question. In the meantime, Robert Murphy had been routinely transferred back to Washington to become a member of the State Department team counseling Jessup. Although Murphy was privy to secret talks, he was forbidden from notifying Clay of their existence.[3]

The US military, unaware of these negotiations and frustrated with the stalemate, again recommended a decision be made regarding Berlin. Secretary of the Army, Kenneth C. Royall, again brought up the armed convoy plan in a memorandum to Acheson as a means to bring the situation to a head. It was either this or withdraw from Berlin, which Royall discouraged.[4]

This proposal was ignored by Acheson as the Jessup-Malik discussions continued. There were several critical negotiations going on in early 1949, and one of historical significance was the North Atlantic Treaty Organization (NATO) pact. After almost a year of diplomatic negotiations, the NATO treaty was ready and the British and French foreign ministers were in Washington during the first week of April 1949, to sign it. It was then that the British and French were first advised of the Jessup-Malik discussions. Although apprehensive about a Soviet trap to sabotage the proposed West German government negotiations, which were also now progressing well, the British and French authorized Jessup to speak for them. On April 5, Jessup read a statement to Malik that the three governments understood that only two points were under discussion: simultaneous lifting of the blockade and counterblockade, and a fixing of a date for a meeting of the Council of Foreign Ministers. However, the three governments would not agree to suspend or postpone their preparations for the formation of a West German government pending a meeting of the Council of Foreign Ministers.[5]

The Western Powers reached a wide-ranging agreement on a large number of issues concerning the formation of the West German government and issued a communique concerning this agreement on April 8. Two days later, Malik advised Jessup that the Soviet Union understood there would be no provisional West German government established before or during a scheduled Council of Foreign Ministers meeting. Under instructions, Jessup diplomatically rejected this Soviet interpretation, but indicated that if they acted quickly, the provisional West German govern-

(*Top*) US Sector workers toiling without heat during the winter of 1948-1949 due to the shortage of coal. (*Left*) General Howley examines cameras manufactured in Berlin. (*Right*) More as a sign of pride and determination than of economic viability, workers stencil "Made in blockaded Berlin" on outbound freight.

# A Blockaded City Helps Itself

Before World War II, Berlin's industry dominated many fields but war's end found 85 percent of the production facilities in the city destroyed. By 1948, Berlin's industrial capacity was well on the way to normalcy when access to its western Sectors was shut off by the Soviets. Cut off from its markets and sources of supply in the surrounding Soviet Zone, and plagued by frequent power shortages, industry in the blockaded city quickly withered.

Goods from Berlin (*top*) being loaded aboard a C-47 in April 1949 and (*bottom*) awaiting shipment to the Free World.

A special meeting of the Berlin City Assembly to mark the lifting of the blockade, 12 May 1949. General Clay (second from left in the front row) and the other Allied Military Governors listen to Franz Neumann at the podium.

ment would not be in existence at the time of the Council of Foreign Ministers meeting because various steps were still necessary before this situation could occur.[6]

It was not until a week later that the Department of Defense and Clay were formally advised of the Jessup-Malik negotiations. Although Clay had got wind of the negotiations informally, he was annoyed about being kept in the dark. Clay was also frustrated with the restrictions placed on him by the State Department in negotiating with the Germans on their provisional constitution or Basic Law. Although the date of his departure from Germany had now been set for May 15, 1949, Clay became so angered at instructions from the State Department which he claimed would violate his principles that he requested he be allowed to leave and retire immediately. The matter eventually resolved itself and Clay agreed to stay on until May 15.

Of some significance to the settlement of the Berlin problem was the announcement by the Soviet government on March 29, 1949, that Marshal Sokolovsky was being replaced as the Soviet Military Governor of Germany. Sokolovsky, who had been highly regarded by Clay through the early years of the Allied occupation of Germany, had since early 1948 followed a hard-line policy on Germany and Berlin. Although undoubtedly carrying out instructions from his government, Sokolovsky had become the symbol of Soviet policy on Germany and now, quite unexpectedly, he was replaced. Was this another signal from the Soviets of their desire to solve the Berlin crisis?

As the Jessup-Malik negotiations to lift the Berlin blockade progressed during the last week of April, there were several flare-ups which threatened to scuttle any planned diplomatic settlement. The British desired specificity regarding the restrictions to be lifted and written agreement on Western Power access to Berlin, while the United States, supported by the French, desired a broad statement on lifting restrictions and silence on access. The US position was based on the experience of the Military Governors negotiations during the first week of September 1948, which had bogged down on specifics. The British eventually relented.

After further negotiations between US, British, and French representatives at the UN with Soviet representative Malik on May 2 and then again on May 4, agreement was finally reached and a Four Power communique was issued on May 5, 1949. The Soviet Union agreed to lift the blockade of Berlin and the Eastern Powers agreed to lift the counterblockade as of May 12, 1949. A meeting of the Council of Foreign Ministers would convene in Paris on May 23, 1949, to "consider questions relating to Germany and problems arising out of the situation in Berlin, including also the question of currency in Berlin."[7]

Shortly after midnight on Thursday, May 12, 1949, the barriers for road, rail, and barge traffic to Berlin were raised and supplies began arriving in the city by means other than airplanes for the first time in almost eleven months. Although the Four Power agreement was tentative, history would show that the blockade of Berlin had ended. Temporary interruptions and delays would periodically occur, but the Soviet Union has not resorted to the failed policy of total blockade in 40 years.

Although many accounts of the Berlin airlift tie Clay's departure from Berlin with the end of the blockade, cable

traffic between Washington and Berlin disclose that Clay's plans were formalized before the announcement of May 5. There had been a plan in early 1948 for the US Army to turn over the administration of Germany to the State Department by June 1948, by which time Clay would have departed Germany to retire. Even prior to the blockade, the crisis situation in Germany caused a change in this plan and Clay agreed to stay on. By the beginning of 1949, Clay was again pressuring the Army to allow him to retire. April 15 was the date set for departure from Germany, but he agreed to stay on until May 15 to complete the negotiations on the provisional German constitution. The end of the Berlin blockade on May 12 turned out to be a happy and fitting coincidence and climax for the soldier-statesman who had

Delegation heads at the 1949 Council of Foreign Ministers meeting (left to right) Dean Acheson for the United States, Andrei Vyshinsky for the Soviet Union, Robert Schuman for France, and Ernst Bevin representing Great Britain.

guided US policy in occupied Germany for almost four years.

Clay and Berlin had become symbols of the Western Powers' resolve. Clay, who came as a conqueror, left as a hero. Thereafter, when Soviet threats again endangered Berlin, other US presidents wisely used Clay as an ambassador to show the Berliners and to signal to the Soviet Union that the United States had no intention of surrendering the principle of their presence and right to be in Berlin.

Upon learning of the Soviet agreement to end the blockade, Clay advocated that the airbridge at least not be abandoned prior to and throughout the meeting of the Council of Foreign Ministers. Clay did not believe the Soviets would reinstitute the blockade, but he believed the continuation of the airlift to build up reserves of food and fuel was sound policy, and this was agreed to by Washington.[8]

Clay, however, wrongly believed Soviet tactics in Germany had radically changed. He believed they would now accept a solution to unify Germany as a buffer state and attempt to prevent it from becoming oriented to the West by making promises and concessions to the Germans which could later be exploited. Clay feared the Soviets would call for a complete withdrawal of all occupation forces and a proposal for the Germans to work out a constitutional solution. Such a proposal would have great popularity and appeal to many Germans. However, the Soviets would only have to withdraw to Germany's eastern borders, while the United States and Great Britain would probably return their forces home, leaving a still-weak France as the only nearby Western Power.[9]

The Soviets, however, had no intention of permitting the reunification of Germany unless they could be absolutely certain of its orientation. A reunified Germany oriented to the West would cause a significant threat to the Soviet Union because there would undoubtedly be a continuing political pressure in Germany as it grew stronger to reclaim East Prussia and other former eastern German territories. The Soviets, after their experiences in World Wars I and II, had great respect for Germany's martial ability. Because of their harsh occupation policies in 1945, the imposition of the Berlin blockade, and the German Communist operations in the Soviet Zone and Berlin, the Soviet Union had no chance of winning the hearts and minds of the Germans in a free democratic election.

Apparently deciding not to give back anything they already had, the Soviet Union decided to cut its losses in Berlin and that half a loaf was better than none. The formalization of the division of Germany which had begun in 1948 was finalized in 1949 with the formation of the Western Zones into the Federal Republic of Germany and of the Soviet Zone into the German Democratic Republic. The meeting of the Council of Foreign Ministers called for by the May 5 agreement which some, including Clay, thought might be the most important of any previous such meeting, turned out to be anti-climatic.

The conference commenced on May 23, 1949, in Paris, with delegations headed by Acheson for the United States, Bevin for Great Britain, Robert Schuman for France, and Andre Vyshinsky, who had replaced Molotov, for the Soviet Union. Although the expressed purpose of the meeting was to discuss the entire German question, including Berlin, the Western Powers and the Soviet Union came to the conference table with positions that almost guaranteed the division of Germany. Both sides publicly trumpeted their respective plans for the reunification of Germany.

The goal of the Soviet Union was to halt the formation of the West German government and it proposed a "return to Potsdam," the reestablishment of the Allied Control Council, and the requirement of unanimity on all proposals

(*Top*) A pair of US Navy R5D aircraft (the naval version of the C-54) flank an Air Force Skymaster while awaiting takeoff from Rhein-Main. The Navy loaned two transport squadrons to the airlift. (*Left*) Chief Aviation Machinist's Mate Paul E. Palmer testing the lashings on a load of coal. (*Right*) Ensign Harry Madsen accepts "a bite of chow" from Inga Grockers in one of Tempelhof's mobile lunch wagons, 9 January 1949.

# Here Comes the Navy

relating to Germany. This was, naturally, unacceptable to the Western Powers.

The Western Powers, while apparently proposing a solution that would reunify Germany, wanted to hasten the formation of the West German government. Speaking for the Western Powers, Bevin proposed incorporation of the Soviet Zone into the framework of the West German model, abolition of zonal borders, adoption of a single currency, free elections, and replacement of military governors by a Four-Power High Commission having supervisory powers under a majority vote. Not surprisingly, this solution was rejected by the Soviet Union.

Regarding Berlin, Vyshinsky proposed a return to the Four-Power Kommandatura, acting, as previously, on the basis of unanimity. Acheson counter-proposed a new city-wide election and a new city assembly to draft a permanent constitution for the entire city. Both sides ignored the fact the city was split with two rival administrations and two currencies. The Western Powers could not accept a return to the *status quo* with Soviet veto power to stalemate and frustrate. The Soviet Union could not accept city-wide elections which would almost certainly result in an overwhelming rejection of their policies and the defeat of their puppet East Berlin city government.

Berliner's interest in the airlift remained undulled throughout the many months of the Blockade.

With no possibility for a major agreement, Vyshinsky went on a propaganda offensive by proposing a German peace treaty. With no plan agreeable for the future of either Germany, this proposal was strictly for the record and for its emotional appeal to the German people. The Soviet Zone press played this up for several weeks, but it did not have the expected appeal to West Germans as they seemed to understand it was unrealistic.

After a month of agreeing to disagree on all major questions relating to Germany and Berlin, the final Council of Foreign Ministers meeting of the post-World War II era ended. The closing communique of June 20, 1949, acknowledged that no agreement had been reached on the economic and political unity of Germany, but that the occupation powers were duty-bound to take necessary measures which would assure a normal functioning and use of traffic and other communications to and from Berlin.

Thus, the first Berlin crisis was over. The blockade and the counter-blockade were lifted, but no permanent solution was reached. The Western Powers still had no written access rights to Berlin, other than the air corridor agreements of 1946-47. The Soviet Union had not been able to eliminate the Berlin window to the West. Unable to prevent the formation of the West German government and

(*Below*) The three Western Commandants, Generals Bourne of Great Britain, Graneval of France, and Howley of the United States explain the Third Ordinance for Monetary Retorm at a press conference. (*Opposite*) Berliners celebrate the lifting of the blockade.

recognizing that the tide had turned in Western Europe with the Marshall Plan, the NATO treaty, and the failure of the Berlin blockade, the Soviet Union decided to consolidate and solidify its gains in Eastern Europe.

With the adoption of the provisional constitution in May 1949, the Military Governors of the United States, Great Britain, and France were supplanted by an Allied High Commission. Sir Brian Robertson stayed on in this new capacity for the British, while John J. McCloy replaced Clay for the US, and André François-Pincet replaced Koenig for the French. The military government era in West Germany had ended. The three High Commissioners set up shop in Bonn, the provisional West German capital and, after parliamentary elections in August 1949, the Federal Republic of Germany was officially declared on September 15, 1949, with Konrad Adenauer, elected by the *Bundestag*, as the chancellor.

In the meantime, the Soviet Union had been preparing to establish a rival German government in their zone while still attempting to halt the formation of the West German government. With the formation of the Federal Republic, there was no longer any need to postpone and, on October 7, 1949, the formation of the German Democratic Republic was announced. Both governments claimed to be the only legitimate German government.

The East Germans declared Berlin to be their capital, but the Western Powers claimed Berlin was an occupied city under Four Power control. The East Germans set up their government institutions in East Berlin, but the Western Powers chose to ignore this and maintained they would recognize only the Soviet Union as the sovereign power in East Berlin. Under the provisional West German constitution, Greater Berlin was included as an integral entity. This was immediately protested by the Soviet Union.

The Western Powers also had reservations about including Berlin in the West German government based on their continued contention that Berlin was a Four Power occupied city and they decided to suspend this article for the "time being." However, the Western Powers agreed that West Berlin could send representatives to the Bonn parliament. On May 14, 1949, two days after the lifting of the blockade, the Western Powers, in an effort to give West Berlin a larger share in self-government, issued a Statement of Principles governing the relations of Greater Berlin with the Allied Kommandatura. This document gave the West Berliners most of the same liberal measures applicable to West German citizens while reserving certain powers to the Western Allies to maintain the special status of the city.

When the UN committee of experts announced in early February 1949 they could find no solution to the currency problems in Berlin acceptable to all Four Powers, the British dropped their objections to introducing the West Mark as the sole currency for West Berlin and joined the Americans in pressuring the French. Under the threat of bilateral action on this question, the French finally relented and agreed that the West Mark would become the sole legal currency for West Berlin.

After nine months of operating under a dual currency and flirting with making the East Mark the sole currency for all of Berlin, the Western Powers promulgated on March 20, 1949, the Third Ordinance for Monetary Reform which provided for the immediate declaration of the West Mark as exclusive legal tender in the Western Sectors of Berlin. The East Mark, however, was neither "outlawed" nor "barred" from West Berlin, as the West Mark had been in the Soviet Sector and the Soviet Zone. Individuals and businesses desiring to voluntarily use the East Mark in transactions were permitted to do so.

To many Berliners, still uncertain about the Western Powers commitment to their city, this step of tying their currency to West Germany was more important than any

statement from Western political leaders and their confidence in the future grew. The city government agencies could now budget on a firm foundation, but the fragile West Berlin economy would require financial support from the Western Powers and West Germany for many years.

As spring arrived in Berlin, rumors began to circulate about the possibility of the blockade being lifted, but each report proved false until the Four Power communique on May 5 confirming the blockade would end on May 12. During the week of May 5-12, reporters and photographers converged on Berlin to record every aspect of the end of the blockade. They covered the *Autobahn* at both ends to record the lifting of the barriers at the West German end and the tumultuous greeting by Berliners at the other. They covered the first departure of interzone passenger and freight trains and the gathering of some 200,000 West Berliners in front of the Schöeneberg borough town hall on May 12 to celebrate and listen to speeches by their leaders.

(*Top*) The first vehicle to travel the land route between the US Zone and the Western Sectors of Berlin, 12 May 1949. (*Left*) The press filming the first buses leaving Berlin for western Germany. (*Right*) Arrival of the first supply trucks at the Autobahn Bridge in Berlin.

Mayor Ernst Reuter welcomed the end of the blockade and declared:

> The attempt to force us to our knees has failed, frustrated by our steadfastness and firmness. It failed because the world heard our appeal and came to our assistance." He then ended with a familiar phrase for Berliners "*Berlin bleibtdoch Berlin*" (Berlin will always remain Berlin).[10]

Clay, in a farewell speech before a special session of the Berlin City Assembly, stated, "There are two classes of airlift heroes, first, the pilots who flew the planes to Berlin in every kind of weather; and secondly, the population of Berlin, who, after having chosen freedom were also prepared to make the necessary sacrifices to uphold it."[11] Reuter, speaking on behalf of the West Berlin city government,

(*Top*) Passenger truck leaving for Hannover in the British Zone, 12 May 1949. (*Left*) The first barge traffic to reach Berlin since the lifting of the blockade, 14 May 1949. (*Right*) "Bananas!" Another rarity during the blockade makes its first appearance on store shelves, 30 June 1949.

thanked the military governors of the Western Powers and their governments and all Germans in Western Germany for aiding Berlin and added, "The airlift was the most impressive demonstration of the firm determination of the whole world to shield us from the destiny to which we otherwise would have fallen prey."[12]

Special tribute was paid to those who gave their lives during airlift operations. A resolution was passed to erect a monument in the square facing Tempelhof airfield and to rename this square *Platz der Luftbruecke* (Airlift Square).

As was customary in Berlin in 1949, a retreat ceremony was held each Sunday evening at the US headquarters on *Kronprinzen Allee*. In some manner, Berliners learned that Clay would make his final appearance at the retreat cere-

(*Top*) Railroad strikers at the *S-Bahn* station in Charlottenburg in the British Sector and (*bottom*) East Sector police leaving the station, 22 May 1949.

Mail truck backs up to a waiting C-54 at Tempelhof to unload its cargo, 3 June 1949. The mail had only recently begun traveling to western Germany by train again but the *S-Bahn* strike prevented all rail traffic from entering and leaving Berlin.

mony on Sunday, May 15. Thousands of ordinary citizens gathered to pay their respects as Clay departed en route to Tempelhof airfield and the United States. This was a spontaneous and moving tribute by the usually mundane Berliners who can be very sentimental about those leaders they respect and honor.

Clay was afforded another honor seldom bestowed on a foreign military leader. A month after he departed Berlin, the City Assembly voted to rename *Kronprinzen Allee*, the wide boulevard that passes in front of the US headquarters in Berlin, *Clay Allee*. In doing so, Reuter declared, "General Clay entered Berlin as a victor. He left as our friend."[13]

No sooner was the blockade lifted than a new crisis struck in Berlin when on Friday, May 21, 1949, the railroad workers went out on strike. The Allied Control Council had given the Soviets the authority to operate the railroads and the *S-Bahn* (the elevated commuter lines that served Berlin and its suburbs) in 1945. A large number of the railroad workers resided in West Berlin and had been hard hit by the first currency reform of June 1948 because the State Railroad Authority (*Reichsbahndirecktion*), controlled by the Soviets, refused to pay them 25 percent of their wages in West Marks as employers in the Western Sectors were required.

The currency reform of March 1949, which made the West Mark the sole legal currency for West Berlin, made the situation intolerable for those railroad workers residing in West Berlin. They were being paid solely in East Marks,

Berlin housewives look at shop windows offering meat and sausage products seldom seen during the blockade.

when it took four East Marks to buy one West Mark, but were required to pay rent and utilities in West Marks. Many had also joined the Western sponsored union. This had been formed to oppose the Communist union organization which had dominated until 1948 and many were discharged solely for this reason.

The strike disrupted rail traffic to and from Berlin just when it had started up again. Efforts to get the Soviet controlled State Railroad Authority to negotiate with the workers were unsuccessful. Soviet Sector transportation police had been allowed to patrol railroad properties in West Berlin and when they would not allow peaceful picketing, violence broke out. The Western Sector commandants then ordered the Soviet Sector police out of West Berlin. After extended negotiations, the strike was finally settled on June 28, 1949, with a tentative agreement that railroad workers residing in West Berlin would receive 60 percent of their wages in West Marks and that they would not be persecuted for their strike.

This strike and other periodic interruptions of road, rail, and barge traffic to and from Berlin during May, June, and July 1949, showed the foresight of the Western Powers in continuing the airlift after the blockade had officially ended. The airbridge was not only kept in place, but maintained at its record high of April 1949. The airlift delivered 250,818 tons in May; 240,325 in June; and set an all-time monthly record with 253,090 tons in July.

By the end of July 1949, the Western Powers determined that they had stockpiled sufficient supplies in Berlin as a hedge against any new Soviet blockade. They felt the situation on the land, rail, and water routes into Berlin had normalized to the extent that they could start winding the airlift down.

On July 30, 1949, an official announcement was made by the Combined Airlift Task Force that the airlift would be terminated at the end of October 1949. During August and

The last Vittles flight left Rhein-Main Air Base on September 30, 1949 at 1845 hours as sister planes of the airlift flew overhead in formation, marking the end of a dramatic chapter in air history.

September the phase-out began with the departure of the US Navy VR-6 and VR-8 squadrons, the return of a number of C-54s to the United States, and the closing down of bases at Fassberg, Wunsdorf, and Celle. The first day of September saw the joint British-American CALTF headquarters inactivated and on Friday, September 30, 1949, the last US C-54 made the run to Berlin. The British made their last flight on Thursday, October 6, and so the airlift ended almost a month ahead of schedule.

An important chapter in aviation history had been written. The proponents of air power had proven that it could be used not only to destroy an enemy in wartime, but that a large civilian populace could be totally supplied by air to preserve the peace.

On September 15, 1949, the US State Department officially took over the administration of Germany from the Department of the Army. This changeover coincided with official establishment of the Federal Republic of Germany. The Office of Military Government became the Office of High Commissioner for Germany. Most of the military government offices and personnel were transferred to Frankfurt Main with reduced responsibilities. General Maxwell Taylor replaced General Howley as US Commander, Berlin, and was given the additional duties of serving as the representative of the US High Commissioner for Germany in Berlin.

The crisis situation in Berlin gradually cooled. The Berliners attempted to normalize their daily lives and to rebuild their city. It was obvious, though, that nothing lasting had been resolved and that the time bomb that was Berlin was still ticking.

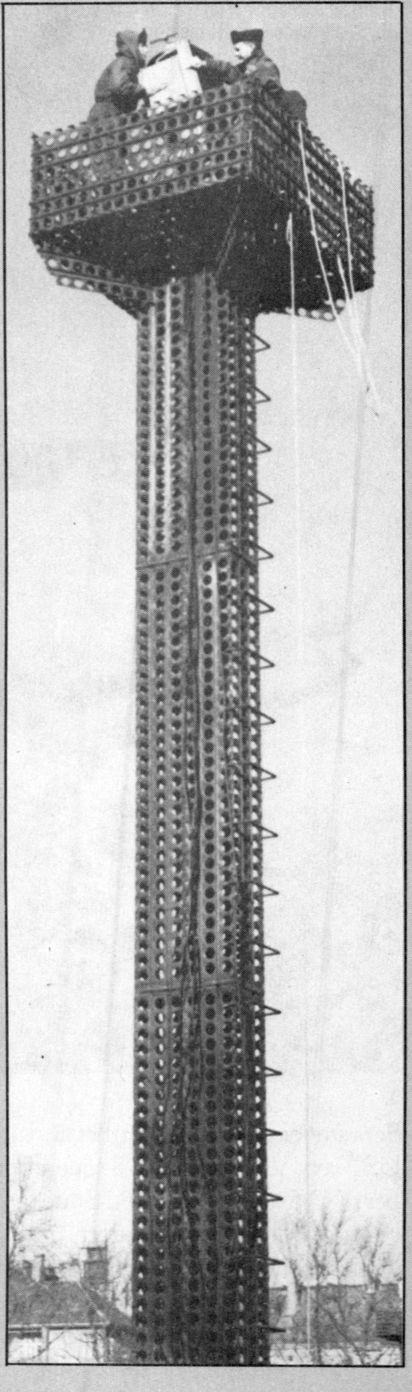

## Air Traffic Control Revolutionized

Bringing the airplanes in and out of Tempelhof, Gatow, and Tegel airfields in Berlin at three minute intervals in all kinds of weather was one of the most difficult and stressful jobs of the entire airlift operation. This job fell to the military air traffic controllers and communication specialists of the US and British Air Forces, plus many civilian specialists brought over to assist. In 1948-49, these units were known in the US Air Force as Airways and Air Communication Services. They supplied the radio navigation aids, manned the control towers, radio ranges, radio beacons, radar equipment, and air traffic control facilities. Although much of the technology used then

(*Opposite top*) A Controlled Approach unit at Tempelhof designed in sections to facilitate movement. (*Opposite bottom*) Air traffic controlers at Tempelhof. (*Opposite*) One of forth ights placed in two, 20-lights, parallel rows lighting a 3000 foot approach to the main runway at Tempelhof. The towers used as platforms for the lights were manufactured from runway matting. The reason for its great height is so the approach lights are not blocked from sight by the tall buildings around the airport. (*Below*) The Tempelhof Flight Operations Desk.

has been overtaken by the revolutionary developments in electronics in the 1960s and 1970s, the procedures developed during the Berlin Airlift became a vital building block for the modern air traffic control system as we know it today.

As after most military operations, there were numerous "after action" reports and "lessons learned" studies with emphasis on how best to set up another airlift operation in the event the Soviets reimposed a blockade on Berlin or somewhere else. Just as General Tunner had been able to use some of the experiences and techniques learned from the "Hump" operation in Asia during World War II during the Berlin Airlift, some of the techniques learned during the airlift were applicable to air supply operations during the Korean War.

The Berlin Wall shortly after its construction.

# EIGHT
# Aftermath

The city of Berlin is located 110 miles from the borders of the newly established Federal Republic of Germany, in what US soldiers euphemistically call "Injun territory," and this fact of geography presents some problems. While in 1949 there seemed to be little question over the Western Powers' rights in Berlin being guaranteed by earlier Four Power accords, the agreements covering the actual access to the city were just as weak as before the airlift.

When the Council of Foreign Ministers meeting in Paris during May and June 1949 failed to resolve either the German question or the problems facing Berlin, the Western Powers had little alternative other than to maintain the position that had served them well throughout the Berlin crisis of 1948-49. That position was and still remains that all of Berlin is an occupied city; that US, British and French rights and position in the city are guaranteed by wartime agreements among "allies," including the Soviet Union; and that no single power can unilaterally take action to change this status without the agreement of the other "allies."

West Berliners were anxious to be included within the constitutional structure of the emerging Federal Republic and, from a sentimental standpoint, the Western Allies had to agree that this was a quite natural desire. The Soviet Union, however, did not recognize the western Federal Republic just as the Western Allies did not recognize the eastern Democratic Republic. The two Germanys did not recognize each other. Access to Berlin and the freedom of its people in the West Sector rested solely on Four Power agreements. Any actions demonstrating that another power (for example, the West Germans) was in control could be used by the communists as an excuse to terminate access.

The Basic Law of the Federal Republic treated West Berlin as a *land* (state) of the Federation. The Western Allies, though, still retained supreme authority in West Germany and forced a suspension of that portion of the law regarding Berlin. While they would allow the representatives of Berlin to attend the legislative bodies meeting in the temporary capital city of Bonn and perform all the lobbying and consultive functions of *Land* representatives, they could not vote since that could call into question Allied jurisdiction in Berlin.

In addition, Federal laws and treaties could only be adopted in the city if the Berlin Chamber of Deputies passed a *Mantelgesetz* (cover law) legislating their enactment in the city. Even then, the Western Sector commanders retained the legal right to suspend or declare laws

Care packages being distributed to Berliners

as invalid. The Federal Constitutional Court was barred from the city and, after the Federal Republic established an army and joined the North Atlantic Treaty Organization (NATO), the new West German armed forces could not enter the city nor could the residents of the city be drafted into the *Bundeswehr* (Federal Army).

Marshall Plan Aid and the free market economic system, introduced by Minister of Economics, Ludwig Erhard, propelled the new Federal Republic into a period of spectacular growth and revitalization. Erhard's "Free Market Economy" was based on liberal trade laws, tariff reductions, cheap imports (while boosting exports) and an almost religious avoidance of labor disputes. The income of the average West German rose 12 percent a year between 1950 and 1955 and unemployment plummeted by almost two-thirds. West Germans were allowed to "work off an immense surplus of energy in order to buy the . . . consumer goods which they so badly wanted, after six prewar years of Nazi austerity, six years of war and four years of postwar want."[1] By the time the occupation of Germany formally ended in May of 1955, the nation was already the most prosperous country in Europe.

Initially, the economic recovery of West Germany was of little value to Berlin and "German leaders were not in a position to do much about Berlin."[2] Even before the "economic miracle" was well underway, productivity and living standards across West Germany were generally meeting or even surpassing prewar levels by 1950 while Berlin's production index showed the city wallowing at only a third of its 1936 level.

While Berlin had suffered as much or more war damage as other German cities, it had additionally borne the brunt of Soviet dismantling, losing more than 500 factories of all sizes and types. Moreover, Berlin could no longer exercise

Schloss Strasse in the US Sector from the top of Wertheim's Department Store, 27 August 1952. As late as 1946 this street was half filled with rubble with only one lane open to traffic.

the traditional functions of a capital city and roughly 175,000 public sector jobs simply no longer existed. Other associated industries normally located in a capital such as import, export, the wholesale trades, advertising, printing, finance, banking, insurance, the stock market, and the hotel catering trades, all moved west to greener (and safer) pastures. They took well over half a million jobs with them. Then came a ruinous year-long blockade which essentially stopped the modest recovery efforts that had made some headway in 1947 and early 1948. Even with the city's population reduced to 3 million from its prewar height of almost 4.5 million, 300,000 West Berlin workers were still unable to find a job in 1950.

Two years later, as the world marveled at the bounding West German economy, the average number of unemployed in West Berlin had decreased by only 25,000. In 1952, important steps were taken to put Berlin back on its feet. On January 4, the Federal Parliament in Bonn passed the "Third Transference Law" in which West Berlin was incorporated into the financial and legal system of the Federal Republic. West Berlin was now able to receive annual subsidies from the federal treasury and the city legislature no longer had to debate every federal law and treaty before they became applicable in Berlin. As before, though, the three Western Commandants still retained their supreme authority.

1952 also saw all the US State Department's work on Germany and Berlin concentrated in the German Office with Eleanor Lansing Dulles* being charged with finding out what the United States could do about Berlin. Dulles worked to expand and develop the complicated working ar-

*Eleanor Lansing Dulles was the sister of Allen W. Dulles and ambassador at large, John Foster Dulles. The following year, brothers Allen and John would become heads of the Central Intelligence Agency and State Department, respectively.

rangements between Bonn, Washington and Berlin and ended up making more than two dozen round trips across the Atlantic.

Dulles later found that her passport showed more than thirty trips into Berlin as she "went back and forth from the Federal Republic to tie together negotiations there, with arrangements made in Berlin for various programs of construction and support." Such globe-trotting was necessary because "the three-cornered financing of many projects and the psycological subtleties of the resistance to Communist harassment called for a more responsive understanding of the moods and attitudes which could not be easily reflected in cables."[3]

There was great concern in Washington over Berlin's fate. Dulles points out that:

> In 1953 the economy of the city was faltering, and production was at a low level. Some thought there could be only a small amount of improvement. Using a more optimistic approach, a many-sided program was initiated. This included continuing aid to industry, building up the stockpile, subsidizing housing for refugees in Berlin and in the Federal Republic, improving public relations, and varied measures not developed under other aid programs. The new attention to the city of Berlin was to be so comprehensive as to give a clear impression of the usefulness of an imaginative American and German approach to the needs and support which could be given. . . . .
>
> Some of the "impact projects" met with initial resistance from [Berlin officials] and from some financial officers in Bonn. They were obliged to ration sparingly the supporting German budget funds. We Americans, on our part, had to stress the over-all needs of the economy and the long-run interests of the city as well as propaganda and political issues. Without impairing these various considerations, consulting together, we developed a balanced and dependable program.[4]

Reconstruction in West Berlin was accelerated and the standard of living brought up to par with that in West Germany. By 1957, unemployment had dropped below 100,000 and in five more years, would drop to almost 10,000.

The great strides being made in West Germany could hardly be concealed from those living in the east and, when coupled with increasing communist repression, served as a magnet for East Germans wanting a better way of life. In 1959, the Association of Free Jurists in West Berlin, which had amassed voluminous material on violations of human rights in East Germany, published a summary of events on the occasion of the tenth birthday of the German Democratic Republic:

> 1950: A Ministry of State Security was created, in order to take over the antidemocratic police powers hitherto exercised by the Russians. A "single-list" election for the new "People's Chamber" (*Volkskammer*) took place, with a 99.7 per cent vote for the selected candidates. During the year, 197,788 East Germans fled to the West.
>
> 1951: The Ministry of State Security was hard at work. In a single trial nineteen young people (some of them still at the secondary school of Werdau and seven of them under eighteen) were sentenced to a total of one hundred and thirty years' imprisonment. The workers lost their right to negotiate wage agreements. . . . That year 165,648 East Germans fled to the West.
>
> 1952: A "security zone" and a "death strip" were established along the interzonal frontier. A law was passed providing for the confiscation of all property belonging to people who "fled from the Republic." Nevertheless, 182,393 East Germans fled to the West during 1952.
>
> 1953: The East German Government raised compulsory work norms by 10 per cent, with no increase of pay. This led directly to the strike of the Stalinallee building-workers in east Berlin, and to the national uprising of June 17 against the regime. Afterwards eighteen people were sentenced to death, and roughly twelve hundred people were sentenced to a total of four thousand years' imprisonment. That year 331,390 East Germans fled to the West.
>
> 1954: The second "People's Chamber" was elected, again on a "single-list" system, by a 99.46 per cent vote. The first youth-initiation committees were formed and the Communist campaign against religious teaching in the schools and the homes was under way. During that year 184,198 East Germans fled to the West.
>
> 1955: The Communist campaign against private industry moved into top gear, while steady progress was made in the formation of the State co-operatives on the land. During that year 252,870 East Germans fled to the West.
>
> 1956: The first trials took place of people who had "encouraged flight from the Republic." In a test trial, two men and one woman were all sentenced to life imprisonment for this "crime." The regime introduced its new method of destroying private firms by "offering" State participation in management

(*Top*) A demonstration passing under the Brandenburg Gate. (*Bottom*) Berliners scatter as Soviet tanks erupt onto Potsdamer Platz.

# The June 1953 Uprising

On June 16, 1953, the East Berlin building workers went on strike against a 10 per cent increase in work quotas. One day later, the protest developed into a large demonstration and spread throughout the Soviet Zone. Within a short time, the strike assumed the character of a popular uprising, a manifestation against the existing regime and in favor of free and secret elections. The Ulbricht Regime, unable to cope with the situation, was saved by the Soviet occupation forces when Russian troops, supported by tanks, went into action and were ultimately successful in stifling the uprising.

Soviet troops returning to their sector after a ceremony at the Soviet War Memorial, 9 May 1952. Nearly a decade later, the Berlin Wall was erected roughly half way between where the British soldier is standing guard and the Brandenburg Gate.

and financing. During that year 279,189 East Germans fled to the West.

1957: A new passport law provided for three years' imprisonment for anyone making an unauthorized journey outside the borders of East Germany. . . . During 1957, however, 261,622 East Germans fled to the West.

1958: Under a new law criticism of the regime could be regarded as "slandering the State." Nineteen students from Jena University were sent to prison for breaking this law. Compulsory "polytechnical" education was introduced; it meant that all school children had to work for stated periods in industry and agriculture. During that year 204,092 East Germans fled to the West.

1959: The Ministry for Cultural Affairs ordered a purge of the Universities and technical colleges. At Dresden five students were given sentences totaling 37½ years' imprisonment. Members of the "People's Chamber" received instructions relating to their "duty" to explain and justify every act of the regime to the population. It was not their duty to "represent" the wishes of constituents.[5]

The "security zone" established by the East Germans along their border with West Germany greatly lessened the flow of refugees along the frontier and the refugee centers at Ulzen and Giessen have had fewer customers ever since. The opposite was true for the Marienfelde center in West Berlin. With the city still under military control and no travel restrictions between the four occupation sectors, an East German or East Berliner could simply walk into one of the West sectors or, if the refugee had much baggage to lug around, take the *U-Bahn* or *S-Bahn* to freedom.

During this period, not all the actions taken by the West were without some degree of provocation. The controversial Food Project Program, a joint Central Intelligence Agency (CIA)-State Department operation, was viewed by the Soviets as being a direct threat to stability in East Germany. Initiated on the heals of the unsuccessful June 1953 uprising, Eleanor Lansing Dulles relates that:

> The thought was, somehow, to make a gesture to demonstrate our concern for those whose homes and jobs were in the Soviet zone.
>
> Fifteen million dollars were allocated for this general purpose in July. The method adopted was to give out food packages to all who came to get them. To permit immediate action the supplies were borrowed from the stockpile already in Berlin, later replaced by shipments from America. The people who streamed into the city during the next weeks were making a gesture of solidarity with the West. They came in many cases from afar. Their expenses often exceeded the value of the gift.
>
> The Communists, faced with this act of defiance, hestitated to impose obstacles for those seeking food, but they finally decided to harass, and even arrest, many of those traveling to Berlin. It was decided to halt the program to lessen the danger to the residents of the Zone. The funds remaining were spent in other ways for their benefit. Some of the subsequent programs were classified.[6]

Being the only hole in the iron curtain, Berlin became "the listening post of the west." The refugee stream was a constant source of valuable information for Western intelligence attempting to piece together what was going on in Eastern Europe. It was also a lucrative recruiting ground for some willing to return before their absence was noticed in exchange for financial assistance immediately and again later when they came back to stay. Or, the information supplied by refugees pinpointed someone still in place willing to furnish information for any of a variety of reasons.

Possibly the most well publicized intelligence gathering effort was the Berlin tunnel operation. Constructed by the CIA under the East Sector of the city to monitor telephone calls, the operation "produced literally tons of trivia and gossip, but provided little in the way of high-grade secret in-

The Soviet delegation arrives for a session of the Four-Power Conference of Foreign Ministrs, 1 February 1954. Foreign Minister Molotov, at far right, leads the way followed by Jacob Malik and Andrei Gromyko.

formation that could be used by the agency's intelligence analysts."[7] In the end, the primary value of the tunnel operation ended up being the embarrassment it caused the Soviet Union and its intelligence agency, the *Komitet Gossudarstvennoi Bezopasnost* (KGB)

The oft repeated Soviet charges that West Berlin was a "nest of spies" was, however, not unlike the pot describing the color of the kettle. The refugee stream also provided ample cover for trained Communist agents to infiltrate the West German infrastructure. Using hundreds of low-level agents to tie-up Western counter-intelligence, the well-documented high-level agents with detailed "cover" easily made their way to West Germany and gradually attained access to the highest of political, military, and economic levels. The effectiveness of these "moles" is attested by he fact that many were not uncovered until the 1970s and 1980s. One such operation brought down the government of Chancellor Willy Brandt in 1979 when it was discovered that his personal advisor, Günther Guillaume, was an East German spy.

The vast number of diplomatic notes, conferences, and propaganda campaigns that centered around the questions of Berlin and German unification throughout the 1950s are too long to recount here and, in any event, are heavily documented elsewhere. A brief look at certain highlights is instructive, however, in understanding how Berlin has fit into the pattern of East-West relations.

In the early 1950s, the Soviet Union still believed that West Germany was not yet firmly aligned with the West and most of their efforts were aimed at preventing the Federal Republic from becoming part of the Western Alliance. Numerous Soviet proposals were put forth which purported to favor making all of Germany one nation again. All proposals were finely attuned to the Soviets' perception of German public opinion and their longing for reunification of the country. And all were structured in such a way as to create a neutralized German state which, deprived of its ability to form political or defensive alliances with other nations, would have been hard pressed to resist Soviet domination.

The Soviet note of March 10, 1952, for example, contained the draft of a peace treaty which included a provision that all foreign troops would leave the reunified German

Chancellor Konrad Adenauer, holding hat, and Defense Minister Theodor Blank inspecting 1,500 army, navy and air force personnel of the emerging West German armed forces.

nation within one year. But while the six US divisions stationed in West Germany would presumably withdraw across the Atlantic, the estimated 22 Soviet divisions would pull back to Poland where they would sit menacingly along the German border. Since the proposed treaty had a ban on entering into military alliances, even asking the United States or other European powers for support against possible Soviet aggressions could be used as a pretext to invade the country.

Another note submitted on August 15 of that year suggested that a future German government could be formed by the parliaments of the two Germanys. Thus, the 500 handpicked members of the East German "People's Chamber," who met two or three times a year in one day sessions to cast unanimous votes, were equated with freely elected representatives of West Germany. No mention was made in the note of free elections, in which the Soviets knew the East German regime would fare disastrously, but it was suggested that the parliament should do their work "with the broad participation of democratic organizations." In Communist parlance "democratic" means Communist or at minimum pro-Communist. William Henry Chamberlin, who served as a Moscow correspondent for over a decade, wrote:

> Decisive proof that the Soviet Government has never been interested in German reunification in freedom . . . was furnished at a four-power conference on Germany which took place in Berlin from January 25 until February 18, 1954. At this meeting British Foreign Secretary Anthony Eden put forward the following scheme for German unity:
>
> (1) Free elections throughout Germany.
>
> (2) The convocation of a national assembly on the basis of these elections.
>
> (3) The drafting of a constitution and the preparation of negotiations for a peace treaty.
>
> (4) Adoption of the constitution and formation of an all-German government, responsible for the negotiation of a peace treaty.
>
> (5) Signing and entering into force of the peace treaty.
>
> The Federal Republic accepted these proposals. The Soviet Government rejected them. It is also noteworthy that Soviet notes proposing German reunion were regularly and obviously timed to obstruct the progress of the negotiations that led to German integration with the West. . . .
>
> After the Federal Repubic joined NATO, the Soviet Government ceased to pay even lip service to the desirability of a

Nikita Khrushchev addressing the General Assembly of the United Nations, 23 September 1960.

united Germany. One exception to this rule may be noted: At the Geneva conference of heads of government in July, 1955, Nikolai Bulganin, then Soviet prime minister, signed a joint direction to the foreign ministers of the four powers (the United States, the Soviet Union, Great Britain, and France) to settle "the reunion of Germany by means of free elections." But this promise was quickly broken. For at the subsequent conference of foreign ministers Molotov stubbornly adhered to the position that there are two German states, which must settle the problem of reunion between themselves.[8]

The prospect of German reunification, dangled so tantalizingly by the Soviets, was desired by almost all Germans. But as Wilhelm Grew, who later became West Germany's ambassador to the United States, observed, "The goal of German foreign policy is not mere reunion, but reunion in freedom. A reunion which would lead to a Communist-ruled all-Germany, or to a type of all-German state for which Sovietization would be only a question of time would be no worthwhile object of German policy."[9]

After Joseph Stalin's death in 1953, the Kremlin saw many old faces come and go during a power struggle that would last five years. Nikita Khrushchev, who had successfully ousted numerous rivals, including Molotov, rose to the premiership in 1958, after forcing Bulganin to resign.

Khruschev immediately embarked upon a campaign to enhance the power and stature of the Soviet Union and fixed on Berlin, which he described as "the testicles of the West," as being the focal point of his efforts. "When I want the West to scream," he later said, "I squeeze on Berlin."

In a report produced for the RAND Corporation think tank, Hans Speier related that:

> After some preliminary storm signals in September and October, 1958, and following Khrushchev's speech of November 10, the Soviet Government presented diplomatic notes to the three Western powers and the Federal Republic on November 27, 1958, proposing a radical change in the four-power status of Berlin. The Soviet Government declared that it regarded the international agreements of September 12, 1944, and May 1, 1945, concerning the zones of occupation in Germany and the administration of Greater Berlin as no longer having any validity. After speaking of "the unlawful occupation of West Berlin" and of "the severe abuse of the occupation rights" by the Western powers for the purpose of damaging the Soviet Union, the German Democratic Republic, and the other socialist countries, the Soviet Government proposed the "demilitarization" of West Berlin, that is, the withdrawal of all military forces from the city, and the establishment of West Berlin as a "Free City."
>
> . . . .
>
> The Soviet Government declared its readiness to negotiate with the Western powers about its proposal . . . but added three important stipulations. First, it intimated that the period allowed to attain four-power agreement on the Soviet proposal should be limited to six months. The Soviet Government declared that it would not change the existing procedure for military traffic of the United States, Great Britain, and France between West Germany and West Berlin for this period of six months, that is, until May 27, 1959.
>
> Second, the Soviet Government declared that if the Russian proposal were unacceptable to the Western powers, no four-power negotiations on the status of Berlin could take place.
>
> In this case, as its third stipulation, the Soviet Government would conclude an agreement with the East German Government bestowing full sovereignty upon the latter, "on land, on water, and in the air," that is, including the approaches to Berlin.[10]

The Western powers viewed the Soviet note as nothing short of an ultimatum and insisted that the Soviet Union could not unilaterally repudiate its earlier agreements over the Western presence in the city in exchange for the huge portions of East Germany occupied by the US and British forces at the end of World War II. The signing of a peace treaty between the East German government would, in the Soviet view, free them from their earlier obligations regarding the occupation of Germany and would thus remove the only means of legal access to the city deep in East German territory.

As for the idea of establishing a "Free City," such an entity with few, if any, ties to West Germany would have been even more susceptible to Soviet threats and intimidations than before. The Soviets backed the claim of the East German regime that the Western Sectors of the city were a part of their sovereign territory. The proposed entity would not have included the Soviet Sector and, as East German officials described it in a note to the Soviet Union on January 7, 1959, was in reality, "the Free City of West Berlin."

A new arrangement guaranteed by the four powers, but not including East Berlin, would almost certainly entail a Soviet military presence in the part of the city they had left 14 years before.* Apparently, the time-honored Soviet diplomatic formula of "What's mine is mine; what's yours is negotiable" was still held in high regard.

When it became apparent that the Western powers would not be bullied into accepting such an agreement, Khrushchev conceded, during a March 18 press conference, that the Western powers had "lawful rights for the deployment of troops in Berlin as occupiers" and that his original six months deadline was only approximate. For the time being, Khrushchev settled down to attempting to undermine the Western Alliance by portraying West German leaders as intransigent and their country's policies as a threat to peace. Hans Speier wrote:

> The Communist attack on [Chancellor Konrad] Adenauer and [West Berlin mayor Willy] Brandt, and on General Hans Speidel and Defense Minister Franz Josef Strauss, followed the familiar pattern of political warfare, in which the opposing coalition is weakened by the creation of schism in its ranks. The Soviet Government tried to bring about a situation in which the three Western powers might tire of the abnormal difficulties involved in protecting West Berlin against conversion into a Free City as well as Adenauer's intransigence. Soviet invitations to the West to conclude the last war by a peace treaty, to trade, to exchange visits, to coexist, and to disarm may all be regarded as instrumental in bringing about such a situation.
>
> But in this general effort toward *détente*, the Soviet denial of Adenauer's right to concern himself with West Berlin was the most interesting, and potentially the most dangerous, aspect of the new Soviet tactic. It was dangerous to the economic well-being of the city, which depends on its ties with West Germany, and to the Western presence in Berlin and thus to Berlin's political freedom. It also endangered, by implication, the cohesion of NATO, since West Germany would be a less reliable ally if it felt that the major NATO powers had not adequately protected their interest in West Berlin.[11]

During this time, numerous efforts were also made to erode the Western Powers legal position in Berlin or increase the East German regime's status to the detriment of the West's access routes. Early in 1959, the Soviets attempted to enforce a flight ceiling of 10,000 feet in the air corridors running between Britain and West Germany. The US' reply on April 13 was sharp and immediate: "The United States never has recognized and does not recognize any limitations to the right to fly any altitude in the corridors."[12]

Professor Paul R. Voitti of the US Air Force Academy explains that:

> From time to time, typically or allegedly due to military exercises, the Soviets have either closed one or more corridors for a brief time or offered such compensatory arrangements as allowing the Western allies 5,000 to 12,500 feet in lieu of the customary 2,500 to 10,000 feet. Although such compensation may appear reasonable, in fact it positions the Soviets as authoritative actor, dictating the terms under which the Western allies may use the corridors. The October 1946 Flight Rules do address the possibility of imposing "airspace restriction," but the "appropriate authority" is left unspecified. Because the Western allies view use of the corridors as their right, they have been somewhat reluctant to take "privileges" offered by the Soviets (flying above 10,000 feet when, indeed, they have never conceded their right in principle to fly above that altitude); particularly when taking such "privileges" could establish de facto the authority of the privilege granter.[13]

In February of 1960, the Soviet representative at the Berlin Air Safety Center (BASC) approved the application of a Scandinavian airline for commercial flights through the Hamburg air corridor. Western representatives discovered, however, that the Soviet member had entered a notation stating that he had previously obtained the consent of East German authorities before making his decision. The Western representatives then turned the application down

---

*Soviet troops do, however, continue to conduct vehicle patrols in the three West Sectors just as the Western Allies conduct similar patrols in theirs. Soviet troops also stand guard at their war memorial near the *Reichstag* in the British Sector.

A US Army convoy heading to Berlin (left) is blocked by Soviet armored vehicles at the Soviet/East German checkpoint at Babelberg, East Germany, 12 October 1963. An outbound US convoy is voluntarily remaining in place until the other convoy is cleared. Note the Soviet vehicles on the side road.

and directed one of the airline's incoming planes to Schönefeld Airport located outside Berlin, but within the Four Power "Berlin Circle" used by aircraft landing at West Berlin airfields.

Another incident occurred early that year when, according to Speier:

> The passports issued by the Soviet commander to the members of the Western military missions in Potsdam were suddenly changed to read that their bearers were registered residents of the German Democratic Republic. These missions in Potsdam, like the Soviet military missions in Frankfurt, Bünde, and Baden-Baden, had been established at the end of World War II by special agreement among the four supreme commanders in accordance with the then-prevailing plan for a common administration of the whole of Germany.
>
> While the issue did not directly involve Western occupation rights in Berlin, acceptance of the new passports would have meant a *de facto* recognition of the prerogative of the Pankow regime to change a four-power agreement. The Western military commanders wrote to the Soviet commander in Potsdam that they would under no circumstances accept the new documents.[14]

But while the Soviet Union could try to erode the Western positions on Berlin and East German recognition, East Germany itself was deflating like a balloon as refugees spilled into Berlin by the thousands each week. Between the establishment of the German Democratic Republic in 1949 and August of 1961, roughly three million people fled the "workers paradise" thus bestowing on East Germany the dubious distinction of being the only country in the world to suffer a population decrease in the 1950s.

Although the East Germans who made their way to the Marienfelde refugee center in West Berlin came from all walks of life, an inordinately large portion of them were people the Soviet sponsored East German government was depending on to build the first German Socialist state. More than half of the refugees were under 25 years old and most of the rest were under 45. They included more than 16,000 engineers, 5,000 doctors, dentists and veterinari-

(*Left*) British Prime Minister Harold MacMillan and President John F. Kennedy, 4 April 1961. (*Right*) A lonely flight across the border.

ans, almost 1,000 university professors along with more than 15,000 elementary and high school teachers. The entire law faculty of the University of Leipzig trekked west as well as the chief physicians at numerous hospitals and even some of their appointed replacements.

As East-West tensions mounted and rumors began to circulate in the East that the gateway to freedom would soon be closed forever, the refugee stream increased. By mid-Juy 1961, more than 1,000 people a day were filing for refugee status, in spite of the fact that arrests were increasing as the East German *Vopos* (short for *Volkspolizisten*, or People's Police) increased their efforts to separate would-be refugees from the normal cross sector traffic. It was apparent that the Soviet Union could not let East Germany continue to hemmorage.

In the early hours of a warm Sunday morning, August 13, 1961, the *Vopos* began to erect barbed wire barricades along the entire length of the West Sector boundaries. East German party chief Ulbricht had given his protégé, Erich Honecker, the task of building the wall and five months of secret preparations paid off as bewildered Berliners watched the feverish activity under the glare of floodlights. Meanwhile, the teletype machines of the Western news agencies

chattered with the official announcement drawn up at the Warsaw Pact meeting held during the previous week in Moscow.

"In the face of the aggressive aspirations of the reactionary forces of West Germany and its NATO allies," according to the turgid East German officialese, "necessary steps" were being taken to ensure that, "reliable safeguards and effective control be established around the whole territory of West Berlin."

The administration of US President John F. Kennedy had engaged in extensive contingency planning for a Soviet blockade, similar to the kind which took place in 1948, but the construction of a barrier to physically restrain would-be refugees was never looked upon as a serious possibility. Once construction started, the administration did nothing about the wall. Kennedy thought that an aggressive response would help precipitate what they believed would be the *real* crisis which was sure to come with a squeeze on the Berlin access routes.

While the United States was willing to go to great lengths to preserve the freedom of West Berlin, neither the United States, Great Britain nor France were willing to risk a wider confrontation over the post-World War II occupation statutes which allowed all Germans unhindered pas-

(*Top*) West Berlin children look across communist barricades at their former playmates. The barbed wire was soon replaced by a concrete block wall. (*Bottom*) East Berliners being kept back from the wire by the People's Police.

# The Wall

Following Land Registery records precisely, the Wall cut off sidewalks from their streets, blocked trolley lines and ran through buildings. Below, French soldiers patrolling the boundary in armoured cars. The houses are in the Soviet sectors. Doors and windows in the mezzanine floor are walled up; in the first floor the forcibly evacuated homes now accommodate guards who prevent East Berliners from escaping through the windows. Waving to their relations in West Berlin is the only means of communication left to the upper story tenants.

(*Top*) The Wall is strengthened by adding concrete slabs, 16 April 1964. (*Left*) A portion of the neatly manicured "death strip" created along the Wall. (*Right*) People's Police carry away a dying youth they had shot nearly an hour earlier. The 18 year old construction worker, Peter Fechter, was one of the first East Berliners killed while attempting to flee to the West.

(*Top*) US and Soviet tanks face each other across the sector boundry at Checkpoint Charlie, 24 August 1961. (*Bottom*) After several of their buses had been stoned by West Berlin young people, the Russians took to changing the guard at the Soviet war memorial with armored cars. The vehicles were stopped at the checkpoint and were then escorted by US Military Police to the Soviet War Memorial which is in the British Sector. The British Military Police then escorted the Soviet vehicles back to the checkpoint where they reentered East Berlin, 25 August 1962.

(*Top*) Khrushchev visits the Wall and pronounces it "a great and heroic Socialist achievement," 17 April 1963. Wearing a fedora at upper left is SED first secretary, Walter Ulbricht. (*Bottom*) Kennedy and West Berlin mayor Willy Brandt at the Wall, 26 June 1963.

sage from one sector of Berlin to another. The unrestricted construction of a wall which, in effect, turned East Germany into the world's largest prison camp, profoundly shocked West Germans.

As it became more and more apparent that a crisis of confidence was building in West Germany and, especially, West Berlin, Kennedy sent Vice-President Lyndon Baines Johnson and General Clay to the city along with 1,500 troops to add to the US contingent in Berlin. Clay stayed on as Kennedy's personal representative in the city and, with Kennedy's reluctant blessing, proceeded to make sure that no additional ground was lost to the Communists. Clay's repeated use of armed patrols to escort US diplomat Allan Lightner past East German guards demanding to see his passport horrified Kennedy's top-ranking advisors.

"But Clay, taking full advantage of his position as the president's personal representative, was operating on a totally different wavelength," said Norman Gelb, a reporter covering the unfolding story in Berlin.

> [Clay] placed great importance on the fact that by long-standing agreement to which the Soviets were a party,

Lightner had as much right to move about freely in East Berlin as in the western sectors of the city. The general was a devout adherent of the theology of the Berlin situation in which unrestricted access to the East for Allied personnel, the refusal to show passports, and other seemingly trivial observances were symbols of the entire structure of established relationships, a structure that would collapse—jeopardizing the American position—if the symbols were disregarded.[15]

Other incidents occurred and eventually US and Soviet tanks were virtually snout to snout at the Checkpoint Charlie Sector crossing. Kennedy continued to back Clay over the strenuous objections of senior civilian and military advisors and Allied prerogatives in Berlin were not further eroded. But while Clay had certainly won few friends in Washington and at NATO headquarters in Paris, where it was felt he had unnecessarily "exposed the United States to the possibility of having to back down in the face of far superior fire power. . . . West Berliners had been delighted that the Americans had demonstrated that they were prepared to defend them, by force if necessary. And the Soviets had learned that the changes they wished to impose on the situation would no longer draw only routine protests from the United States."[16]

Throughout the 1960s, morale in Berlin had its ups and downs but generally remained high. Financial advantages were given to firms opening subsidiaries in the city and the economy boomed. West Berlin, which had 300,000 unemployed just over a decade before, had actually developed a labor shortage by 1965. The access routes across East Germany remained open despite delays on the *Autobahns* and the potentially disastrous buzzing of commercial aircraft and blinding of the BASF radar system during Warsaw Pact maneuvers.

While construction of the "Wall of Shame" across Berlin was—and to a certain degree still is—a propaganda nightmare for the East German government, it did put a stop to the exodus of young and highly skilled workers. Within a fairly short period of time, East Germans began to achieve a relatively high level of prosperity when compared with other Communist block nations. Consequently, the successful Hallstein Doctrine,* by which West Germany threatened to break off diplomatic and trade relations with any state recognizing Ulbricht's German Democratic Republic, became harder to enforce and Willy Brandt's *Ostpolitik* became official West German policy when he won the chancellorship in 1969.

Brandt promptly enunciated the new government's *Ostpolitik* (eastern policy)—a new approach to East-West *détente. Ostopolitik* focused on the *Deutschlandproblem* (German problem) and approved recognition of East Germany as the necessary precondition for peaceful relations with Eastern Europe. Normalization of relations between the two Germanys, it was expected, would foster progress toward future reunification. Brandt's proposed formulation—"two states of one German nation"—affirmed the unique relationship of the two German States. The Federal Republic continued to regard the two polities as constituent parts of a single nation, sharing a common language, culture, and tradition. The special category of "inter-German relations" was devised for diplomatic contacts.[17]

A series of treaties negotiated and ratified in the early 1970s formed the heart of *Ostpolitik*. The Moscow Treaty of August 1970, between the Soviet Union and West Germany, guaranteed the existing borders of all European states including the two Germanys. The Warsaw Treaty signed by Poland and West Germany four months later confirmed the loss of Germany's pre-World War II territories turned over to Poland by the Soviet Union. The signing of the Basic Treaty in 1972 by the East and West German governments removed the last obstacles to each country's membership in the United Nations which they joined the following year. By the terms of the Basic Treaty, both Germanys "pledged mutual respect for each other's independence and autonomy in the conduct of internal and external affairs. West Germany rejected the idea, however, that East Germany constituted foreign territory. The exchange of diplomatic missions was promised, as were further treaties to establish trade, travel, and communications relations."[8]

In the meantime, enough important aspects of the Berlin issue—which had been the final obstacle to a treaty between the two Germanys—were worked out between Britain, France, the United States and the Soviet Union that an accord was able to be signed in September 1971. The Four Power Agreement on Berlin "guaranteed that ties and links between Bonn and West Berlin would be maintained and developed. The Federal Republic was prohibited, however, from incorporating West Berlin despite the fact that East Berlin had been de facto made part of East Germany. West Berliners were promised the right to visit

*Named after its author State Secretary for Foreign Affairs, Walter Hallstein.

Erich Honecker, May 1971.

East Berlin and East Germany and to improve communications with those areas. The Western powers retained authority in West Berlin and responsibility for its defense.[19]

The three *Ostpolitik* treaties were only ratified by the West Germans after prolonged and continuous struggle and, even once the Basic Treaty was passed, it was unsuccessfully challenged in the Federal Constitutional Court by its opponents. In East Germany, the prime opponent to *Ostpolitik*, Walter Ulbricht, was elbowed out of his leadership position because he had become an impediment to Soviet *détente* with the West.

The new first secretary, (later changed to general secretary), Erich Honecker, went along with the temporary spirit of *détente*, but only to the extent that it would gain more recognition for the East German state. Honecker's polity of *Abgrenzung* (demarkation) allowed increased trade with West Germany, but East Germany would follow its own path toward economic, political and social development. In the beginning at least, he appeared to be less rigid in his approach to the state-party system. There was even a brief flowering of the arts and literature before the institution of more stringent censorship laws and the exiling of several authors from the Writer's Union, along with other critics, brought things back to normal.

In the 1970s and 80s, the East German Communists have had some degree of success in maintaining the complacency of their subjects through strenuous efforts to satisfy consumer demands. This effort, of course, was not new and moves in this direction were first seriously introduced in 1953 under Ulbricht, but did the Communists little good until the last escape route to the West was closed with the sealing off of Berlin. Today there is undoubtedly more of an "East German consciousness" than ever before, but it remains under siege as the death strip along the inter German border and the Berlin Wall are not barriers to West German and West Berlin television programming.

> Time was when East German Communist youth groups climbed rooftops to haul down any television antennae oriented to the West. Grade-school teachers would ask their classes to sketch the TV logo they recalled seeing on their home screens, and any child who innocently drew the west German logo instead of the East German one earned for his parents harassment and warnings.
>
> Such measures were "senseless," said [prominent East German television official] Kurt Ottersberg, and besides, they didn't work. These days, the GDR strategy is simply to try to create programs that will be more popular than those from the West. Out of that confrontation has grown some of the best television in Europe—drama, ballet, cabaret, sports coverage. "Some evenings they're better, some evenings we're better," said Ottersberg. And with a smile: "We would prefer to have a neighbor not so sophisticated in television."[20]

Well aware of the fact that they enjoy the highest standard of living in Eastern Europe (including the Soviet Union), it remains painfully obvious to East Germans that they still lag far behind their brethren in the West. Moreover, the increasing contacts that Honecker has allowed between people of the two German states only serves to reinforce this.

Seven to eight million West Germans and West Berliners visit family and friends across the border each year and two million East Germans—more than 10 percent of the country's population—were allowed to visit the West in 1981. West Germans shell out well over a billion and a half dollars a year for the privilege of retaining these contacts through transportation agreements, interest-free credits and currency exchange requirements at the border which amount, in effect, to transit fees. As for the East Germans, most of those allowed to visit the West are elderly pensioners whom the Communists would be just as happy to have stay in West Germany so as to no longer be a burden on the treasury of the socialist workers state. Emigration restrictions have also been eased slightly so that "malcontents" foolish enough to not want to be a part of the "workers paradise" also find it easier to leave, thus removing a potential pool of troublemakers from East Germany.

For many, though, becoming a target for repression by putting one's name on an emigration list seems more risky than making the deadly crossing that has seen a minimum of 70 people killed since the building of the wall. While a large portion of the two to three thousand East Germans who flee to the West each year are the aforementioned elderly pensioners who never make the return trip home, a surprisingly large number of younger Germans continue to escape to the West by innovative methods including flying

(*Top*) East German guards peer at a memorial to Peter Fechter who was shot and killed at this spot while attempting to flee to the West on 17 August 1962. By March 1964, when this photo was taken, the barrier was being improved by the demolition of buildings in the background to form an improved firing line for the *Vopos*. (*Bottom*) The same portion of the Wall today, almost twice the height and with a slick rounded top too large for an arm to stretch around.

The system of concrete block and wire fence barricades erected by the East Germans on the Soviet side of Checkpoint Charlie are designed to prevent high speed escapes. The area at upper left showing crossed I-beam vehicle traps behind a high white screen is typical of the inner section of the Wall facing East Berliners. Tourists entering and leaving East Berlin are directed to the large white customs shed between the inner and outer portions of the Wall.

over the border in light planes, powered hang-gliders and even balloons, while others swim across the Havel Lake and Spree River into West Berlin or the Elbe River southeast of Hamburg; or scale the border fences which some have apparently learned to climb without setting off alarms.

But for every East German who makes it across, an unknown number fail, often at the cost of their lives. In the summer of 1986, a man driving a gravel filled dump truck with his girlfriend and her child aboard, smashed through the concrete barriers at Checkpoint Charlie. The next two similar attempts by East Germans ended in failure. Interestingly enough, the *Vopos* have always made up a large portion of the refugees since they are on the border regularly and can plan an escape with relative ease. After the building of the Berlin Wall, many *Vopos* fled to the West singly or in groups which reached company strength in 1964. Orders went out that the *Vopos* would henceforth patrol in teams, in effect putting a guard on each guard. The result has been fewer defections, but when they come over now, they are usually in pairs.

For Honecker, the sheer numbers of people wanting to get out of his country and its long-held economic position of being the best of the worst in Europe, has led to a realization that closer ties with West Germany are essential to East Germany's stability and prestige. After the July 1984, signing of a $330 million West German loan to East Germany in exchange for an easing of humanitarian contacts between the two Germanys, it was announced that Honecker would visit Bonn that fall. However, when the Soviets began to grumble loudly and publicly over the visit, the Kremlin's pressure unnerved the East German Communists and the trip was cancelled.

In 1987, Honecker was more successful in gaining Soviet support for a visit and the Western press expended much newsprint over what it all meant. But for Honecker's old comrad in arms, Wolfgang Leonard the matter was simple: "East Germany desperately seeks legitimacy as a sovereign state. The visit will inevitably upgrade its reputation and Honecker will repay this with certain concessions in human rights."[21]

While West German politicians still insist that there is only one German nation—even if it is currently divided into two states—and do not recognize the sovereignty of the German Democratic Republic over its land and people, they were more than willing to go through the Alice-in-Wonderland protocol of receiving Honecker with all the pomp and ceremony of a genuine head of state if it would help open ties to East Germans. When Honecker stepped fom his plane through the West German looking glass, the man whose Free German Youth mobs once broke up Berlin city council meetings during the airlift and who later personally oversaw the construction of the Berlin Wall, could see the East German flag flying at the airport.

West Berlin youths toss a giant blue balloon on the lawn of the Reichstag. (*Below*) West Berlin police sift through the rubble for clues to the 5 April 1986 bombing of a disco frequented by Americans.

NINE

# Berlin Today

Every year that passes pushes events in the 1940s, 50s and early 60s further into the dim recesses of the past. The reasoning behind the Western Allies strict legalism, which seemed so clear when the Communist threat to Berlin was more apparent, seems rather senseless to many Germans who have come of age during the last 25 years of relative *détente*. But 40 years after the Berlin Airlift, and just over 15 since the series of agreements which brought stability to its access routes, the Soviet Union and East Germany still continue to aggressively test the West's resolve in maintaining the city's fragile legal position. Three recent events illustrate this:

After the April 5, 1986 bombing of the La Belle discotheque, in which two people were killed and 230 others were injured, the Kommandantura directed the West Berlin police to expell certain suspected terrorists as well as tighten controls at Western entry points into the city. East Berlin, though, presented a problem. Along the seven entry points through the Wall between East and West sectors, *Vopos* check passports to prevent East Germans from passing into the West, while the British, French, and American guards allow people to pass unimpeded since they don't view East Berlin as a foreign territory. A situation was thus created where potential terrorists finding some access restrictions from the West could move into the city from East Berlin where the Syrians, Lybians, Iranians, and Palestine Liberation Organization all maintain diplomatic missions.

The US Embassy in East Berlin contacted their Soviet counterparts, who maintain a discrete presence at the sector crossings, and asked for assistance in combating terrorism in the city. As is normal in cases like this, East German assistance was not requested directly, since the Western stance is that the East Germans have no sovereignty in a city that is still under Four Power jurisdiction. The communist response was to have the border guards attempt to check the passports of *Western* diplomats moving between East and West Berlin since *they* might be terrorists who "forged" the simple East German identity cards carried by all diplomatic personnel. The diplomats refused, but if they had shown their passports to the *Vopos*, it could be construed that they recognized the Wall as the international border of East Germany. This was judged by the Western governments as being the true motive behind the move.

Diplomats of the four Powers making up the Kommandantura were exempt from the new rule and could proceed normally, but diplomats from other NATO countries, including Italy, Denmark, the Netherlands, and West Germany, had to take long detours around the outskirts of the city to avoid being forced to show their passports at the sector crossings. When the East Germans saw that the ploy was not working, they relented and stated they would issue new identity cards that were "secure" against forgery. The fact, though, that they may have been willing to escalate the situation to include the Kommandantura members if the other Western diplomats broke the ice by relenting to East German demands was borne out by the comments of *Vopos* at the sector crossings that British, French and US diplomats would soon be required to present passports as well.

Another interesting move to undermine the West's position in the city was initiated by Honecker himself later that year when he asked the mayor of West Berlin, Eberhard Diepgen, to attend East Berlin festivities marking the 750th Anniversary of the city in 1987.

The *Economist's* correspondent in Berlin related the story with wonderful clarity:

> Mr. Diepgen would like to go. He is keen to seize every chance to reopen connections between the two halves of a city which has been divided since the Berlin wall went up (under Mr. Honecker's supervision) in 1961.
>
> But, like so much about Berlin, the invitation is less straightforward than it looks. It refers to East Berlin as "capital of the German Democratic republic." The three western allies argue tht, if Mr. Diepgen accepts, this will undermine their insistence that all Berlin, East and West, remain under the control of the four victors of 1945, by an agreement reached with the Russians. The point looks legalistic, but the western allies are convinced that their protective role in the western part can stay credible only if the city's four-power status is firmly upheld. If it is not, then West Berlin, isolated 100 miles behind the East German border, will be helpless if the Communists choose to put pressure on it again.
>
> The western allies therefore indicated that they would prefer Mr. Diepgen to turn down the invitation. The western side's decisions on Berlin are normally reached in the so-called "Bonn Group,"[*] made up of representatives in Bonn of the three western allies in consultation with the West German government.
>
> Contacts with the West Berlin city government are close: usually only a friendly allied nudge, rather than an outright order, is enough to get the Bonn Group's policy carried out. Certainly neither side has anything to gain from a public row. But in this case Mr. Diepgen, a forthright and ambitious Christian Democrat who has been in office since 1984, has not taken the hint.
>
> He has gone on publicly insisting that no visit of his to East Berlin can change the city's status. He also invited Mr. Honecker to come over for next week's party in West Berlin.
>
> After a lot of dithering, the East German leader finally said no on April 13 [1987]. Berlin-watchers reckon that, just as the prospect of a Diepgen trip eastwards worries the western allies, so the Russians were not keen on a Honecker visit westwards on April 30th. They emphasize that under the four-power Berlin agreement of 1971 they and the western allies agreed that West Berlin is not part of West Germany. They do not want Mr. Honecker implicitly suggesting a connection by crossing the wall for celebrations attended by West German notables like the federal chancellor, Mr. Helmut Kohl.[1]

Another clever assault on Berlin's legal position was buried by all the hubbub over Mikhail Gorbachev's Washington visit to sign the Intermediate-range Nuclear Forces (INF) Treaty in December 1987. The 56-page treaty contains numerous protocols covering the mechanics of the verification process in third-party countries where Soviet or US missiles are located. There were, for example, as many as 77 medium-range SS-20 missiles based in East Germany and Czechoslovakia at the time of the signing. Various Soviet-American "working groups" negotiated the details of these protocols as well as other matters such as the

*The "Bonn Group" consists of the ambassadors of Great Britain, France and the United States along with the West German foreign minister. As a practical matter, however, day to day affairs are handled by lesser diplomats of the respective embassies and West German foreign ministry.

wording of the final summit statement and groundwork for future negotiations.

During work on the East German protocol, the question arose of where the US verification team would enter the country. The Soviet negotiator informed his US counterparts that the East German government would allow the US team to enter the German Democratic Republic at Schönefeld Airport. Of all the airfields in their country to choose from, the East Germans picked the one lying just outside Berlin, but well within the agreed upon confines of the Four Power Berlin Control Zone, or "Berlin Circle," eminating for 20 miles around Tempelhof.

Neither air traffic controllers at Schönefeld nor East Block aircraft using the airport coordinate with Four Power representatives at the Berlin Air Safety Center so landing the US verification team there was unacceptable to the United States. The Soviet negotiators knew this ahead of time but made the proposal anyway apparently believing that the US would not let such an "inconsequential" matter get in the way of signing the INF Agreement. The US members of the working group, however, would and did with the blessing of US Secretary of State George Shultz and the White House was briefed on the problem.

The Soviets held firm as well in the face of US "suggestions" that other airports would not jeopardize either sides' view of Berlin and that they should come up with another location. This and other problems held up finalization of the agreement and negotiators worked well into the night to hammer things out. Talks resumed on Thursday morning, December 10 and by the time Gorbachev arrived at the White House — late because of his plunge into crowds of shoppers — the working group still had not settled the Schöenfeld/Berlin question. Just barely in time for Gorbachev's scheduled departure from Washington, Soviet negotiators finally relented, stating that the East Germans would agree to the US teams entering the German Democratic Republic at Leipzig.

While this strict Allied adherence to the theology of Berlin is reassuring to its Western citizens, many of these same Berliner's will often tell you that it proves very restrictive when West Berlin must deal with matters concerning East Berlin such as operation of the city's subway system. West Berliners point out that East Germany continuously flouts the 1971 Four-Power Agreement reaffirming that the

*Vopos,* who used to regularly paint over graffiti on the Wall, rarely bother to do so now. One item that was recently removed and hauled back to East Berlin was a urinal affixed by an artist. Its removal prompted one observer to remark that shortages were still a problem in the East.

(*Left*) The US side of Checkpoint Charlie. (*Right*) Scouts from the US Army's Berlin Brigade check on activity on the communist side of the Wall during a patrol.

city is still under the jurisdiction of the British, French, Soviets, and Americans and wonder why the treaty provision stating that ties between Wester Berlin and West Germany "will be maintained and developed" can't be interpreted a bit more expansively.

The obvious answer, of course, is that the current resurgence of *détente* is not likely to last forever and no amount of *glasnost* is going to remove the 110 miles of East German territory separating the city from West Germany. Little nibbles into the Western Powers legal position today could well open West Berlin up to enormous problems in the not too distance future and be crucial in any potential international court of law ruling on the legal status of the city. While it is highly unlikely that either side would abide by any adverse opinion on such a crucial question, both sides are mindful of "world opinion" and both are courting the German people.

The Allied presence in the city is maintained by 6,000 US, 3,500 British, and 2,800 French troops who are, in turn, ringed by the tank and motorized divisions of the Soviet 20th Guards Army. Referred to now as a "protective" rather than occupation force, the Western Allies keep a low profile except along the border areas abutting East Germany and East Berlin. Following the 1987 death of Rudolph Hess, who had been the only inmate under Four Power jurisdiction at Spandau Prison since 1966, the facility reverted to British control. The remaining Four Power contact between the Western and Soviet military forces in the Berlin area is maintained at the US, British and French military missions in Potsdam, the Soviet War Memorial and at the Berlin Air Safety Center (BASC) located in the former Allied Control Authority Building.

Paul R. Viotti, who served as a political advisor to the US European Command and is currently a professor at the US Air Force Academy, described the continuing operation of these post-war institutions in a 1984 article:

> Established by agreements signed in 1947 and 1948, each of the four allies has liaison missions attached to the command

Soviet soldiers stand ceremonial guard at the Soviet War Memorial located inside the British Sector. Because of a shooting incident between a West German youth and guards, the memorial can now only be viewed from passing cars and busses.

headquarters of the other. Thus, a Soviet military liaison mission, located in Frankfurt since its establishment, is accredited to the U.S. Army Headquarters in Heidelberg. Similar Soviet missions are attached to French and British headquarters in their "former" zones of occupation. American, French, and British missions are maintained in Potsdam, accredited to the Soviet general staff.

The military liaison missions were originally established for the recovery of war dead and to provide a communications link between heads of occupying forces. Important as these missions still are for maintaining communication, viewed by some as prototypical confidence-building institutions, they are indeed an anomaly, existing as they do within two separate, otherwise sovereign states. Western military liaison officers have right of movement throughout the GDR except in certain specified restricted areas; the same right is accorded their Soviet counterparts in the FRG. With respect to maintaining Berlin access, the right of movement enjoyed by Western allied officers is particularly convenient when problems occur on the highway or railroad connecting Berlin with the FRG. Ill passengers aboard the troop train can be brought to a local hospital under escort of a military liaison officer. "Lost" drivers who, contrary to regulations, have strayed from the *autobahn* may be pursued by liaison officers beyond the more limited jurisdiction of allied military police officers who do not have authority to move beyond the immediate confines of the highway.[2]

Voitti also described how things are handled on the political side of the fence:

Although [the US] embassy is located physically in East Berlin (as are the British and French embassies), the United States continues to deny the East German claim that Berlin is the capital of the GDR. From the American perspective, the embassy is accredited to the GDR and merely happens to be located in a city still under occupation.

Accordingly, East German authorities sometimes refer to Western embassies in East Berlin matters associated with their presence as part of the allied occupation. In turn, the embassies routinely defer these issues to military authorities or to their national missions in West Berlin that have responsibility for occupation matters. To do otherwise would undermine the Western claim to occupation rights; dealing with such matters through an embassy accredited to the GDR would use a channel external to the occupation regime and be supportive of East German claims to authority. . . .

The Kurfürstendamm, West Berlin.

In this regard, the Soviet embassy in East Berlin is the principal point of contact for the Western missions. Occupation "business"—overseeing arrangements between German authorities in eastern and western sections of the city for underground (*U-Bahn*) and surface (*S-Bahn*) transit systems as well as handling protests, denials, and other communications—is conducted among the Western allied missions in coordination with West Berlin authorities, and between the Western allies and the Soviet embassy in East Berlin.[3]

It is this last matter, the inability of the East and West Berlin city governments to work together directly on mat-

Havel Lake, once the scene of hurried airlift operations, offers enjoyment and beauty to West Berliners.

ters affecting both of them, that is so galling to West Berlin authorities and their East German counterparts work subtly and efficiently to promote dissention. As a purely practical matter, though, "the Western Allies" according to the *Economist*, "have probably gone about as far as they can in developing authority to the mayor and his colleagues without jeopardizing their own status as protecting powers."

Most West Berliners continue to feel that the Allied presence in their city, not treaties with East Germany or the Soviet Union, is the best guarantee of their city's freedom. According to a poll conducted by SFB, the city's main broadcast organization, this belief cuts across all age groups and all party lines from the right of center, Christian Democrats through the anti-establishment Alternative List. The main question among Berliners centers mostly on just how many Allied troops are actually needed in the city with almost 70 percent of these under 30 believing that only a "symbolic presence" is needed to ensure Berlin's safety from Communist blackmail.

The overwhelming preoccupation of the majority of West Berliners over the past 40 years has been their security. Although they have demonstrated their continued desire for freely elected democratic government, their principal fear is that some unthinking Western leader might, in word or deed, undermine their freedoms. Therefore, Berliners need constant reinforcement from Western political leaders in the form of statements of support and personal visits. Every American president since Truman has made the standard required commitment to defend Berlin, but those who visit and make catchy symbolic statements (Kennedy: "I am a Berliner" or Reagan: "Tear down this

San Francisco? Kansas City? Boston? East Berlin youths on skateboards and roller skates enjoy some free time in a local park. Such behavior is referred to as "malignant hooliganism" by East German officials.

wall") win the devotion of Berliners as few German leaders could ever hope to attain. This is simply because the politically sophisticated Berliners understand the American president, as leader of the Western world, holds the key to the future of their city.

On the other side of the Wall, East Berlin looks better than it ever has. Areas that once lagged far behind West Berlin's reconstruction efforts, like along the Unter den Linden, have been almost completely restored although wandering a block or two from the main streets still puts one face to face with the bullet-scarred ruins of 1945. A frequent complaint, long voiced by both foreign visitors and Berliners' alike, concerned the lack of good places to eat in East Berlin, outside of the hard currency restaurants in some hotels. Even that now is beginning to change with the appearance of "tolerable" bars and cafes.

One of the more interesting developments in East Berlin has to do with the young people of the city. Communist officials who once took great delight in sneering at West Berlin youth for taking on the trappings of a "decadent American culture" (while simultaneously cheering on the raucous student protests of the 1960s and '70s) have found themselves facing an increasingly independent-minded group of young people who have literally grown up with Western television.

During the three-night rock concert celebrating the 750th anniversary of Berlin, held on the grounds along the West side of the wall adjacent to the old *Reichstag* building, more than 3,000 East German youth attempted to converge on their side of the Brandenburg Gate where they could hear the bands. The crowds were peaceful and unaggressive until stopped by East German police from getting close enough to hear "their" music. Then, what started out as catcalls and whistles at the police soon saw objects being thrown.

The three nights of unrest that followed culminated on the night of June 8-9 when dozens of demonstrators were rounded up and chants of "Freedom," "Down with the wall" and "We want Gorbachev" echoed down the Unter den Linden. The spectacle of East German youth calling on a Soviet leader to support their bid for more freedom was gleefully received by the Soviet Embassy personnel and ignored by East German officials who, true to form, attempted to deny that absolutely anything was going on along the Wall. The old demon of Western television, however, again reared its glowing head and simply ran replays and additional footage of the tumultuous events for viewers on both sides of the border.

The old Anhalter train station, where Berliners with bags and suitcases in hand once milled about apprehensively when the routes to the West were clamped shut in 1948, has long since been demolished. Only the massive five-story portal remains, its two stone figures still patiently waiting for travelers who will never arrive. Today, the spacious vacant lot that was once covered by track, waiting halls and platforms has been reclaimed by nature, and urban naturalists have detected many varieties of endangered plants and insects among the chunks of a concrete, broken bricks, and weeds.

Most of the earlier debris that clogged West Berlin streets and sidewalks after the war was passed piece by piece back

The view looking south from the Reichstag in the British Sector to the Brandenburg Gate behind the Berlin Wall. The expanse of open ground beyond the gate once contained a number of important government buildings during the Nazi era — all of which covered an extensive complex of underground bunkers and passageways. The bunker where Adolph Hitler committed suicide was located under a portion of the treed area at left. Today a series of barriers making up the Wall stretch across the area and the many trees planted there after the war were cut down to give guards an unobstructed view. The first few rows of buildings in the

background are in the Soviet Sector with Potsdamer Platz at the extreme right. The buildings of newer construction lie in the US Sector.

into the shells of the buildings it came from by the *Trümmerfrauen* or rubble women. When the pace of recovery quickened in the 1950s and whole city blocks were demolished to make way for new construction, the war rubble was gathered together in various parts of the city into huge heaps called *Trümmerbergen.* These mountains of rubble vary greatly in size and, more often than not, these mounds are now used as city parks. The largest *Trümmerberge* has a volume of over 34 million cubic yards and towers 377 feet over the Grunewald Forest in the Wilmersdorf District. Berliners, being a particularly clever segment of the human race, use it as a perch for hang-gliding in the summer and as a ski slope in the winter. As for the *Trümmerfrauen* who gathered most of this material together in the first place, a 1987 law of the Federal Republic made them eligible to receive a pension for their postwar work.

Berliners on both sides of the wall have generally learned to live with the abnormal situation fate has thrust upon them. Every day 90,000 West Berlin subway riders pass under the Wall as they travel between the French Sector buroughs of Wedding and Reinickendorf in the north and the US Sector boroughs of Keuzberg, Tempelhof and Neukölln to the south. Jutting between them is the Soviet Sector borough of Mitte where most of Berlin's most historic sites are located.

Rolling slowly through the tunnels, trains on West Berlin's *U-Bahn* Lines 6 and 8 pass a dozen unused stations that were sealed shut in 1961 to prevent East Berliners from escaping to the West. Through the dim station lights, one can make out crumbling plaster, a few East German guards patroling the platform with automatic weapons, and almost 3 decades worth of grime covering the floor and walls. Only at Friedrichstrasse Station are the West Berlin trains allowed to stop for the riders with business in the East who exit the cars and head for the border control checkpoint with their passports.

The question often posed is, how long can this seemingly unnatural situation of a divided city with a wall down its middle endure? Even if the wall were to come down tomorrow, the city would remain, as before the Wall was erected in 1961, divided. There is no immediate short-time solution to the status of Berlin. Nor, barring war or some radical change in the balance of power, is there any long-term solution. As long as Germany remains divided along the current political schisms, so will Berlin.

# Notes

**Chapter 1**

1 *A Special Study of Operation "Vittles"*, Aviation Operations, April 1949 (New York, NY, Connover-Mast Publications), p. 9

2 Milovan Djilas, *Conversations with Stalin* (Harmondsworth, England, Penguin, 1962), p.90

3 Georg Von Rauch, *A History of Soviet Russia* (New York, NY, Frederich A. Praeger, 1957), p. 391

4 Churchill, *op. cit.*, pp. 440-442

5 *Ibid.* pp. 226-228

6 *Ibid.* pp. 571-572

7 John H. Backer, *The Decision to Divide Germany* (Durham, NC, Duke University Press, 1978) pp. 19-22

8 Franklin M. Davis, Jr., *Come as a Conqueror, The United States Army's Occupation of Germany 1945-49* (New York, NY, The Macmillan Company, 1967), pp. 76-77

9 *Ibid.* pp. 78-79

10 Ibid., pp. 81-83

11 Protocol of European Advisory Commission, dated September 12, 1944

12 Churchill, *op. cit.*, p. 510

13 Davis, *op. cit.*, pp. 86-87

14 Protocol of European Advisory Commission, dated November 14, 1944

15 Churchill, *op cit.*, pp. 251-261

16 Russell D. Buhite, *Decisions at Yalta* (Wilmington, Del, Scholarly Resources, Inc., 1986), pp. 28-29

17 Official Gazette of the Control Council, Supplement 1 Lucius D. Clay, *Decision in Germany* (Garden City, NY, Doubleday & Company 1950) pp. 13-15

18 Churchill, *op. cit.*, p. 353

19 Official Gazette of the Control Council, Supplement 1 Clay, *op. cit.*, pp. 20-23

20 Clay, *op. cit.*, pp. 24-27

**Chapter 2**

1 Douglas Botting, *From the Ruins of the Reich*, (New York, Crown Publishers Inc., 1985), pp. 179-92 from data originally published in *Documentation on the Expulsions of the German Population from East Central Europe* (Bonn, West Germany, Federal Ministry for Expellees, Refugees and War Victims).

2 Wolfgang Leonhard, *Die Revolution Entlaesst Ihre Kinder* (Cologne, Germany, Verlag Kiepenhauer & Witsch, 1955)

3 Koppel Pinson, *Modern Germany* (New York, NY, Macmillan, 1954), p. 417

4 Leonhard, *op. cit.*, pp. 380-391

5 *Ibid.*, pp. 348-358

6 *Ibid.*, pp. 389-390

7 *Current Biography Yearbook, 1972,* D. H. W. Wilson Co., New York, 1972

8 John H. Backer, *Winds of History, The German Years of Lucius Dubignon Clay (New York, NY, Van Nostrand Reinhold Company, Inc., 1983), p. 87*

9 *Ibid.*, p. 97

10 *The Historical Encyclopedia of World War II* (New York, NY, Facts on File, Inc., 1980), p. 291

11 *Backer, Winds of History, op. cit.*, p. 3

12 *Ibid.*, p. 104

13 Avi Shlaim, *The United States and the Berlin Blockage 1948-49* (Berkeley, California, University of California Press, 1983), pp. 99-100

14 *Ibid.*, p. 102

15 Backer, *Winds of History, op. cit.*, pp. 85-89

16 *Ibid.*, pp. 89-90

17 Edward N. Peterson, *The American Occupation of Germany, Retreat to Victory* (Detroit, Michigan, Wayne State University Press, 1978), p. 119

18 Buhite, *op. cit.* pp. 32-37

19 Backer, *The Decision to Divide Germany, op. cit.*, p. 89

20 *Ibid.*, pp. 90-91

21 *Ibid.*, pp. 93-95

22 *Ibid.*, pp. 97-98

23 *Ibid.*, pp. 97-99

24 Edward A. Tenenbaum, *Military Government and Monetary Reform, Chapter 12* (Unpublished manuscript, Truman Library), p. 200

25 *Report of the Military Governor # !*, August 1945, p. 5

26 Jack Bennett, "The German Currency Reform". *Annals of the American Academy of Political and Social Science,* Vol. 267 (January 1950), p. 44

27 Tenenbaum, *op. cit.*, p. 201

28 *Ibid.*, pp. 202-203

29 *Ibid.*, p. 206

30 *Ibid.*, p. 206

31 *Ibid.*,p. 209 *Robert Murphy stated the printing order was not placed until after the Council of Foreign Ministers meeting in London in December 1947 (Robert Murphy, *Diplomat Among Warriors* (Garden City, NY, Doubleday & Company, 1964), pp. 312-313

32 Leonhard, *op. cit.* pp. 425-426

33 *SBZ von 1945 bis 1954*, p. 29

34 Terence Prittie, *Willy Brandt, Portrait of a Statesman* (New York, NY, Schocken Books, 1974). p. 74

35 *Ibid.*, p. 75

36 Walter Hammer *Hohes Haus in Henkers Hand* (Frankfurt/Main, Germany, Europaeische Verlangsanstalt, 1956), p. 84

37 Prittie, *op. cit.*, p. 72

38 Murphy, *op. cit.*, p. 211

39 *Ibid.*, pp. 277-279

40 Backer, *Winds of History*, op. cit., p. 57
41 Delbert Clark as quoted in Backer, *Ibid.*, pp. 87-88
42 Charles E. Bohlen *The Transformation of American Foreign Policy* New York, NY, W. W. Norton & Company, 1969), p. 86
43 *Ibid.*, pp. 87-88
44 Murphy, *op. cit.*, p. 308

**Chapter 3**

1 Clay, *op. cit.*, p. 174
2 U.S. Department of State, *Germany 1947-49: The Story in* Documents (Washington, D.C., U.S. Government Printing Office, 1950), p. 12
3 Clay, *op. cit.*, p. 176
4 *Ibid.*, p. 176
5 *Ibid.*, pp. 178-79
6 *Ibid.*, p. 350
7 *Ibid.*, p. 394
8 Shlaim, *op. cit.*, p. 34
9 Clay, *op. cit.*, pp. 398-400
10 *Ibid.*, pp. 408-412
11 *Ibid.*, p. 349
12 *Ibid.*, pp. 350-51
13 Davis, *op. cit.*, p. 200
14 Clay, *op. cit.*, pp. 355-56
15 Truman, Harry S., *Memoirs,* Volume II (Garden City, NY, Doubleday & Company, Inc., 1956), pp. 121-22
16 Smith, Jean Edward, editor, *The Papers of General Lucius D. Clay: Germany, 1945-1949* (Bloomington, Indiana, Indiana University Press, 1974), Vol 2, pp. 600-606
17 *Ibid.*, p. 607
18 *Ibid.*, pp. 622-23
19 Shlaim, *op. cit.*, pp. 137-38
20 Tenenbaum, *op. cit.*, p. 211
21 Bennett, *op. cit.*, pp. 48-49
22 *News of Germany # 133*, June 17, 1948
23 Clay, Lucius D., *Germany and the Fight for Freedom,* (Cambridge, Mass., Harvard University Press, 1950), p. 36
24 Taegliche Rundschau, May 30, 1948
25 Tenenbaum, *op. cit.*, p. 206
26 *Ibid.*, p. 210
27 *Ibid.*, pp. 209-10
28 Murphy, *op. cit.*, p. 383
29 Shlaim, Avi, *The United States and the Berlin Blockade, 1948-1949* (Berkeley, California, University of California Press, 1983), pp. 151-56
30 *Report of the Military Governor # 36*, June 1948, p. 2
31 *Report of the Military Governor # 37*, July 1948, p. 1
32 Shlaim, *op. cit.*, p. 157
33 *Ibid.*, pp. 151-52
34 Tenenbaum, *op. cit.*, p. 246
35 *Ibid.*, pp. 247-48
36 *Ibid.*, p. 249
37 *Ibid.*, pp. 249-50 and Bennett, *op. cit.*, pp. 51-52

**Chapter 4**

1 Smith, *op. cit.*, p. 622
2 *Ibid.*, p. 677
3 *Ibid.*, p. 692
4 Frank Howley, *Berlin Command* (NY, NY, G. P. Putnam's Sons, 1950), p. 200
5 Shlaim, *op. cit.*, p. 200
6 Smith, *op. cit.*, pp. 699-704
7 *Ibid.*, p. 697
8 Shlaim, *op. cit.*, p. 202
9 *Ibid.*, p. 203
10 Truman, Vol. 2, *op. cit.*, p. 123
11 Shlaim, *op. cit.*, p. 205
12 Smith, *op. cit.*, pp. 707-08
13 Walter Millis, editor, *The Forrestal Diaries* (NY, NY Viking Press 1951), pp. 452-54
14 Shlaim, *op. cit.*, p. 220
15 *Ibid.*, p. 227
16 Department of State Bulletin, July 4, 1948, p. 54
17 Shlaim, *op. cit.*, p. 233
18 *Ibid.*, p. 252
19 *Ibid.*, p. 262
20 National Security Council Minutes, July 22, 1948
21 New York Times, July 24, 1948
22 Documents on Germany, pp. 63-72
23 *Ibid.*, pp. 63-72
24 A Special Study of Operation "Vittles", *op. cit.*, p. 8
25 *Berlin Airlift*, A USAFE Summary, p. 16
26 A Special Study of Operation "Vittles", *op. cit.*, pp. 54-58
27 The New York Herald Tribune, European Edition, July 12, 1948
28 *Ibid*
29 Richard Collier, *Bridge Across the Sky,* (NY, NY McGraw-Hill Book Company, 1978), p. 79

**Chapter 5**

1 William H. Tunner, *Over the Hump,* (NY, NY, Duell, Sloan and Pearce, 1964), p. 161
2 Curtis E. LeMay with MacKinlay Kantor, *Mission with LeMay* (Garden City, NY, Doubleday & Company, Inc., 1965) p. 416
3 Tunner, *op. cit.*, p. 166
4 *Ibid.*, pp. 167-68

5 *Ibid.*, pp. 152-53
6 A Special Study of Operation "Vittles", *op. cit.*, pp. 60-65
7 Shlaim, *op. cit.*, pp. 337-41
8 Smith, *op. cit.*, p. 763
9 Shlaim, *op. cit.*, p. 309
10 *Ibid.*, pp. 337-41
11 *Ibid.*, pp. 747-48
12 Smith, *op. cit.*, p. 747
13 *SBZ von 1945-1954* (Bonn, West Germany, Bundesministerium fuer Gesamtdeutsche Fragen, 1956) p. 94
14 Ibid., p. 95; Clay, *op. cit.*, p. 377
15 *Report of the Military Governor No. 39*, September 1948, Office of Military Government, Berlin
16 Smith, *op. cit.*, pp. 844-45
17 Clay, *op. cit.*, p. 377; Smith, *op. cit.*, pp. 856-57
18 Telegraf, dated September 9, 1948
19 SBZ von 1945-1954, *op. cit.*, p. 95
20 Smith, *op. cit.*, pp. 856-57

**Chapter 6**

1 Tunner, *op. cit.*, p. 205
2 *Berlin Airlift*, USAFE Summary, p. 29
3 *A Four Year Report,* Office of the Military Government, U.S. Sector, Berlin, July 1, 1945–September 1, 1949 (Berlin, Deutsche Verlag, 1949), p. 20
4 *Ibid.*, p. 78
5 Collier, *op. cit.*, pp. 84-86
6 A Four Year Report, *op. cit.*, p. 20
7 Shlaim, *op. cit.*, p. 366
8 Smith, *op. cit.*, p. 986

**Chapter 7**

1 Tunner, *op. cit.*, pp. 221-22
2 Smith, *op. cit.*, p. 860
3 Shlaim, *op. cit.*, pp. 381-82
4 *Ibid.*, p. 383
5 *Ibid.*, pp. 384-85
6 Alan Bullock, *Ernest Bevin, Foreign Secretary, 1945-1951*, NY & London, W. W. Norton & Company, 1983), p. 669
7 Department of State Bulletin, May 15, 1949, p. 631
8 Smith, *op. cit.*, pp. 1137-39
9 *Ibid.*, pp. 1137-39
10 *Airlift Berlin,* (Berlin, Arani Verlag G.m.b.H., 1949) pp. 78-79
11 *Ibid.*, p. 79
12 *Ibid.*, p. 79
13 Paul Fisher, "The Berlin Airlift," *The Bee-Hive*, Volume XXIII, Number 4, Fall 1948, pp. 26-27

**Chapter 8**

1 Terence Pritte, *Germany Divided, The Legacy of the Nazi Era* (Boston, Mass, Little, Brown and Company, 1960) pp 31-32
2 Eleanor Lansing Dulles, *Berlin, The Wall Is Not Forever* (Chapel Hill, University of North Carolina Press) p. 37
3 *Ibid.*, pp 10-11
4 *Ibid.*, p. 10-13
5 Pritte, *op. cit.*, p. 16
6 Dulles, *op. cit.*, p. 16
7 Victor Marchetti and John D. Marks, *The CIA and the Cult of Intelligence* (New York, Dell Publishing Co., 1974) p. 34
8 William Henry Chamberlin, *The German Phoenix* (New York, Duell, Sloan & Pearce, 1963) pp. 147-49
9 *Ibid.*, p. 149
10 Hans Speier, *Divided Berlin, The Anatomy of Soviet Political Blackmail* (New York, Frederich A. Praeger, 1962) pp. 9-11
11 *Ibid.*, pp. 65-66
12 *Ibid.*, p. 95
13 Paul R. Viotti, *Berlin and Conflict Management with the USSR*, Orbis, Fall 1984, p. 588
14 Speier, *op. cit.*, pp. 93-94
15 Norman Gelb, *The Berlin Wall* (New York, Times Books, 1986) p. 253
16 Gelb, *op. cit.*, pp 257-58
17 *Federal Republic of Germany, A Country Study,* (Washington, DC, Department of the Army, 1983) p. 52
18 *Ibid.*, p 54
19 *Ibid.*, pp. 53-54
20 Neil Hickey, "TV Is Opening up the Soviet Block Nations — Whether They Like It Or Not," *TV Guide*, August 22, 1987, p. 7
21Christine Toomey Wiebelskirchen, "Honecker Goes Over the Wall For Pomp and Home Cooking," *The Sunday Times* (London), September 6, 1987, p. 17

**Chapter 9**

1 "Why They're Sulking As Well As Celebrating in Berlin," *The Economist*, April 25, 1987, p. 43
2 Viotti, *op. cit.*, p. 568
3 Viotti, *op. cit.*, pp. 586-87
4 "West Berlin, Looking For a Future," *The Economist*, May 10, 1986, p. 51

# Index

# Photo Credits

**US Army:** 1, 2, 3, 4, 5, 6, *7, *9, *11 (bottom), 13, 15, 17, 18, 19, 20, 21, 22, 23, 24, 25 (inset), 27, 29, 30, 33, 34 (top left & right), 36, 37, 39 (bottom), 40 (bottom), 41, 42, 45, 46 (bottom), 51, 52, 56, 61, 64 (right top & center), 66, 71, 78, 79, 80, 81, 83, 84, 85, 91, 92, 114 (top), 136 (bottom), 138, 139, 140, 161 (top right), 167 (top), 168, 173 (right), 174, 175, 179, 180, 184, 185 (bottom), 186, 191, 193 (top & bottom right), 195, 196, 201, 203, 204, 208, 209, 213, 215, 217, 218, 222, 223, 226, 228, 229, 230.
**From newsreel footage supplied by the Soviet Government after World War II.*
**US Air Force:** 89, 93, 94, 95, 99, 100, 101, 103, 104, 105, 106, 107, 108, 109, 110, 111, 112 (center & right), 117, 118, 121, 122, 123 (top), 123-124, 125, 126, 127, 128, 129, 130, 133, 134, 145, 146, 147, 148, 149, 150, 151, 153, 154, 155, 157, 158, 159, 160, 161 (top left), 162, 163, 164, 172, 176, 177, 181, 185 (top), 189-190, 198, 199, 200.
**US Navy:** 178 (top), 188.
**Federal Ministry for All-German Affairs**: 215 (bottom), 216.
**Press and Information Office of Berlin**: 43-44, 63, 104 (inset), 141, 206 (bottom), 219 (top).
**Landesbildstelle Berlin**: 39 (top), 40 (inset), 47, 48, 49, 50, 53 (bottom), 57, 58, 62, 64 (left), 86, 102, 112 (top), 113, 115, 116, 119, 132, 135, 166, 167 (bottom), 169, 170, 171, 173 (left), 182, 192, 193 (left), 194, 197, 206 (top), 207, 221, 231, 232.
**Bettmann Archives**: 31, 32, 34 (bottom), 46 (top), 59, 60.
**National Archives**: 8 (top), 38, 64 (bottom right), 69, 143-144, 161, (bottom), 187.
**Soviet Military Review**: 11 (top), 12.
**Cotton Coulson**: 225.
**US Information Agency**: 178 (bottom), 210, 214.
**Greek Ministry of National Defense**: 67-68.
**Harry S Truman Library**: 67 (inset), 74, 183.
**Patrick Piel, Gamma Liaison**: 233.
**John F. Kennedy Library**: 219 (bottom).
**United Nations**: 211.
**New York Times via National Archives**: 25-26, 75, 76, 87, 136 (top), 165.
**Der Tagesspiegel**: 142.
**Imperial War Museum**: 8 (center & bottom).
**Major Carlton F. Schwan**: 54.
**Ullstein**: 136.
**The authors**: 53 (top), 88.

# Presidio Press Books In Print Through January 1989

**ACE!**
A Marine Night Fighter Pilot in World War II
Colonel R. Bruce Porter with Eric Hammel
$22.95 - Cloth

**AIRBRIDGE TO BERLIN**
The Berlin Crisis of 1948, Its Origins and Aftermath
D.M. Giangreco and Robert E. Griffin
$14.95 - Paper

**AIRLIFT**
A History of Military Air Transport
David Wragg
$25.00 - Cloth

**ALPHA BUG**
a novel
M.E. Morris
$14.95 - Cloth

**AMBUSH AT OSIRAK**
a novel
Herbert Crowder
$18.95 - Cloth

**AMERICANS AT WAR, 1975-1986**
An Era of Violent Peace
Daniel P. Bolger
$24.95 - Cloth
November 1988

**ANATOMY OF A DIVISION**
1st Cav in Vietnam
Shelby L. Stanton
$17.95 - Cloth

**AUGUST 1944**
Robert A. Miller
$17.95 - Cloth

**BATTLE FOR HUE**
Tet 1968
Keith William Nolan
$14.95 - Cloth

**BEFORE THE BATTLE**
A Commonsense Guide to Leadership and Management
Lt. Gen. Edward M. Flanagan, Jr., USA (Ret.)
$10.95 - Paper

**BILL MAUDLIN'S ARMY**
Bill Maudlin's Greatest World War II Cartoons
Bill Maudlin
$12.95 - Paper

**BRENNAN'S WAR**
Vietnam 1965-69
Matthew Brennan
$17.95 - Cloth

**BURMA**
The Untold Story
Won-loy Chan
$14.95 - Cloth

**COMMON SENSE TRAINING**
A Working Philosophy for Leaders
Lt. Gen. Arthur S. (Ace) Collins, Jr., USA (Ret.)
$9.95 - Paper

## CONCISE GUIDE SERIES

**AXIS AIRCRAFT OF WORLD WAR II**
David Mondey
$12.95 - Paper

**COMMERCIAL AIRCRAFT OF THE WORLD**
David Mondey
$12.95 - Paper

**MILITARY AIRCRAFT OF THE WORLD**
Edited by Chris Chant
$12.95 - Cloth

**CORREGIDOR**
E.M. Flanagan
$18.95 - Cloth

**DEATH VALLEY**
The Summer Offensive I Corps, August 1969
Keith William Nolan
$17.95 - Cloth

**DEFEAT OF THE WOLF PACKS**
Geoffrey Jones
$16.95 - Cloth

**THE DEFENSE OF HILL 781**
Lt. Col. James McDonough
$15.95 - Cloth

**DEVIS BOATS**
The PT War Against Japan
William Bruener
$16.95 - Cloth

**DRAGONS AT WAR**
2-34th Infantry in the Mojave
Daniel P. Bolger
$18.95 - Cloth

**THE EASTER OFFENSIVE**
Vietnam, 1972
Col. G.H. Turley, USMCR, (Ret.)
$18.95 - Cloth

**ESCAPE FROM LAOS**
Dieter Dengler
$9.95 - Paper

**FIRE ARROW**
a novel
Franklin Allen Leib
$18.95 - Cloth
August 1988

**FIREPOWER**
R.P. Hunnicutt
$40.00 - Cloth

**FOLLOW ME**
The Human Element in Leadership
Maj. Gen. Aubrey S. Newman, USA (Ret.)
$9.95 - Paper

**FROM OSS TO GREEN BERETS**
The Birth of Special Forces
Col. Aaron Bank, USA (Ret.)
$16.95 - Cloth

**GASTON'S WAR**
The True Story of a Hero of the Resistance in World War II
Allan Mayer
$17.95 - Cloth

**GEORGE S. BROWN**
General, U.S. Air Force Destined for Stars
Edgar F. Puryear, Jr.
$16.95 - Cloth

**GREEN BERETS AT WAR**
U.S. Army Special Forces in Asia 1956-1975
Shelby L. Stanton
$18.95 - Cloth

**THE GRUNTS**
Charles R. Anderson
$14.95 - Cloth

**GUARDIANS**
Strategic Reconnaissance Satellites
Curtis Peebles
$28.95 - Cloth

**THE HALDER WAR DIARY, 1939-1942**
Edited by Charles Burdick and Hans-Adolf Jacobsen
$35.00 - Cloth
November 1988

**HAMBURGER HILL**
May 11-20, 1969
Samuel Zaffiri
$18.95 - Cloth
September 1988

**HEADHUNTERS**
Stories from the 1st Squadron, 9th Cavalry, in Vietnam 1965-1971
Matthew Brennan, Editor
$18.95 - Cloth

**HELL ON WHEELS**
A History of the 2d Armored Division
Donald E. Houston
$12.95 - Paper

**THE HISTORY OF THE BRITISH ARMY**
Charles Messenger
$25.00 - Cloth

**HISTORY OF THE ROYAL NAVY**
In the Twentieth Century
Anthony Preston
$25.00 - Cloth

**"HOWLIN' MAD" vs THE ARMY**
Conflict in Command, Saipan 1944
Harry A. Gailey
$17.95 - Cloth

**THE ICEMEN**
a novel of Antarctica
M.E. Morris
$17.95 - Cloth
August 1988

**THE INFLUENCE OF SEA POWER**
Alfred Thayer Mahan
$40.00 - Cloth

**INSIDE THE GREEN BERETS**
The First Thirty Years
A History of the U.S. Army Special Forces
Col. Charles M. Simpson III, USA (Ret.)
$16.95 - Cloth

**INTO LAOS**
The Story of Dewey Canyon II/Lam Son 719, Vietnam 1971
Keith William Nolan
$18.95 - Cloth

**LEADERS AND BATTLES**
The Art of Military Leadership
William J. Wood
$16.95 - Cloth

**THE LIBERATION OF GUAM**
21 July-10 August 1944
Harry Gailey
$16.95 - Cloth
October 1988

**LINE DOGGIE**
Foot Soldier in Vietnam
Charles Gadd
$15.95 - Cloth

**THE LOS BANOS RAID**
The 11th Airborne Jumps at Dawn
Lt. Gen. E.M. Flanagan, Jr., USA (Ret.)
$17.95 - Cloth

**LOST VICTORIES**
Erich von Manstein
$22.50 - Cloth

**THE MAKING OF A ROYAL MARINE COMMANDO**
Nigel Foster
$25.00 - Cloth
November 1988

**MASTER OF AIRPOWER**
General Carl A. Spaatz
David Mets
$22.50 - Cloth
December 1988

**MEN OF THE LUFTWAFFE**
Samuel W. Mitcham, Jr.
$18.95 - Cloth
November 1988

## MILITARY UNIFORMS IN AMERICA

**Volume I**
The Era of the America Revolution, 1755-1795
$40.00 - Cloth

**Volume III**
Long Endure:
The Civil War Period, 1852-1867
$40.00 - Cloth

**Volume IV**
The Modern Era, From 1868
$40.00 - Cloth

**MOSCOW: 1941**
The Frozen Offensive
Janusz Piekalkiewicz
$20.00 - Cloth

**MOTIVE FOR A MISSION**
The Story Behind Rudolf Hess's Flight to Britain
James Douglas-Hamilton
$15.95 - Cloth

**MUSTANG**
A Combat Marine
Gerald P. Averill
$18.95 - Cloth

**THE MY LAI INQUIRY**
Lt. Gen. W.R. Peers, USA (Ret.)
$12.95 - Cloth

**NAPOLEON'S INVASION OF RUSSIA**
George F. Nafziger
$45.00 - Cloth
September 1988

**NATO AIR POWER**
Robert Jackson
$25.00 - Cloth

**NINETEEN STARS**
A Study in Military Character and Leadership
Edgar F. Puryear, Jr.
$12.95 - Paper

**NUCLEAR FACTS**
A Guide to Nuclear Weapon Systems and Strategy
Christy Campbell
$18.95 - Cloth

**OBA, THE LAST SAMURAI**
Saipan 1944-1945
Don Jones
$16.95 - Cloth

**ON STRATEGY**
A Critical Analysis of the Vietnam War
Harry G. Summers, Jr., Colonel of Infantry
$14.95 - Cloth

**ON THE BANKS OF THE SUEZ**
An Israeli General's Personal Account of the Yom Kippur War
Avraham (Bren) Adan
$16.95 - Cloth

**OPERATION BARBAROSSA**
Strategy and Tactics on the Eastern Front, 1941
Bryan I. Fugate
$22.50 - Cloth

**OPERATION CITADEL**
Kursk and Orel, the Greatest Tank Battle of the Second World War
Janusz Piekalkiewicz
$25.00 - Cloth

**OPERATION DRAGOON**
**Tha Allied Invasion of the South of France**
William B. Breuer
$17.95 - Cloth

**ORDER OF BATTLE:**
**U.S. Army, World War II**
Shelby L. Stanton
$60.00 - Cloth

**OUR ENDLESS WAR**
**Inside Vietnam**
Tran Van Don
$10.95 - Paper

**PAVN: PEOPLE'S ARMY OF VIETNAM**
Douglas Pike
$22.50 - Cloth

**PACIFIC STARS AND STRIPES**
**The First Forty Years, 1945-1985**
Edited by Hal Drake
$14.95 - Paper

**THE PARAS**
Frank Hilton
$18.95 - Cloth

**PATTON**
**A History of the American Main Battle Tank, Volume I**
R.P. Hunnicutt
$60.00 - Cloth

**PEACE WITH HONOR?**
**An American Reports on Vietnam 1973-75**
Stuart A. Herrington
$15.95 - Cloth

**PHANTOM OVER VIETNAM**
**Fighter Pilot, USMC**
John Trotti
$17.95 - Cloth

**PLATOON LEADER**
James R. McDonough
$15.95 - Cloth

## THE PRESIDIO POWER SERIES

**AIRBORNE**
**Assault from the Sky**
Hans Halberstadt
$12.95 - Paper
Landpower Book #3001

**C-130**
**The Hercules**
M.E. Morris
$12.95 - Paper
Airpower Book #1009
January 1989

**CV: CARRIER AVIATION**
Peter Garrison
Photography by George Hall
$12.95 - Paper
Airpower Book #1001

**GREEN BERETS**
**The U.S. Army Special Forces**
Hans Halberstadt
$12.95 - Paper
Airpower Book #3002

**MARINE AIR: First to Fight**
John Trotti
Photography by George Hall
$12.95 - Paper
Airpower Book #1005

**RED FLAG**
**Air Combat for the '80s**
Michael Skinner
Photography by George Hall
$12.95 - Paper
Airpower Book #1003

**SAC: A Primer of Modern Strategic Air Power**
Bill Yenne
$12.95 - Paper
Airpower Book #1004

**SPACE SHUTTLE**
**A Quantum Leap**
George J. Torres
$12.95 - Paper
Airpower Book #1006

**STRIKE**
**U.S. Naval Strike Warfare Center**
John Joss
Photography by George Hall
$12.95 - Paper
Airpower Book #1008
January 1989

**TOP GUN**
**The Navy's Fighter Weapons School**
George Hall
$12.95 - Paper
Airpower Book #1007

**USAFE**
**A Primer of Modern Air Combat in Europe**
Michael Skinner
Photography by George Hall
$12.95 - Paper
Airpower Book #1002
September 1988

**USCG**
**Always Ready**
Hans Halberstadt
$12.95 - Paper
Seapower Book #2002

**USN: Naval Operations in the '80s**
Michael Skinner
$12.95 - Paper
Seapower #2001

**RED ARMY ORDER OF BATTLE**
**In the Great Patriotic War**
Robert G. Poirier and Albert Z. Conner
$22.50 - Cloth

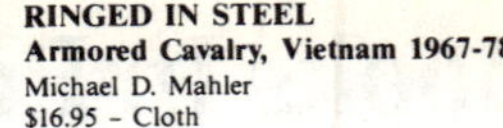

**RINGED IN STEEL**
**Armored Cavalry, Vietnam 1967-78**
Michael D. Mahler
$16.95 - Cloth

**THE RISE AND FALL OF AN AMERICAN ARMY**
**U.S. Ground Forces, Vietnam: 1965-1973**
Shelby L. Stanton
$22.50 - Cloth

**ROYAL AIR FORCE**
**The Aircraft in Service Since 1918**
Paintings by Michael Turner
$20.00 - Cloth

**ST. NAZAIRE COMMANDO**
Stuart Chant-Sempill (OBE MC)
$16.95 - Cloth

**SEACOAST FORTIFICATIONS OF THE UNITED STATES**
**An Introductory History**
Emanuel Raymond Lewis
$9.95 - Paper

**THE SECRET WAR WITH GERMANY**
**Deception, Espionage and Dirty Tricks, 1939-1945**
William B. Breuer
$17.95 - Cloth

**76 HOURS**
**The Invasion of Tarawa**
Eric Hammel
John E. Lane
$22.95 - Cloth

**SHERMAN**
**A History of the American Medium Tank**
R.P. Hunnicutt
$60.00 - Cloth

**SILENCE WAS A WEAPON**
**The Vietnam War in the Villages**
Stuart A. Herrington
$15.95 - Cloth

**SMALL UNIT LEADERSHIP**
**A Commonsense Approach**
Col. Dandridge M. (Mike) Malone, USA (Ret.)
$8.95 - Paper

**SOLDIERING**
**The Civil War Diary of Rice C. Bull**
Editor, K. Jack Bauer
$9.95 - Paper

**SOVIET AIRLAND BATTLE TACTICS**
Lt. Col. William P. Baxter, USA (Ret.)
$18.95 - Cloth

**STARS IN FLIGHT: A Study in Air Force Character and Leadership**
Edgar F. Puryear, Jr.
$14.95 - Cloth
$ 8.95 - Paper

**STRATEGY FOR DEFEAT**
**Vietnam in Retrospect**
Adm. U.S.G. Sharp
$11.95 - Paper

**SUMMONS OF THE TRUMPET**
**U.S.-Vietnam in Perspective**
Dave Richard Palmer
$17.95 - Cloth

**TANK SERGEANT**
Ralph Zumbro
$16.95 - Cloth

**TEAM YANKEE**
**a novel of World War III**
H.W. Coyle
$17.95 - Cloth

**THREE WAR MARINE**
**The Pacific, Korea, Vietnam**
Col. Francis Fox Parry, USMC (Ret.)
$22.95 - Cloth

**VIETNAM: The Other War**
Charles R. Anderson
$13.95 - Cloth

**VIETNAM AT WAR**
**The History 1946-1975**
Gen. Phillip B. Davidson, USA (Ret.)
$27.50 - Cloth

**VIETNAM TRACKS**
**Armor in Battle 1945-75**
Simon Dunstan
$20.00 - Cloth

**WAHOO**
**The Patrols of America's Most Famous WWII Submarine**
R. Adm. Richard H. O'Kane, USN (Ret.)
$18.95 - Cloth

**WAR BRIDES OF WORLD WAR II**
Elfrieda Shukert and Barbara Scibetta
$18.95 - Cloth

**WAR WINNERS**
Ronald W. Clark
$14.95 - Cloth

**THE WARRIORS**
**The United States Marines**
Sgt. Karl C. Lippard
$34.95 - Deluxe Hardcover Binding

**WELCOME TO VIETNAM, MACHO MAN**
**Reflections of a Khe Sanh Vet**
Ernest Spencer
$15.95 - Cloth

**WHAT ARE GENERALS MADE OF?**
Maj. Gen. Aubrey S. Newman, USA (Ret.)
$18.95 - Cloth

**WINGS OF THE LUFTWAFFE**
Capt. Eric Brown, Royal Navy (Ret.)
$20.00 - Cloth

**WITH THE OLD BREED AT PELELIU AND OKINAWA**
Eugene B. Sledge
$15.95 - Cloth

**WOMEN IN THE MILITARY**
**An Unfinished Revolution**
Maj. Gen. Jeanne Holm, USAF (Ret.)
$12.95 - Paper

**Presidio Press books are available through fine bookstores everywhere. You may also order any of our books in print directly from Presidio. Please include $2.00 for shipping and handling. California residents add 6% state sales tax.**

***Guarantee:*** **Our high standards of editorial care, quality printing and binding, and overall excellence assure your satisfaction. If for any reason you are not completely satisfied, return the book with invoice number to Presidio Press, 31 Pamaron Way, Novato, CA 94949, within 15 days after you receive it, and we'll refund your full purchase price.**